SIGN RE[...]
(signs used in the [...])

Good footpath – – – – – – – – – –
(sufficiently distinct to be followed in mist)

Intermittent footpath – – – – – – –
(difficult to follow in mist)

**Route recommended
   but no path** · · ·>· · · · · · · · · · · ·>· · ·
(if recommended one way only, arrow indicates direction)

Wall ∞∞∞∞∞∞∞∞   **Broken wall** ∘∘∘∘∘∘∘∘∘∘∘∘

Fence ++++++++++   **Broken fence** ''''''''''''''''''

Marshy ground ⁖⁖⁖⁖⁖   **Trees** 🌳🌳🌳🌳

Crags ⛰⛰⛰   **Boulders** ∘◇◇∘

Stream or River
     (arrow indicates direction of flow)

Waterfall ⌇   **Bridge** ⌇

Buildings ▪▫▪   **Unenclosed road** ▭▭▭▭

Contours (at 100' intervals) ·····1900·····
                                  ·····1800·····
                                  ·····1700·····

Summit-cairn ▲   **Other** (prominent) **cairns** △

THE
WESTERN
FELLS

REVISED EDITIONS

PUBLISHER'S NOTE

Fell walking can be dangerous, especially
in wet, windy, foggy or icy conditions.
Please be sure to take sensible precautions
when out on the fells. As A. Wainwright himself
frequently wrote: use your common sense
and watch where you are putting your feet.

A PICTORIAL GUIDE
TO THE
LAKELAND FELLS

SECOND EDITION

REVISED BY CHRIS JESTY

being an illustrated account
of a study and exploration
of the mountains in the
English Lake District
by

AWainwright

BOOK SEVEN
THE WESTERN FELLS

Frances Lincoln Limited
4 Torriano Mews
Torriano Avenue
London NW5 2RZ
www.frances.lincoln.com

First edition published by Westmorland Gazette, Kendal, 1966
First published by Frances Lincoln 2003
Second (revised) edition published by Frances Lincoln 2009

Printed and bound in Thailand

A CIP catalogue record is available for this book
from the British Library.

ISBN 978 0 7112 2199 4

9 8 7 6 5 4 3 2 1

THIS REVISED AND UPDATED EDITION PUBLISHED BY
FRANCES LINCOLN,
LONDON

FOREWORD
BY BETTY WAINWRIGHT

FOREWORD

The Pictorial Guides have never before been revised, for the reasons given by AW in his concluding remarks to the third volume, *The Central Fells*, where he wrote that by the time he had finished Book Seven, age would prevent him undertaking the 'joyful task' of revising the series himself. He went on to write:

> ... Substantially, of course, the books will be useful for many years to come, especially in the detail and description of the fell tops, while the views will remain unaltered for ever, assuming that falling satellites and other fancy gadgets of man's invention don't blow God's far worthier creations to bits. But, this dire possibility apart, the books must inevitably show more and more inaccuracies as the years go by. Therefore, because it is unlikely that there will ever be revised editions, and because I should just hate to see my name on anything that could not be relied on, the probability is that the books will progressively be withdrawn from publication after a currency of a few years.

This was written in 1958, when the oldest volume was only three years old and by the time he had completed Book Seven in 1965 he was even more conscious of the little things that had gone out of date in the previous volumes — cairns demolished or built, screes eroded, woods felled or grown up, new paths made. As the years passed and it became apparent that the books were still in demand, despite these inaccuracies, he was occasionally approached by people asking for revised editions. But the core of the problem was that, as old age approached, he knew he could not undertake the changes himself, nor did he trust anyone to do the work as he would have wished.

When, in 1980, Chris Jesty broached the idea to him, he was told 'after my lifetime'. This was half the battle won — AW knew Chris's work well, and did trust him. Now, given the continuing popularity and use of the Pictorial Guides, I am delighted that, due to Chris's commitment, the guides are being revised and I give them my blessing. It is with pleasure that I picture Chris re-walking and checking and, where necessary, correcting every route, every ascent and every path. Although most of the individual corrections are minor, the overall impact is huge, and I feel proud and confident — as I am sure AW would be too — that the revised guides will satisfy the needs of the 21st-century walker.

Betty Wainwright
Kendal, January 2005

Betty Wainwright, AW's beloved wife,
companion, chauffeur and soulmate,
died in August 2008.

INTRODUCTION
TO THE
SECOND EDITION
BY CHRIS JESTY

INTRODUCTION TO THE SECOND EDITION

In 1959 I went on an Outward Bound course at Eskdale Green, which involved a lot of walking in the mountains. I found that the depiction of paths on Ordnance Survey maps left definite room for improvement, and I had the idea of producing a guide book that would make it easier for people to find their way around. But in 1961 I was given one of Wainwright's Pictorial Guides to the Lakeland Fells and discovered that he had beaten me to it.

It occurred to me that one day the books would become out of date, and that, as I was presumably much younger than the author, the time might arrive when I would be allowed to revise them. It has taken more than forty years for that dream to turn into a reality.

In the meantime I had made the acquaintance of the author. I collaborated with him on *A Guide to the View from Scafell Pike*, and later on, when his eyesight was failing, I drew the maps for two of his other books (*Wainwright in the Limestone Dales* and *Wainwright's Favourite Lakeland Mountains*). Shortly before he died he requested that if ever the Lakeland Guides were to be revised I should be offered the job.

When, in 2003, following a change of publisher, the proposal was revived, I threw myself into the job with enthusiasm. I had a number of advantages over the author. I had a car, I had satellite navigation equipment, I was able to work on enlargements of the pages, and as I didn't have a job I was able to devote all my time and all my energy to this vast project.

Every feature on the maps and ascent diagrams and every word of text have been checked, but I have not checked every recommended route without a path. Descriptions of natural features and views are virtually unaltered, but the number of changes that have been made to maps and ascent diagrams is enormous. The decision was taken to print the paths in a second colour so that they stand out from other details, and also so that readers can tell at a glance that it is the revised edition they are using.

Summit altitudes have been corrected where they differ by five feet or more from the latest Ordnance Survey figures. Parking information has been added where appropriate. I have also taken the liberty of adding other information that seems to me to be of interest. No changes have been made to drawings of landscapes, natural features or buildings, or, of course, to Wainwright's 'Personal Notes in conclusion'.

Occasional references will be found in the books to Bartholomew's maps. These are still available but they are now published by Collins.

Revising these books has been immensely satisfying, but it has not been without its problems. It has often been difficult to fit the new text to the space occupied by the old text, and sometimes it has been difficult to fit new detail to the maps. On Gowbarrow Fell in Book One, for example, there is a path from Aira Force to the car park on Park Brow. I could get it to fit at the western end, or I could move the path down and get it to fit at the eastern end, but to get it to fit at both ends I had to completely realign the main road.

Another problem involves the forestry plantations. Instead of bringing the plantations to an abrupt end the Forestry Commission have started to plant the trees progressively farther apart near the boundaries so that they gradually fade away. This has the effect of making the forest appear more natural, but it makes life difficult for the cartographer.

In Book Seven three routes recommended in the first edition have been removed at the request of the landowners. These are Lamplugh to Burnbank Fell, Low Lorton to Fellbarrow and Croasdale to Gavel Fell.

INTRODUCTION TO THE SECOND EDITION

This has meant condensing the rest of the relevant chapters to produce an even number of pages in each case.

Most of the changes have been very small, but there have been a few major developments, such as the closing of the railway from Keswick to Threlkeld and its conversion to an excellent footpath. Now there are plans to reopen the railway, which means that the text on Blencathra 8 may have to be revised again one day.

The areas I have most enjoyed working in are the low-lying places on the fringes of the Lake District, and this is the sort of terrain I expect to encounter in my next assignment, the revision of *A Coast to Coast Walk*. After that I hope to revise *The Outlying Fells of Lakeland*, and eventually, if all goes well, *Pennine Way Companion*.

In order to keep the books as accurate as possible and in anticipation of future revised editions, readers are invited to write to me (c/o the publishers) about any errors they find in the revised Pictorial Guides. Emails to chrisj@frances-lincoln.com and letters sent to me c/o Frances Lincoln, 4 Torriano Mews, Torriano Avenue, London NW5 2RZ, will be passed on regularly. Amendments and information about changes that have taken place since publication are available on the Frances Lincoln website (www.franceslincoln.com).

Chris Jesty
Kendal, May 2009

BOOK SEVEN
is dedicated to

ALL WHO HAVE HELPED ME

sometimes with advice, sometimes with information,
sometimes with no more than a friendly nod or smile.
They are too many to be named, and indeed some are
unknown, anonymous fellow-walkers who pass the time
of day and are gone. I must, however, thank my wife,
for not standing in my way, and a few special friends
who would not ask for identification here, for making
the way easier for me to travel.   It has been a long
and lonely way, but I have trodden it increasingly
aware of the goodwill and encouragement of many
kind people, most of whom I shall never meet. And
now, after thirteen years, I have come to the end of it
and my final task, a difficult one, is to find words
adequate to express my appreciation to everybody
who has helped.   The least I can do, and the most I
can do, is to acknowledge my debt by this dedication.

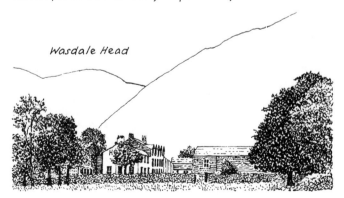

Wasdale Head

Classification and Definition

Any division of the Lakeland fells into geographical districts must necessarily be arbitrary, just as the location of the outer boundaries of Lakeland must always be a matter of opinion. Any attempt to define internal or external boundaries is certain to invite criticism, and he who takes it upon himself to say where Lakeland starts and finishes, or, for example, where the Central Fells merge into the Southern Fells and *which* fells *are* the Central Fells and which the Southern and *why* they need be so classified, must not expect his pronouncements to be generally accepted.

Yet for present purposes some plan of classification and definition must be used. County and parochial boundaries are no help, nor is the recently-defined area of the Lakeland National Park, for this book is concerned only with the high ground.

First, the external boundaries.   Straight lines linking the extremities of the outlying lakes enclose all the higher fells very conveniently. There are a few fells of lesser height to the north and east, however, that are typically Lakeland in character and cannot properly be omitted : these are brought in, somewhat untidily, by extending the lines in those areas. Thus:

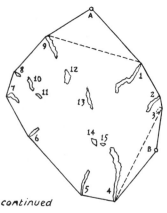

1 : *Ullswater*
2 : *Hawes Water*
3 : proposed *Swindale Resr*
4 : *Windermere*
5 : *Coniston Water*
6 : *Wast Water*
7 : *Ennerdale Water*
8 : *Loweswater*
9 : *Bassenthwaite Lake*
10 : *Crummock Water*
11 : *Buttermere*
12 : *Derwent Water*
13 : *Thirlmere*
14 : *Grasmere*
15 : *Rydal Water*
A : *Caldbeck*
B : *Longsleddale* (church)

continued

Classification and Definition

continued

The complete Guide includes all the fells in the area enclosed by the straight lines of the diagram. This is an undertaking quite beyond the compass of a single volume, and it is necessary, therefore, to divide the area into convenient sections, making the fullest use of natural boundaries (lakes, valleys and low passes) so that each district is, as far as possible, self-contained and independent of the rest.

This division gives seven areas, each with a well-defined group of fells, and each area is the subject of a separate volume

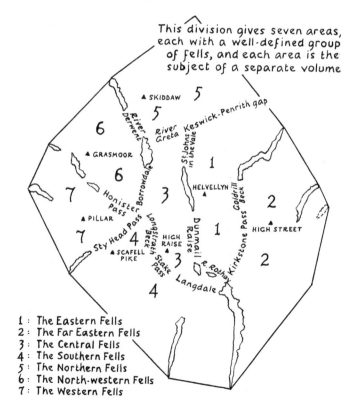

1 : The Eastern Fells
2 : The Far Eastern Fells
3 : The Central Fells
4 : The Southern Fells
5 : The Northern Fells
6 : The North-western Fells
7 : The Western Fells

INTRODUCTION

Notes on the Illustrations

THE MAPS.................. Many excellent books have been written
about Lakeland, but the best literature of all for the walker
is that published by the Director General of Ordnance Survey,
the 1" map for companionship and guidance on expeditions, the
2½" map for exploration both on the fells and by the fireside.
These admirable maps are remarkably accurate topographically
but there is a crying need for a revision of the paths on the hills:
several walkers' tracks that have come into use during the past
few decades, some of them now broad highways, are not shown at
all; other paths still shown on the maps have fallen into neglect
and can no longer be traced on the ground.

The popular Bartholomew 1" map is a
beautiful picture, fit for a frame, but this
too is unreliable for paths; indeed here the
defect is much more serious, for routes are
indicated where no paths ever existed, nor
ever could — the cartographer has preferred
to take precipices in his stride rather than
deflect his graceful curves over easy ground.

Hence the justification for the maps in this book: they have
the one merit (of importance to walkers) of being dependable as
regards delineation of paths. They are intended as supplements
to the Ordnance Survey maps, certainly not as substitutes.

THE VIEWS............... Various devices have
been used to illustrate the views from the
summits of the fells. The full panorama
in the form of an outline drawing is most
satisfactory generally, and this method
has been adopted for the main viewpoints.

THE DIAGRAMS OF ASCENTS................... The routes of ascent
of the higher fells are depicted by diagrams that do not pretend
to strict accuracy: they are neither plans
nor elevations; in fact there is deliberate
distortion in order to show detail clearly:
usually they are represented as viewed
from imaginary 'space-stations.' But it is
hoped they will be useful and interesting.

THE DRAWINGS....... The drawings at least are honest attempts
to reproduce what the eye sees: they illustrate features of
interest and also serve the dual purpose of breaking up the
text and balancing the layout of the pages, and of filling up
awkward blank spaces, like this:

Thirlmere

THE
WESTERN
FELLS

If Lakeland can be thought of as being circular in plan, the Western Fells may be described as being contained within a wide sector, the apex driving deep into the heart of the district at Sty Head and the boundaries running therefrom northwest along the valley of the Cocker, jewelled by the lovely lakes of Buttermere and Crummock Water, and southwest along Wasdale towards the sea.

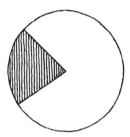

If Lakeland can be thought of as a wheel, the Western Fells may be likened, simply yet appropriately, to two spokes (the Pillar and High Stile ranges) radiating from a central hub (Great Gable), with Ennerdale between the spokes and the two valleys of the Cocker and Wasdale bordering them.

In this area is a wide diversity of scenery. The section nearest to and including the hub is entirely mountainous, crowded with fine peaks although none quite attain 3000 feet. Here is the hoary old favourite, Great Gable, and the magnificent Pillar, the fascinating Haystacks and the exhilarating spine of the High Stile ridge: a rugged territory of volcanic rock and syenite. Further west the slopes are smooth and rounded, characteristic of the underlying slate; towards the arc of the circle they decline into low grassy foothills and rolling sheep pastures, a splendid walking country but comparatively unexciting and unfrequented.

Valley and lake scenery is of the very best vintage, excepting Ennerdale, where natural beauty has been sacrificed to material gain, an irretrievable mistake. There is water extraction from some of the lakes, a process carried out by the responsible authorities unobtrusively and with due regard to amenities.

There are no centres of population within the area, and only hamlets and small villages around the perimeter; most of them cater for visitors but accommodation is necessarily restricted. Buttermere and Wasdale Head in particular are popular resorts.

The western boundary of the area described in this book is fairly well defined by the fells themselves, although lesser hills continue into the industrial belt of West Cumbria. This arbitrary boundary coincides, in places, with that of the Lake District National Park but is generally within it.

Lorton

Mosser

Loweswater

Lamplugh

Ennerdale
Bridge

Croasdale

Ennerdale Water

Calder

The
Western
Boundary

plantations

Greendale

Wast Water

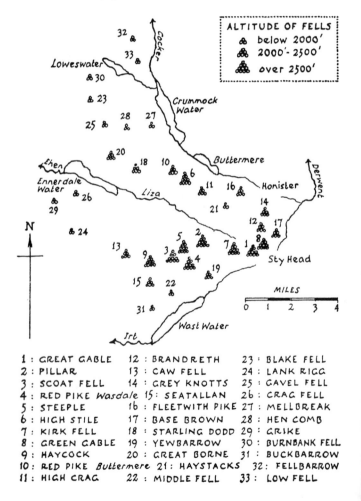

THE WESTERN FELLS
Natural Boundaries

ALTITUDE OF FELLS
♠ below 2000'
♠ 2000'- 2500'
♠ over 2500'

MILES
0 1 2 3 4

1 : GREAT GABLE	12 : BRANDRETH	23 : BLAKE FELL
2 : PILLAR	13 : CAW FELL	24 : LANK RIGG
3 : SCOAT FELL	14 : GREY KNOTTS	25 : GAVEL FELL
4 : RED PIKE *Wasdale*	15 : SEATALLAN	26 : CRAG FELL
5 : STEEPLE	16 : FLEETWITH PIKE	27 : MELLBREAK
6 : HIGH STILE	17 : BASE BROWN	28 : HEN COMB
7 : KIRK FELL	18 : STARLING DODD	29 : GRIKE
8 : GREEN GABLE	19 : YEWBARROW	30 : BURNBANK FELL
9 : HAYCOCK	20 : GREAT BORNE	31 : BUCKBARROW
10 : RED PIKE *Buttermere*	21 : HAYSTACKS	32 : FELLBARROW
11 : HIGH CRAG	22 : MIDDLE FELL	33 : LOW FELL

THE WESTERN FELLS

in the order of their appearance in this book

Reference to map opposite: over 2500'	2000-2500'	below 2000'		Altitude in feet
	17		BASE BROWN	2120
		23	BLAKE FELL	1878
	12		BRANDRETH	2344
		31	BUCKBARROW	1410
		30	BURNBANK FELL	1558
	13		CAW FELL	2288
		26	CRAG FELL	1716
		32	FELLBARROW	1363
	16		FLEETWITH PIKE	2126
		25	GAVEL FELL	1726
	20		GREAT BORNE	2019
1			GREAT GABLE	2949
8			GREEN GABLE	2628
	14		GREY KNOTTS	2287
		29	GRIKE	1601
9			HAYCOCK	2618
		21	HAYSTACKS	1959
		28	HEN COMB	1670
	11		HIGH CRAG	2443
6			HIGH STILE	2644
7			KIRK FELL	2630
		24	LANK RIGG	1775
		33	LOW FELL	1352
		27	MELLBREAK	1676
		22	MIDDLE FELL	1908
2			PILLAR	2927
	10		RED PIKE *Buttermere*	2479
4			RED PIKE *Wasdale*	2707
3			SCOAT FELL	2760
	15		SEATALLAN	2266
	18		STARLING DODD	2077
5			STEEPLE	2687
	19		YEWBARROW	2058
9	11	13		
33				

Each fell is the subject of a separate chapter

Base Brown

Seatoller •
• Seathwaite
BASE ▲ BROWN

▲ GREAT GABLE
// Sty Head Pass

MILES

0   1   2   3

from the Borrowdale Yews

NATURAL FEATURES

Base Brown marks the end of roads and farmsteads, of woods and green pastures, as one proceeds into the upper recesses of Borrowdale. It marks the beginning of wildness and desolation. It is the first of the rough and rugged heights extending to and around Wasdale, and introduces its hinterland excellently, being itself of striking appearance, gaunt, steep-sided, a pyramid of tumbled boulders and scree, a desert abandoned to nature. It is a cornerstone, walkers' paths to Sty Head curving around its base below sixteen hundred feet of chaotic fellside scarred by gully and crag and strewn with the natural debris of ages; a stark declivity. The opposite slope, although also rimmed and pitted with rocks, is much shorter, being halted by the hanging glacial valley of Gillercomb. Only along the narrow crest of the fell are walkers likely to venture, and but rarely even here, for the ridge rising from Borrowdale is defended by bristly crags; the continuation beyond the summit, however, to a grassy neck of land linking with Green Gable and overlooking Sty Head on one side and Gillercomb on the other, is much easier, and a new popular path (Seathwaite direct to Great Gable) comes into the scene at this point. Base Brown belongs to Borrowdale exclusively, and its streams, attractively broken by waterfalls and cascades, feed the youthful Derwent only.

Taylorgill Force

Sourmilk Gill

The attention of intrepid
and well-insured explorers
is drawn to the remarkable
cleft vertically splitting the
crag. It is not listed as a
rock-climb, either because it
is too easy or too impossible.
It is certain to be dangerous.
The author, still unnerved
after his climb of Jack's Rake
in 1957, has no information
to impart.

*The East Face
above Taylor Gill*

Hanging Stone

The Hanging Stone is repeatedly featured conspicuously in successive editions of the Ordnance Survey maps, where its name is given as much prominence as that of the fell itself, although its precise location is never pinpointed. The Stone occupies a startling position balanced on the rim of a crag, apparently half its bulk being unsupported and overhanging the void, but it is smaller than one is led to expect (a few tons only) and the special distinction given to it on the O.S. maps is not really merited.

looking steeply upwards

People with bad coughs should keep out of the line of fall

Sixty yards further up the ridge a large rounded boulder has come to rest on a number of small ones.

Fallen Stone

Immediately below the crag is a tremendous mass of rock that must at some time have fallen from it, although silting now gives it the appearance of a natural outcrop. It has been badly fractured in the fall, and identifiable fragments from it can be found lower down the slope.

Near the top end of the rock several large boulders have tumbled together, forming caves and foxholes.

MAP

Seathwaite is provided with a café, a farm shop, a camping site and a trout farm. With 130" of rain a year, this is reputed to be the rainiest inhabited place in England.

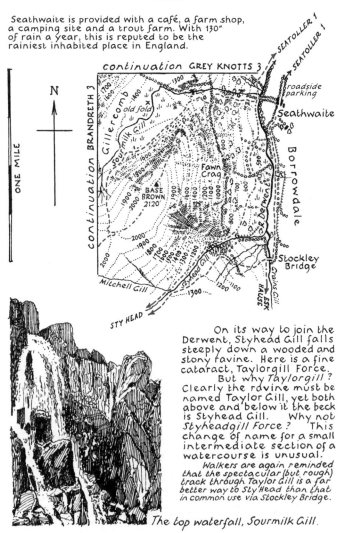

On its way to join the Derwent, Styhead Gill falls steeply down a wooded and stony ravine. Here is a fine cataract, Taylorgill Force. But why *Taylorgill*? Clearly the ravine must be named Taylor Gill, yet both above and below it the beck is Styhead Gill. Why not *Styheadgill Force*? This change of name for a small intermediate section of a watercourse is unusual.

Walkers are again reminded that the spectacular (but rough) track through Taylor Gill is a far better way to Sty Head than that in common use via Stockley Bridge.

The top waterfall, Sourmilk Gill.

ASCENT FROM SEATHWAITE
1750 feet of ascent : 1½ miles

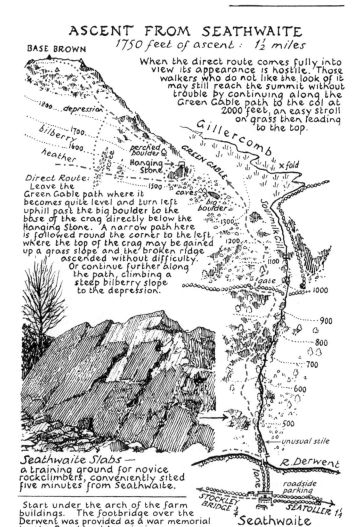

BASE BROWN

When the direct route comes fully into view its appearance is hostile. Those walkers who do not like the look of it may still reach the summit without trouble by continuing along the Green Gable path to the col at 2000 feet, an easy stroll on grass then leading to the top.

1200 .. depression

bilberry ...1700..

..1600..

heather

Gillercomb

perched boulder

Hanging Stone

GREEN GABLE

x fold

scree

Direct Route:
Leave the Green Gable path where it becomes quite level and turn left uphill past the big boulder to the base of the crag directly below the Hanging Stone. A narrow path here is followed round the corner to the left, where the top of the crag may be gained up a grass slope and the broken ridge ascended without difficulty.
Or continue further along the path, climbing a steep bilberry slope to the depression.

..1500.. caves

big boulder

..1300..

..1200..

Sourmilk Gill

..1100..

gate

+1000

900

800

700

600

500

unusual stile

R. Derwent

Seathwaite Slabs —
a training ground for novice rockclimbers, conveniently sited five minutes from Seathwaite.

lane

roadside parking

STOCKLEY BRIDGE ¾

SEATOLLER 1¼

Seathwaite

Start under the arch of the farm buildings. The footbridge over the Derwent was provided as a war memorial by the Ramblers' Association.
There used to be another path on the right of Sourmilk Gill but it has gone out of use and the wall has become impossible to cross. The ascent of Seathwaite Slabs is difficult because there are no handholds, but there is an easier way up on the right.

THE SUMMIT

The summit is out of character, being a broad grassy expanse with no suggestion of the rough craggy slopes that support it. A sprinkling of boulders and some low outcrops do their best to relieve the monotony.

DESCENTS: The eastern slope is excessively steep in all parts, and, above Taylor Gill, positively dangerous. The north-west side overlooking Gillercomb is precipitous.

For Borrowdale the easiest way off, and the best in mist, is to proceed down the gentle slope south-west, there joining the Green Gable - Seathwaite path as it turns to descend into Gillercomb. The direct route of ascent may be reversed in clear weather, but it is advisable NOT to persist in following the ridge to its extremity, which is a 40-foot vertical cliff; instead, turn to the right at the depression down a bilberry slope until a distinct horizontal path is reached, and go along this path, left, to the area of boulders below the 40-foot crag, where a way may be made downhill to the Green Gable-Seathwaite path clearly seen 200 yards below.

If Wasdale is the objective, get Styhead Tarn in view and make a beeline for it, crossing Mitchell Gill; an easy stroll.

RIDGE ROUTE

To GREEN GABLE, 2628': 1 mile : SW

Depression at 1990': 620 feet of ascent

Interest quickens as the walk proceeds.

Soon after leaving the summit south-west the distinct path coming up from Gillercomb is seen in the depression ahead; this is joined and followed up the opposite slope, which becomes stony, to the main watershed and the broad path from Honister 300 yards short of the top of Green Gable.

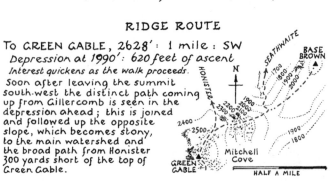

THE VIEW

Higher fells on three sides restrict the open view to the section between north and east, where the village of Rosthwaite and much of Borrowdale are also seen. South is the mountain wall of the Scafells in close detail. West, Pillar and Scoat Fell make an unexpected appearance over Gillercomb Head.

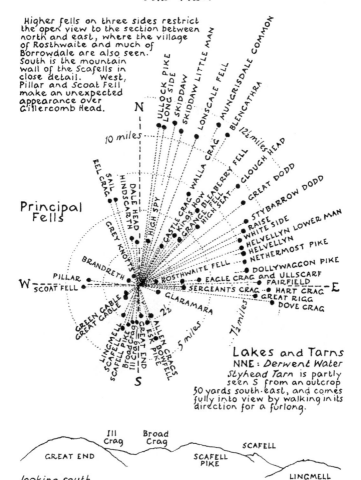

Principal Fells

Lakes and Tarns
NNE: *Derwent Water*
Styhead Tarn is partly seen S from an outcrop 50 yards south-east, and comes fully into view by walking in its direction for a furlong.

looking south

In good lighting conditions this view south to the Scafells calls for a photograph, but before releasing the shutter walk towards the scene until Styhead Tarn appears fully in the middle distance and gives relief to the sombre background. Then do it.

Blake Fell

1878'

Lamplugh   Loweswater
●   ●
BURNBANK FELL
▲ BLAKE FELL

▲ GAVEL FELL
● Croasdale

MILES
0   1   2   3

from Cogra Moss

NATURAL FEATURES

Blake Fell (locally known simply as Blake) is the highest of the Loweswater uplands, overtopping the others considerably and asserting this superiority by a distinctive final upthrust that makes it prominent in views of the group. A long high shoulder, Carling Knott, extends towards Loweswater, hiding the main summit from that valley, but on the opposite western flank, facing industrial Cumbria, a scree-covered declivity drops immediately from the summit-cairn to the hollow of Cogra Moss and encircling arms comprise many subsidiary tops, of which the chief is the shapely peak of Knock Murton. This side of the fell has for long been commissioned to the service of man: here, up to a century ago, were extensive iron-ore mines and a railway to serve them; Cogra Moss has been dammed to make a reservoir, and in the 1960s the Forestry Commission moved in and planted the first trees in a project that has altered the landscape completely. The fell, by reason of its fringe situation, gives the feeling of belonging more to West Cumbria than to the Lake District; more to Lamplugh, where everybody knows it, than to Loweswater, where Mellbreak is favourite. Its waters mainly feed the Derwent.

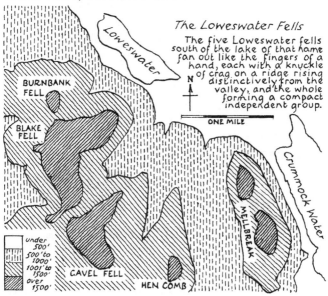

The Loweswater Fells

The five Loweswater fells south of the lake of that name fan out like the fingers of a hand, each with a knuckle of crag on a ridge rising distinctively from the valley, and the whole forming a compact independent group.

ONE MILE

under 500'
500' to 1000'
1001' to 1500'
over 1500'

Blake Fell 3

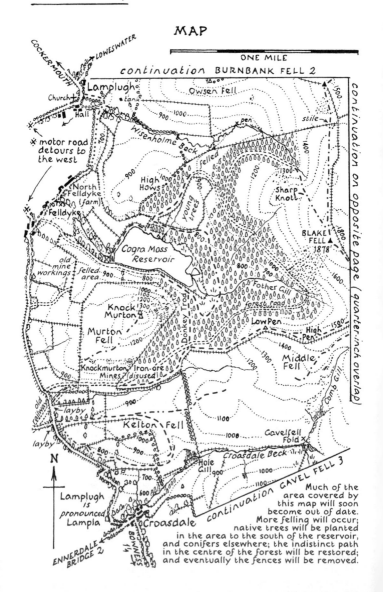

ONE MILE

continuation BURNBANK FELL 2

continuation on opposite page (quarter-inch overlap)

COCKERMOUTH
LOWESWATER

Lamplugh

Church
Hall

* motor road
detours to
the west

North
Felldyke
(farm)
Felldyke

old
mine
workings

felled
area

Knock
Murton

Murton
Fell

Knockmurton Iron-ore
Mines (disused)

old
railway

layby

layby

N

Lamplugh
is
pronounced
Lampla

Croasdale

ENNERDALE
BRIDGE 2

BOWNESS 1¼

Owsen Fell

pen

stile

Wisenholme Beck

felled

High
Hows

young trees

Cogra Moss
Reservoir

Donkey Trod

Sharp
Knott

BLAKE
FELL
1878

Fother Gill

forest road

Low Pen

High
Pen

Middle
Fell

Comb Gill

Kelton Fell

Cavelfell
Fold

Croasdale Beck

Hole
Gill

continuation GAVEL FELL 3

Much of the
area covered by
this map will soon
become out of date.
More felling will occur;
native trees will be planted
in the area to the south of the reservoir,
and conifers elsewhere; the indistinct path
in the centre of the forest will be restored;
and eventually the fences will be removed.

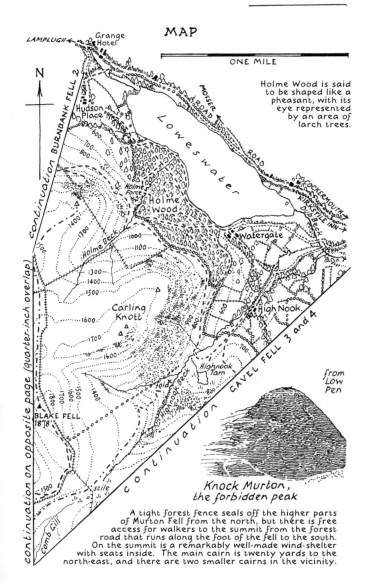

MAP

ONE MILE

Holme Wood is said to be shaped like a pheasant, with its eye represented by an area of larch trees.

LAMPLUGH ←

Grange Hotel

continuation BURNBANK FELL 2

N

Hudson Place

Loweswater

MOSSER ROAD

COCKERMOUTH ROAD

KIRKSTILE INN →

Dub Beck

Holme Force

Holme Wood

Watergate

Holme Beck

continuation on opposite page (quarter-inch overlap)

Carling Knott

High Nook

Highnook Tarn

fold

Highnook Beck

continuation GAVEL FELL 3 and 4

BLAKE FELL 1878

stile

Comb Gill

from Low Pen

Knock Murton,
the forbidden peak

A tight forest fence seals off the higher parts of Murton Fell from the north, but there is free access for walkers to the summit from the forest road that runs along the foot of the fell to the south. On the summit is a remarkably well-made wind-shelter with seats inside. The main cairn is twenty yards to the north-east, and there are two smaller cairns in the vicinity.

ASCENT FROM LOWESWATER
1550 feet of ascent : 3 miles (from Kirkstile Inn)

looking south-west

BLAKE FELL

GAVEL FELL

BURNBANK FELL

stile   1800

1700

grass

stile

1500   1600

1400

grass

grass

1500

Highnook Beck

Black Crag

path disappears

heather

fold X

Carling Knott

grass

Holme Beck

Highnook Tarn

1700

800

700

1500

1400

intake wall

1300   heather

600

1200

bracken

1100

1000

bracken

900   gate

High Nook (farm)

800

700

Holme Force

In mist prefer the easier sheltered route from High Nook (a farm in a sylvan setting): this is a fast way down.

600   700

500

Holme Wood

farm road

Watergate (farm)

Loweswater

KIRKSTILE INN

car park

lane

Dub Beck

ROAD

In clear weather prefer the steep climb over Carling Knott from Watergate via Holme Wood a route of interesting detail and lovely views.

Ancient cairns on Carling Knott

ASCENT FROM LAMPLUGH
1400 feet of ascent : 3¼ miles

BLAKE FELL

1800
1700
1600
1500

High Pen

1500

Middle Fell

1400
1300
Blakefell Screes
1200
Low Pen
1100
forest road

Knock Murton

1200

1100

col

forest road

Fother Gill

Donkey Trod

900

800

old fence

Cogra Moss Reservoir

felled

1000

900

At the col the route crosses the forest road coming up from the disused iron mine on the south side of Knock Murton. At present, this is the only access for vehicles into the new forest. It is not available to private cars.

From the west the approach by Cogra Moss has always been the best. The reservoir is used by the Cockermouth Angling Association. There are two small islands in the lake, namely Blake Island and Knock Island.

At the head of the reservoir turn up Donkey Trod to the col; then follow the fence along the ridge around the hollow to the summit.

It will be seen from the map on page 3 that there are two alternative routes from the west. One crosses the reservoir dam and approaches the summit from Sharp Knott. The other utilises the forest road to the south of Knock Murton.

The reservoir is not a natural lake, having been formed by damming the outflow from Cogra Moss, once a marsh.

dam

Drakegill Beck

800

gate

100

gate

North Felldyke

Felldyke

car park

looking east-south-east

100

A

gate

Church

Lamplugh

B

A : road to LOWESWATER
B : road to COCKERMOUTH

Note the well-preserved sixteenth-century gateway of the former Lamplugh Hall.

At Lamplugh there is room to park opposite the church when it is not in use, but it is difficult to cross the stream and better to start at Felldyke.

THE SUMMIT

HIGH RAISE GLARAMARA HIGH STILE PILLAR SCAFELL Black Crag SCOAT FELL

The summit is well defined by rising ground on all sides, and the large cairn merely emphasises the obvious. It is a fine airy place, overtopping everything around: the highest point of the Loweswater fells. As on Knock Murton, the cairn has been fashioned into an exceptionally well-constructed wind-shelter. A short path heads south-west to a viewpoint from which the Cogra Moss Reservoir is well seen.

A hundred yards east of the summit is an unclimbable wire-mesh fence erected in the 1960s to mark the boundary of the land acquired by the Forestry Commission. It was put up without a stile, so denying to fellwalkers their inherited right to visit the cairn. Two stiles were later provided, one to link with Gavel Fell, the other with Carling Knott. The former has since completely collapsed and the latter looks as though it is about to do so. In 2008, it must have been decided that the fence no longer served a purpose, for gaps were created at both these places. Between the two gaps, in an old sheepfold, is another wind-shelter.

DESCENTS : For Lamplugh or Felldyke follow the ridge over High Pen and Low Pen and cut down to Cogra Moss Reservoir.

If this route has already been used for ascent then follow the route over Sharp Knott to the reservoir dam. For Loweswater, cross the fence 200 yards south of the summit; then follow the ridge over Carling Knott in clear weather, or, in mist, go down the easy tongue west of Highnook Beck. (Note that in one place the path disappears and is hard to find again.)

Summit cairns on Knock Murton

THE VIEW

The view inland, comprising a splendid array of mountains, is excellent; seawards, it extends uninterrupted far across West Cumbria to the Scottish hills.

Principal Fells

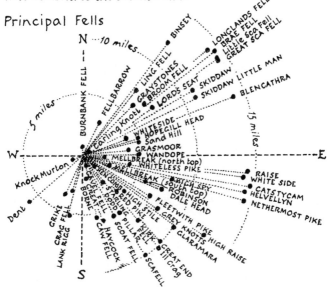

RIDGE ROUTES

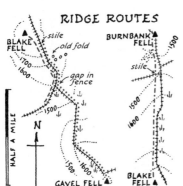

Lakes and Tarns

E: Crummock Water
SE: Buttermere
SSW: Ennerdale Water
SW: Meadley Reservoir
W: Cogra Moss Reservoir
NW: Mockerkin Tarn

TO GAVEL FELL, 1726':
1 mile: SSE
Depression at 1465'
270 feet of ascent

TO BURNBANK FELL, 1558':
1 mile: N, then NNW
Depression at 1470'
150 feet of ascent

Note that no stile is provided on the summit of Burnbank Fell.

Brandreth

2344'

Gatesgarth
Honister Pass

Black Sail Y.H.
▲ GREY KNOTTS
BRANDRETH ▲   Seathwaite

▲ GREEN GABLE
▲ GREAT GABLE

MILES

0   1   2   3

from Base Brown

NATURAL FEATURES

Brandreth is an intermediate height on the broad tilted ridge, almost a tableland, rising gently from the back of Honister Crag and culminating in Great Gable. Its summit is little higher than the general level of the plateau and has nothing of particular interest; indeed, the path along the ridge takes a wide sweep to avoid it, preferring to maintain an easy contour rather than go up-and-down over the top. Brandreth's one claim to distinction is based on its superb view of the High Stile range flanked by the valleys of Ennerdale and Buttermere, a magnificent prospect; but this is a view as well seen from the west slope, around which the path curves, as from the top. This western slope is broad and sprawling, part of it declining to Ennerdale and part re-shaping into the undulating summit of Haystacks; in sharp contrast, the eastern is abruptly cut away in cliffs falling into the great upland basin of Gillercomb. On this side any attempt to determine the boundaries separating this and the adjoining fells of Grey Knotts and Green Gable must be purely arbitrary, the long craggy wall of Gillercomb Head extending the length of all three, but without any dividing watercourses; an unusual arrangement.

Of the fells on this watershed between Windy Gap and Honister, Brandreth is geographically the most important, being the only one to feed three distinct river systems — Derwent, Liza and Cocker.

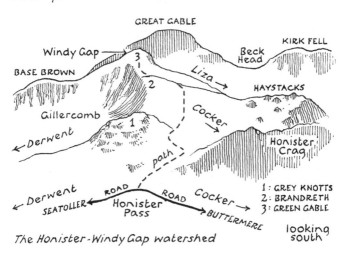

The Honister-Windy Gap watershed

looking south

1: GREY KNOTTS
2: BRANDRETH
3: GREEN GABLE

MAP

The map is extended to the north to include the old quarry tramway, by which the approach from Honister Pass or Gatesgarth is usually made.

N

continuation FLEETWITH PIKE 4

GATESGARTH

HONISTER PASS

foundations of Drum House

Dubs hut Quarry

old tramway

Dubs Bottom

Green Crag

Black Beck

continuation HAYSTACKS 4

1700
1800
1900
2000

continuation GREY KNOTTS 3

Blackbeck Tarn

Great Round How

1600

1700

GREY KNOTTS

tarns

2100

ONE MILE

1800

X post

2200

2300

Brin Crag

Tongue Beck

River Liza

continuation GREEN GABLE 3

1200

1300
1400
1500
1600
1700
1800
1900

The Tongue

Moses Trod

2100

X fold

BRANDRETH
2344

cairned path

1800
1700
1600

Gillercomb

Sourmilk Gill

continuation BASE BROWN 5

2000

2200
2300

continuation GREEN GABLE 3

The three paths on the sprawling western flank of Brandreth are of special interest to walkers.

Starting as one from the Drum House, each has a distinct objective: one aims for Great Gable, another for Wasdale, and the third for Ennerdale. The first is a popular and well-trodden way; the second, less known, is Moses Trod, a very quiet route of great charm; and the third is mainly used by hostellers passing between the Honister and Black Sail Youth Hostels. The point of divergence of the first and third occurs at an angle in the path, a rocky corner with a good view. Moses Trod has no obvious start at its north end, and needs to be hunted; this old pony-track is of unique interest and it is given a page to itself in the Great Gable chapter, page 7

ASCENT FROM HONISTER PASS
1150 feet of ascent : 2 miles

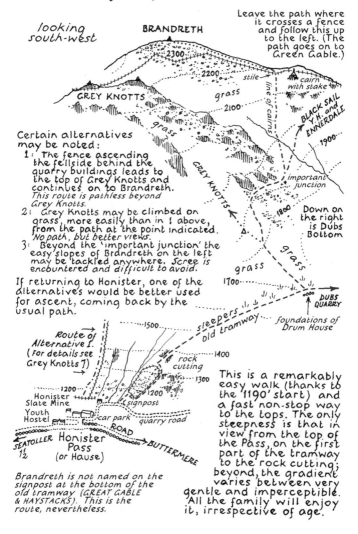

looking south-west

BRANDRETH

Leave the path where it crosses a fence and follow this up to the left. (The path goes on to Green Gable.)

2300

2200

stile · line of cairns

grass

cairn with stake

GREY KNOTTS

2100

BLACK SAIL Y.H. and ENNERDALE

grass

grass

1900

GREY KNOTTS

important junction

Down on the right is Dubs Bottom

1800

grass

1700

grass

DUBS QUARRY

sleepers · old tramway

foundations of Drum House

1500

rock cutting

1400

1300

Certain alternatives may be noted:

1: The fence ascending the fellside behind the quarry buildings leads to the top of Grey Knotts and continues on to Brandreth. *This route is pathless beyond Grey Knotts.*

2: Grey Knotts may be climbed on grass, more easily than in 1 above, from the path at the point indicated. *No path, but better views.*

3: Beyond the 'important junction' the easy slopes of Brandreth on the left may be tackled anywhere. *Scree is encountered and difficult to avoid.*

If returning to Honister, one of the alternatives would be better used for ascent, coming back by the usual path.

Route of Alternative 1. (For details see Grey Knotts 7)

1200

Honister Slate Mine

Youth Hostel

1200

signpost

car park

quarry road

ROAD

SEATOLLER 1½

Honister Pass (or Hause)

BUTTERMERE

This is a remarkably easy walk (thanks to the 1190' start) and a fast non-stop way to the tops. The only steepness is that in view from the top of the Pass, on the first part of the tramway to the rock cutting; beyond, the gradient varies between very gentle and imperceptible. All the family will enjoy it, irrespective of age.

Brandreth is not named on the signpost at the bottom of the old tramway (GREAT GABLE & HAYSTACKS). This is the route, nevertheless.

ASCENT FROM GATESGARTH
2,000 feet of ascent : 3 miles

BRANDRETH

Gillercomb Head

GREAT GABLE

2300

2200

2100

tarns

2000

WASDALE

stile

1900

1800

ENNERDALE

On the final section,
alongside the fence,
three important paths
are crossed. The first is the
Honister-Ennerdale track;
the second, less distinct, is
'Moses Trod', heading for
Wasdale; and the third is
the well-blazed Honister-
Great Gable 'highway'.

awkward
stile

Great
Round How

fine cliffs of
good clean rock

Hereabouts
are many iron posts
embedded in rock and
marking the Lonsdale
Estate boundary.

The wide hollow on this
side is Dubs Bottom.

1600

indistinct
junction

HONISTER

1600

HAYSTACKS

Little Round
How

Green Crag

Dubs
Quarry
(disused)

Dubs
Hut

old
quarry

1400

1200

1100

1000

900

Black Beck

Cross Warnscale Beck
by the footbridge where
Black Beck joins in, and
use the old path on the far
bank, an interesting test in
route-finding over rough
ground. Alternatively the
beck may be crossed by
the stepping stones below
Dubs Hut. In addition there is
a third crossing point between the
two, but this is more difficult. The three
routes unite below Little Round How.
Elsewhere, Warnscale Beck runs deep in
an impassable and dangerous ravine.

falls

Warnscale Beck

800

700

600

500

Warnscale
Bottom

ruin

bracken

looking
south-east

easy level walking

Great Round How

Unlike most mountain climbs,
the interest and excitement
of this walk occur in
the first thousand
feet of ascent.

ROAD

Gatesgarth

car park

HONISTER PASS
SEATOLLER 3

Gatesgarthdale Beck

ASCENT FROM ENNERDALE
(BLACK SAIL YOUTH HOSTEL)
1400 feet of ascent : 1¾ miles

looking east

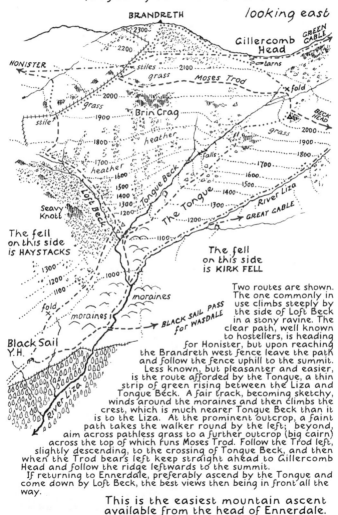

Two routes are shown. The one commonly in use climbs steeply by the side of Loft Beck in a stony ravine. The clear path, well known to hostellers, is heading for Honister, but upon reaching the Brandreth west fence leave the path and follow the fence uphill to the summit. Less known, but pleasanter and easier, is the route afforded by the Tongue, a thin strip of green rising between the Liza and Tongue Beck. A fair track, becoming sketchy, winds around the moraines and then climbs the crest, which is much nearer Tongue Beck than it is to the Liza. At the prominent outcrop, a faint path takes the walker round by the left; beyond, aim across pathless grass to a further outcrop (big cairn) across the top of which runs Moses Trod. Follow the Trod left, slightly descending, to the crossing of Tongue Beck, and then when the Trod bears left keep straight ahead to Gillercomb Head and follow the ridge leftwards to the summit.

If returning to Ennerdale, preferably ascend by the Tongue and come down by Loft Beck, the best views then being in front all the way.

This is the easiest mountain ascent available from the head of Ennerdale.

ASCENT FROM SEATHWAITE
2000 feet of ascent : 2 miles

The hollow of Gillercomb Head contains three small tarns. The regular path from Honister to Great Gable crosses the depression, rounding the tarns in a sharp curve.

GREEN GABLE

BRANDRETH

Gillercomb Head

2300

2200   2100
2200
2100
2000
1900
1800
1700
1600
1500

looking west-south-west

GREEN GABLE

Brandreth does not lend itself to a direct frontal attack from the floor of Gillercomb, its defences being crags and rough scree, but there is one line of weakness — a simple grass rake — not apparent until one is looking straight along it from a point on the Green Gable path soon after passing the last rocks of Base Brown. Here cross the stream where five little tributaries join, and further another meeting-place of streams, the right branch of which sets the direction for reaching the ridge at Gillercomb Head. Follow the fence to the summit.

The ascent of Seathwaite Slabs is difficult because there are no hand-holds, but there is an easier way up on the right, passing to the right of a birch tree and to the left of an oak tree.

The fell on this side is GREY KNOTTS

The big cliff over here is Raven Crag (also known as Gillercomb Buttress)

Gillercomb

The fell on this side is BASE BROWN

Sourmilk Gill

1600

1500
1400
1300
1200
1100
gate   1000
900
800
700
600
500

This is unlikely ever to become a popular climb; from Seathwaite there are several far more desirable objectives. It may be noted, however, that Gillercomb Head, reached as shown here, offers the fastest passage over the tops to Ennerdale.

Seathwaite Slabs

R. Derwent
lane
unusual stile

Seathwaite
ROAD

roadside parking

Gillercomb Head

THE SUMMIT

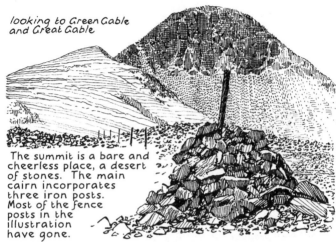

looking to Green Gable and Great Gable

The summit is a bare and cheerless place, a desert of stones. The main cairn incorporates three iron posts. Most of the fence posts in the illustration have gone.

DESCENTS: For HONISTER PASS direct, the fence heading north-east across Grey Knotts is a perfect guide; keep on north-east at a junction of fences. If an easier path is preferred, go down by the western fence for a quarter-mile to join a broad cairned path and turn to the right along it for Honister *via* the Drum House. For BUTTERMERE *via* Warnscale, use this route but turn left at the Drum House. For ENNERDALE, continue along the western fence beyond the first path for another quarter-mile (ignoring a thin track crossing midway) and turn left downhill along a fair path with cairns. For BORROWDALE, head south until the Honister—Gable 'highway' is met and go left along it to the nearby depression of Gillercomb Head, where there are three tarns. Leave the ridge here to go left down a grass slope into Gillercomb and cross the beck to join the Sourmilk Gill path for Seathwaite.

RIDGE ROUTES

To GREY KNOTTS, 2287': ½ mile : NE
Depression at 2250': 50 feet of ascent
Follow the fence north-east and arrival on Grey Knotts is inevitable.

To GREEN GABLE, 2628': 1 mile: S
Depression (Gillercomb Head) at 2160': 450 feet of ascent
Head in a southerly direction to join the Honister—Great Gable path, which is distinct and well-cairned on the long climb to the top of Green Gable.

ONE MILE

THE VIEW

Brandreth's position on the Derwent-Cocker-Liza watershed is sufficient guarantee of a commanding view, and this is extensive in all directions except south, where the two Gables form a near and lofty horizon. Best of all the objects in view are the Grasmoor fells in the north-west, soaring in splendid array from deeply-inurned Crummock Water. Pillar and High Stile are also well displayed. Scafell Pike is hidden behind Green Gable. The conspicuous pyramid on Glaramara, left of the summit, is Combe Head.

For photographic purposes note that the beautiful view north-west is seen to greater advantage from the western slope below the summit. In fine weather, a stroll down by the west fence might well produce the most magnificent picture of the year. Contrast and composition are excellent.

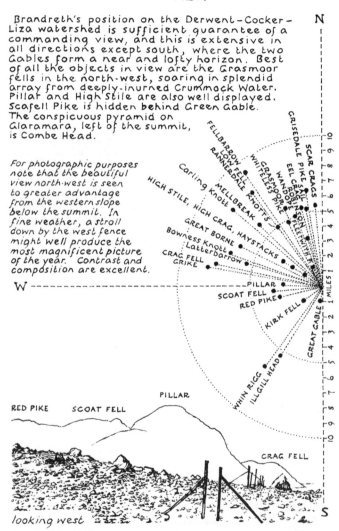

looking west

THE VIEW

Principal Fells

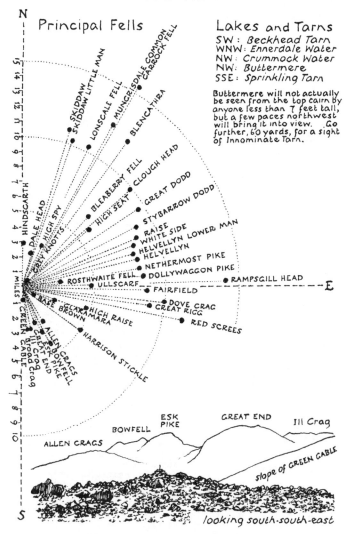

N

15
14
13
12
11
10
9
8
7
6
5
4
3
2
1 MILES
1
2
3
4
GREEN GABLE
5
6
7
8
9
10

S

SKIDDAW
SKIDDAW LITTLE MAN
LONSCALE FELL
MUNGRISDALE COMMON
CARROCK FELL
BLENCATHRA

BLEABERRY FELL
HIGH SEAT
CLOUGH HEAD
GREAT DODD
STYBARROW DODD
RAISE
WHITE SIDE
HELVELLYN LOWER MAN
HELVELLYN
NETHERMOST PIKE
DOLLYWAGGON PIKE
RAMPSGILL HEAD

HINDSCARTH
DALE HEAD
HIGH SPY
GREY KNOTTS

ROSTHWAITE FELL
ULLSCARF
FAIRFIELD
GREAT RIGG
DOVE CRAG
RED SCREES

BASE BROWN
CLARAMARA
HIGH RAISE

ALLEN CRAGS
BOWFELL
ESK PIKE
GREAT END
ILL Crag

HARRISON STICKLE

E

Lakes and Tarns

SW: *Beckhead Tarn*
WNW: *Ennerdale Water*
NW: *Crummock Water*
NW: *Buttermere*
SSE: *Sprinkling Tarn*

Buttermere will not actually
be seen from the top cairn by
anyone less than 7 feet tall,
but a few paces northwest
will bring it into view.   Go
further, 60 yards, for a sight
of Innominate Tarn.

ALLEN CRAGS
BOWFELL
ESK PIKE
GREAT END
Ill Crag

slope of GREEN GABLE

looking south-south-east

Buckbarrow

from Harrow Head

Wasdale Head
▲ SEATALLAN ●
MIDDLE ▲ **Bowderdale**
FELL
▲ BUCKBARROW ●
● Greendale

● Strands
MILES
0   1   2   3   4

Buckbarrow faces the famous Screes across Wast Water and being itself a steep and stony declivity bears some resemblance, if only in miniature. From the road along its base, Buckbarrow seems to be a separate fell, but the name has reference merely to the half-mile rock escarpment, beyond which a grassy plateau is succeeded by a featureless slope rising easily to the top of Buckbarrow's parent fell, Seatallan.

MAP

ONE MILE

N

continuation SEATALLAN 3

continuation SEATALLAN 4

Glade How

BUCKBARROW 1410

fold

1300

1200

1100

800

700

600

500

400

300

Gill Beck

GOSFORTH 4

Harrow Head (farm)

ROAD

Greendale (farm)

WASDALE HEAD 3·4

ASCENT FROM WASDALE
(HARROW HEAD)

1100 feet of ascent: 1 mile

BUCKBARROW

Glade How — 1300

big sheepfold

grass

grass

1200

1100

1000

900

Gill Beck

800

700

600

500

400

GREENDALE

½ mile

pastures

ROAD

Before going on to the highest point turn aside along the top of the craggy spur prominent in the later stages of the climb (for the view)

The front of Buckbarrow is unassailable, but the top of the crags may be reached quite simply by using a convenient path leaving the road alongside Gill Beck 400 yards east of Harrow Head. The path peters out when a stream is reached; cross over the stream and follow it up to the left.

WINDSOR

farm road

Harrow Head

GOSFORTH 4

Tosh Tarn (look over the wall to see it)

This short climb is recommended for its exquisite view of the valley

looking north-east

THE SUMMIT

Sellafield complex
(Calder Hall) ⟶

The highest point in the vicinity of the escarpment is a rocky mound behind the edge of the crags, overlooking the grassy basin below Seatallan. It is undistinguished as a viewpoint in comparison with several less-elevated places along the cliff tops. A quarter of a mile west of north is the prominent cairn on Glade How. (The four cooling towers at Sellafield, shown above, were demolished in 2007.)

DESCENTS : The route recommended for ascent is also the best way down, but if an alternative is wanted it may be found (in clear weather) by skirting the head of Tongues Gills at 1250' to join the path from Greendale Tarn down to the road.

The cairn on Glade How

SCAFELL PIKE

A perched and split boulder (obviously split after perching, probably by frost or lightning)

Buckbarrow from Greendale

THE VIEW

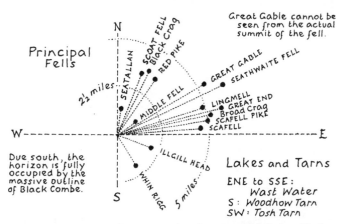

Great Gable cannot be seen from the actual summit of the fell.

Principal Fells

2½ miles

N

SEATALLAN
SCOAT FELL
Black Crag
RED PIKE
MIDDLE FELL
GREAT GABLE
SEATHWAITE FELL
LINGMELL
GREAT END
Broad Crag
SCAFELL PIKE
SCAFELL

W — — — — — — — — — — — — — — — — — — E

Due south, the horizon is fully occupied by the massive outline of Black Combe.

ILLGILL HEAD
WHIN RIGG

S

5 miles

Lakes and Tarns

ENE to SSE:
 Wast Water
S: Woodhow Tarn
SW: Tosh Tarn

It happens frequently that a view from a point below the top of a fell is more attractive than that from the summit, but only rarely that it is more extensive. On Buckbarrow, the best view is obtained from the end of the rocky spur prominently seen in the ascent, this being much finer than that from the summit and actually covering a wider range. Nothing more can be seen from the summit, and a good deal less. The diagrams on this page are based on the end of the spur overlooking Wasdale. The Screes are directly opposite, Wast Water is seen full length and the head of the valley is magnificently closed in by the Scafells.

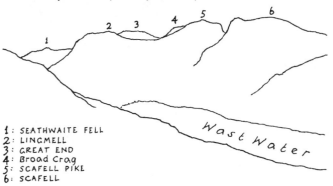

1 : SEATHWAITE FELL
2 : LINGMELL
3 : GREAT END
4 : Broad Crag
5 : SCAFELL PIKE
6 : SCAFELL

The Scafells, from Buckbarrow

Burnbank Fell 1558'

from Waterend

West of Loweswater the high ground of Lakeland gives place to the undulating rural countryside of the quiet Marron valley, and the last height of all is the grassy dome of Burnbank Fell, a cornerstone, a beginning and an end. This is a dull hill, with little to suggest the grandeur of the mountain masses piled inland from it and nothing to divert the attention of a passing traveller. Helped by Holme Wood the northern slope makes a colourful background to Loweswater and has a fine terrace path (not well enough known) contouring high above the lake with charming views, but the sprawling west flank going down to Lamplugh over a lesser height, Owsen Fell, is a moorland lacking interest.

● Mockerkin

Loweswater

Lamplugh ▲

● BURNBANK FELL
▲ BLAKE FELL

MILES

0 1 2 3 4

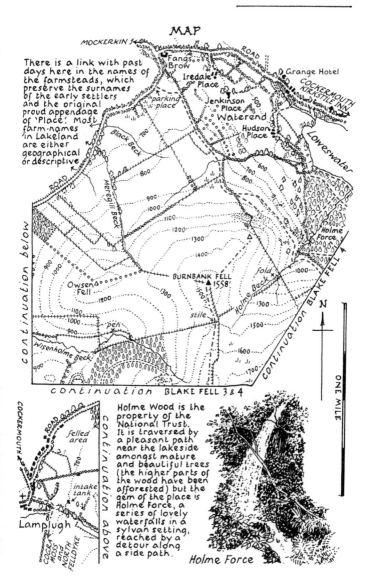

MAP

MOCKERKIN 1

ROAD

There is a link with past days here in the names of the farmsteads, which preserve the surnames of the early settlers and the original proud appendage of 'Place'. Most farm-names in Lakeland are either geographical or descriptive.

Fangs Brow

parking place

Iredale Place

Jenkinson Place

Grange Hotel

COCKERMOUTH
KIRKSTILE INN

Waterend

Hudson Place

Loweswater

Black Beck

700

Meregill Beck

800

1000

700

800

ROAD

continuation below

900

1000

1100

1200

1300

1400

Holme Force

Owsen Fell

1200

1300

1100

1000

900

pen

BURNBANK FELL ▲ 1558

1500

fold

1000

Holme Beck

1300

stile

1500

N

Wisenholme Beck

900

1600

1700

continuation BLAKE FELL 4

continuation BLAKE FELL 3 & 4

ONE MILE

COCKERMOUTH

ROAD

felled area

700

intake tank

continuation above

Lamplugh

COGRA MOSS AND NORTH FELLDYKE

Holme Wood is the property of the National Trust. It is traversed by a pleasant path near the lakeside amongst mature and beautiful trees (the higher parts of the wood have been afforested) but the gem of the place is Holme Force, a series of lovely waterfalls in a sylvan setting, reached by a detour along a side path.

Holme Force

ASCENT FROM WATEREND
1250 feet of ascent : 2¾ miles

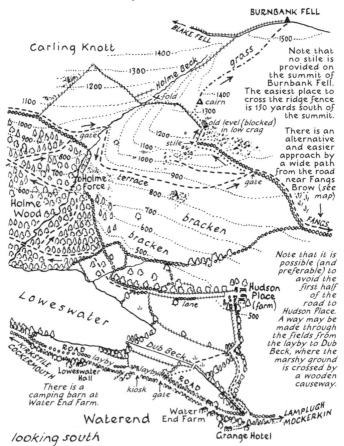

BURNBANK FELL

Carling Knott

Note that no stile is provided on the summit of Burnbank Fell. The easiest place to cross the ridge fence is 150 yards south of the summit.

There is an alternative and easier approach by a wide path from the road near Fangs Brow (see map)

FANGS

BLAKE FELL

grass

Holme Beck

1500

1400

1300

1200

1100

△ cairn 1400
1300

fold

old level (blocked) in low crag

stile

gate

1100
1000

900

800

terrace

Holme Force

700

600

500

Holme Wood

bracken

bracken

Hudson Place (farm)

500

lane

Note that it is possible (and preferable) to avoid the first half of the road to Hudson Place. A way may be made through the fields from the layby to Dub Beck, where the marshy ground is crossed by a wooden causeway.

Loweswater

KIRKSTILE COCKERMOUTH

ROAD

layby

Loweswater Hall

kiosk

Dub Beck

layby

ROAD

gate

Water End Farm

Grange Hotel

LAMPLUGH MOCKERKIN

There is a camping barn at Water End Farm.

Waterend

looking south

This is a dull climb if done straight up the slope, but it can be made interesting and attractive by including in the itinerary a visit to the delightful Holme Force and a stroll along the terrace path. The route recommended is arrowed on the diagram. If views only are the object of the walk there is no point in going on beyond the cairn.

THE VIEW

Landward, the distant view is greatly restricted by the nearby Carling Knott and Blake Fell, which hide all that lies beyond, but seaward there is an uninterrupted panorama from the Isle of Man (seen over St. Bees Head) round to Criffel in Scotland, and nearer the West Cumbrian coastal area is revealed in detail.

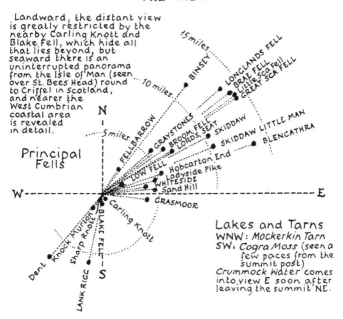

Principal Fells

Lakes and Tarns
WNW: *Mockerkin Tarn*
SW: *Cogra Moss* (seen a few paces from the summit post)
Crummock Water comes into view E soon after leaving the summit NE.

THE SUMMIT

The summit is best described as the gently rounded dome of an upland prairie. An old iron straining post, which has been incorporated into a modern fence, marks the highest point.
DESCENTS : *For Loweswater* follow an indistinct path northeast to a cairn (not seen from the top and sited inconspicuously, yet of some antiquity); below this the slope becomes rough and steeper in the vicinity of old quarries, but after crossing a fence the broad 'terrace' path is joined and a way made down to Hudson Place, or to Watergate through Holme Wood.
For Lamplugh head north and join the bridleway to Fangs Brow. Then follow the road to the left.

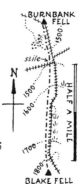

RIDGE ROUTE

TO BLAKE FELL, 1878': 1 mile : SSE, then S
Depression at 1470': 420 feet of ascent

If it is necessary to cross the ridge fence, do so 150 yards south of the summit of Burnbank Fell.

Caw Fell

2288'

Caw Fell, like many of us who lack a good shape and attractive features, objects to having his picture taken and is not at all co-operative as a subject for illustration. From no point of view does the fell look like anything other than a broadly-buttressed sprawling uncorseted graceless lump with a vast flattened summit similarly devoid of a single distinguishing landmark.

In the drawing above, of Caw Fell as seen from Lank Rigg, the great scoop in the western ridge shows prominently. The highest point of the fell occurs above the dark shadow, top left, here seen overtopped by Haycock.

Map

- Ennerdale Bridge
- CRAG FELL ▲
- Gillerthwaite
- LANK RIGG ▲
- CAW FELL ▲
- HAYCOCK ▲
- Thornholme
- Scalderskew
- SEATALLAN ▲
- Calder Bridge
- Greendale
- Gosforth
- Strands

MILES
0 1 2 3 4

NATURAL FEATURES

The magnificent group of mountains between Wasdale and Ennerdale, topped by Pillar and including several other redoubtable peaks, is as rugged and craggy as any in the district, exhibiting steep and precipitous slopes to north and east, where they overlook deep valleys. To south and west, however, this upland area is of entirely different character, declining much more gradually, in easy stages. Mountain gives way to moorland, and the rocky nature of the terrain smooths into wide pastures, slow in descent from the tops and therefore more amiable in gradient; the streams follow long and gentler courses but thread their way through gathering grounds so vast that they quickly assume the proportions of rivers. These are the sheepwalks of Copeland Forest, of Stockdale Moor and of Kinniside Common, rolling grasslands linking the untamed heights with the cultivated valleys — a region uninhabited and unfrequented in this day and age, yet at one time, from evidences that still remain to be seen, the home of primitive man.

Caw Fell occupies much of this territory. It has many unnamed summits, many ridges and many streams. Its ten square miles contain much geographical detail of interest rather than importance, for all its waters ultimately mingle in the Irish Sea off the Seascale coast although to get there they flow in all directions of the compass.

There is not much here to attract walkers whose liking is for rough ground and airy ridges; there is little to excite the senses, nothing of beautiful or dramatic effect. Yet here one can stride out for hour after hour in undisturbed solitude and enjoy invigorating exercise amongst scenery that has not changed since the world began. Only when the lower ground is reached does one become mindful again of the twentieth century; here, spreading like a dark cloak from the valleys are plantations of conifers alongside the ancient settlements of the first Britons.

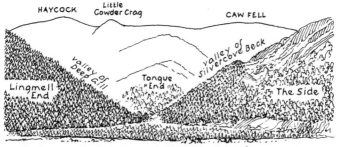

The top of Caw Fell can be seen from a short section only of the walk up Ennerdale, near the first footbridge, where, across the valley, Deep Gill has carved a great opening in the fellside.

Caw Fell 3

MAP

ONE MILE

Caw Fell is a rolling upland of modest height, predominantly grass-covered, and of mainly easy gradients. *But this is a fell that should not be under-estimated.* It is remote from shelter or habitation; in these four pages of maps there is one dwelling only: the isolated farmstead known as Scalderskew. A fair march is needed even to get a foothold on the fell, from any direction, and a long climb follows before the summit is reached. Good advice to those who plan its ascent is to divide the time available by two, and if the top is not gained by half-time *turn back.* An exhausted walker on Caw Fell is in bad trouble. The miles to safety are long and lonely, and the surrounding rivers run wide and fast, unbridged. Before setting out, study the map carefully, noting the many watercourses and ridges that leave the mile-long top, and where they lead in relation to the nearest road, and plan the route in terms of hours. If it is necessary to cross any streams, do so near the source, not lower down. Time spent on a study of the geography on a map, in advance, means time saved on the walk.

N

Ennerdale Water

CONTINUATION CRAC FELL 3

ENNERDALE BRIDGE 4

disused mines

Boathow Crag

stile

gate

Whoap

pool

continuation on opposite page

Red Beck

Short Grain

Red Gill

fold

Worm Gill

Long Grain

old sheepfold

water intake works (disused)

Bleaberry Gill

continuation LANK RIGG 4

Water Intake Works, Worm Gill

continuation on page 5

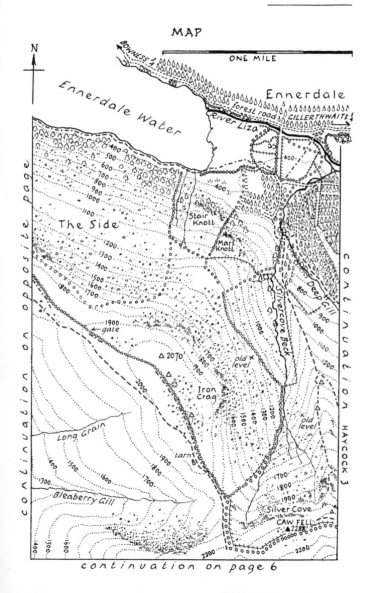

MAP

ONE MILE

continuation on opposite page

continuation HAYCOCK 3

continuation on page 6

Caw Fell 5

MAP

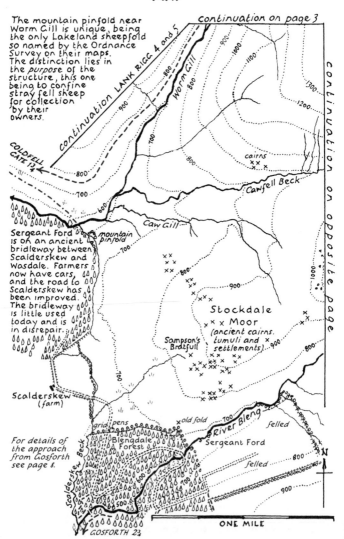

continuation on page 3

The mountain pinfold near Worm Gill is unique, being the only Lakeland sheepfold so named by the Ordnance Survey on their maps. The distinction lies in the *purpose* of the structure, this one being to confine stray fell sheep for collection by their owners.

continuation LANK RIGG 4 and 5

Worm Gill

COLDFELL GATE 13

cairns ××

Cawfell Beck

Caw Gill

Sergeant Ford is on an ancient bridleway between Scalderskew and Wasdale. Farmers now have cars, and the road to Scalderskew has been improved. The bridleway is little used today and is in disrepair.

mountain pinfold

Stockdale Moor (ancient cairns, tumuli and settlements)

Sampson's Bratfull

Scalderskew (farm)

For details of the approach from Gosforth see page 8.

Scalderskew Beck

grid pens

Blengdale Forest

×old fold

River Bleng

Sergeant Ford

felled

felled

continuation on opposite page

N

ONE MILE

GOSFORTH 2½

MAP

continuation on page 4

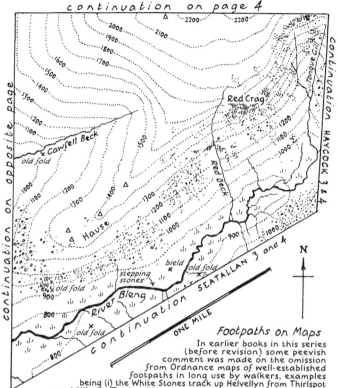

Footpaths on Maps

In earlier books in this series (before revision) some peevish comment was made on the omission from Ordnance maps of well-established footpaths in long use by walkers, examples being (i) the White Stones track up Helvellyn from Thirlspot and (ii) the Taylorgill route to Sty Head from Seathwaite.

In revised editions of the 1" map from 1963 onwards, however, footpaths galore appear for the first time; but, unfortunately, many of them are not visible on the ground: in other words, footpaths are now shown that do not exist, although a right of way is not disputed. For example, without going beyond the environs of Caw Fell, (a) there is no path visible along the north bank of Long Grain; (b) nor on the north bank of the Bleng above Sergeant Ford; (c) nor, continuously, to the ridge from Tongue End; and (d) the paths on the adjacent Tewit How are fictional. Rights of way are all very well, but they cannot be seen and they do not help and guide feet over rough ground.

In this matter of indicating footpaths on maps, most walkers will agree that errors of commission are even worse than errors of omission: it is better for one's peace of mind to find a distinct path one does not expect than to fail to find a path one is told to expect.

A tumulus

The Antiquities of Stockdale Moor

In the uncultivated areas of the Lake District, many evidences remain of the former existence of primitive habitations and settlements, and these are usually to be found on open moorlands around the 900'-1200' contours at the upper fringe of the early forests, lying between the swampy valleys, as they would then be, and the inhospitable mountains. These evidences are very profuse in the area of Stockdale Moor and on the nearby slopes of Town Bank (Lank Rigg) and Seatallan. Here are to be seen the walled enclosures, hut circles, cairns, clearance-heaps, barrows and tumuli of a pre-historic community, with traces of cultivation terraces. This is a great field of exploration for the archaeologist, and much work has been done and recorded, notably in the Transactions of the local Cumberland and Westmorland Antiquarian and Archaeological Society.

Walkers should not visit the area, however, expecting to see a pageant of the past unfold before their eyes. Knowledge and imagination are necessary to recognise and understand the remains. A person both uninformed and unobservant may tramp across Stockdale Moor and notice nothing to distinguish his surroundings from those of any other boulder-strewn upland. Indeed, except for the purposes of a study of the subject, a special visit to the area cannot really be recommended: the scenery is drab and desolate, there is no quick run-off for water on the flattish ground and consequently most of it is marsh; on a wet day the moor is downright depressing.

A cairn

A name that arouses interest on the map of Stockdale Moor is *Sampson's Bratfull*, a concentration of stones dropped from the apron of a giant as he strode across the moor. So legend has it, but learned sources prefer the opinion that this is the site of a tumulus or barrow (a burial place), giving its measurements as 35 yards long and 12 yards wide tapering to the west end.

An enclosure

ASCENT FROM BLENGDALE LODGE
2100 feet of ascent : 5½ miles (7½ from Gosforth)

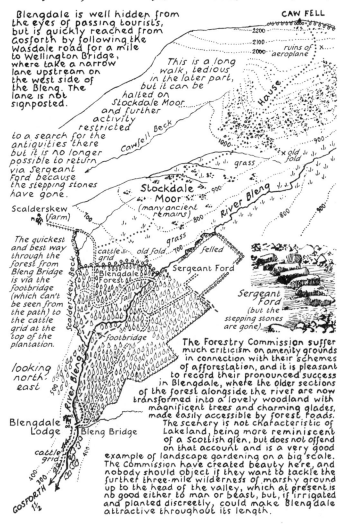

CAW FELL

Blengdale is well hidden from the eyes of passing tourists, but is quickly reached from Gosforth by following the Wasdale road for a mile to Wellington Bridge, where take a narrow lane upstream on the west side of the Bleng. The lane is not signposted.

This is a long walk, tedious in the later part, but it can be halted on Stockdale Moor and further activity restricted to a search for the antiquities there but it is no longer possible to return via Sergeant Ford because the stepping stones have gone.

2200
2100
2000
ruins of ✕ aeroplane

Hause

Cawfell Beck

1000   ✕ old fold   900

grass

Scalderskew (farm)

Stockdale Moor (many ancient remains)

800   River Bleng   800

700

The quickest and best way through the forest from Bleng Bridge is via the footbridge (which can't be seen from the path) to the cattle grid at the top of the plantation.

cattle grid   old fold   700   felled

grass

Blengdale Forest

Sergeant Ford

fall

footbridge

Sergeant Ford (but the stepping stones are gone)

looking north-east

River Bleng

500

Blengdale Lodge   Bleng Bridge

cattle grid

400   300

GOSFORTH 1½

The Forestry Commission suffer much criticism on amenity grounds in connection with their schemes of afforestation, and it is pleasant to record their pronounced success in Blengdale, where the older sections of the forest alongside the river are now transformed into a lovely woodland with magnificent trees and charming glades, made easily accessible by forest roads. The scenery is not characteristic of Lakeland, being more reminiscent of a Scottish glen, but does not offend on that account and is a very good example of landscape gardening on a big scale. The Commission have created beauty here, and nobody should object if they want to tackle the further three-mile wilderness of marshy ground up to the head of the valley, which at present is no good either to man or beast, but, if irrigated and planted discreetly, could make Blengdale attractive throughout its length.

ASCENT FROM KINNISIDE STONE CIRCLE
1850 feet of ascent : 6 miles

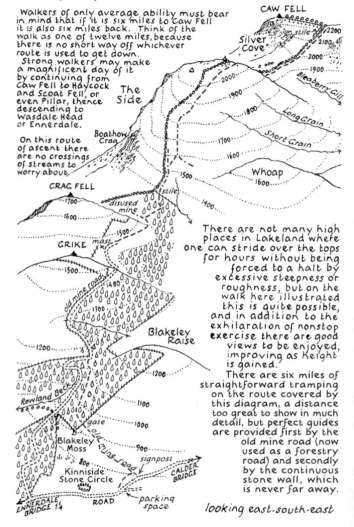

Walkers of only average ability must bear in mind that if it is six miles to Caw Fell it is also six miles back. Think of the walk as one of twelve miles, because there is no short way off whichever route is used to get down.

Strong walkers may make a magnificent day of it by continuing from Caw Fell to Haycock and Scoat Fell, or even Pillar, thence descending to Wasdale Head or Ennerdale.

On this route of ascent there are no crossings of streams to worry about.

CAW FELL

Silver Cove

stile 2200

2100

2000

1900

Bleaberry Gill

Long Grain

Short Grain

The Side

Boathow Crag

2000

1900

1800

1700

1600

1500

Whoap
1600

CRAG FELL

1700

stile

1400

disused mine

1600

1500

GRIKE

mast

1500

1300

old mine road

1400

Blakeley Raise

There are not many high places in Lakeland where one can stride over the tops for hours without being forced to a halt by excessive steepness or roughness, but on the walk here illustrated this is quite possible, and in addition to the exhilaration of nonstop exercise there are good views to be enjoyed, improving as height is gained.

1200

1200

1100

Rowland Beck

gate

1000

old mine road

Blakeley Moss

900

signpost

CALDER BRIDGE

800

Kinniside Stone Circle

parking space

ENNERDALE BRIDGE 14

ROAD

There are six miles of straightforward tramping on the route covered by this diagram, a distance too great to show in much detail, but perfect guides are provided first by the old mine road (now used as a forestry road) and secondly by the continuous stone wall, which is never far away.

looking east-south-east

ASCENT FROM ENNERDALE
(LOW GILLERTHWAITE)
1950 feet of ascent : 2¾ miles

Little Gowder Crag ← HAYCOCK — CAW FELL

2200 — 2100 — 2000 — 1900 — 1800 — 1700

Great Cove — Silver Cove

1500 — × old level

1500 — 1400 — 1300 — 1200 — 1100 — 1000 — 900

heather

Deep Gill

heather

Silvercove Beck

→ Tongue End — falls

This is not only the shortest way from valley-level to the summit of Caw Fell, but the best. The river and woodland and gorge scenery in the vicinity of the confluence of Deep Gill and Silvercove Beck is charming, the more so because the spot is known to very few and rarely visited; indeed, the side opening in which it is situated, being across the valley from the Ennerdale highway, may escape the notice altogether of travellers thereon. The footbridge over the Liza is useful for those coming down the valley from the east or when the Irish bridge is covered in water. The public path leading onto Tongue End from the confluence of Deep Gill and Silvercove Beck is in danger of becoming lost in a jungle of young trees. A stile is provided in the forest fence, but unless the path is kept in use it may be lost.

This route is especially worth noting as a different approach to the main ridge, for the Pillar group. Permitted ways out of the floor of Ennerdale are few and far between since afforestation: this is the easiest route for gradients and certainly the most beautiful.

This plantation has been felled, but natural regeneration has resulted in small trees growing too close to the path.

Here the path encounters a sudden drop that is difficult to negotiate.

Dowdell Beck

forest road — SOUTH SHORE OF ENNERDALE WATER

for additional notes on this route see Haycock 7

Irish bridge (a very low bridge without parapets which serves as a ford when the river is high).

GILLERTHWAITE (and ENNERDALE Y.H.) ← — valley road — → BOWNESS POINT 2

Char Dub (River Liza)

looking SOUTH

THE SUMMIT

The highest of the several tops in the territory of Caw Fell is immediately above Silver Cove, at 2288', on an unattractive stony plateau bisected by the crumbling wall (part of the 'Ennerdale fence') that runs for miles hereabouts along the south Ennerdale watershed and is a depressing ornament in fair weather but a reliable friend in foul. Sharp eyes will discern fragments of an aeroplane a quarter of a mile south of the wall; otherwise there are no items of interest and very little to warrant a prolonged halt.

DESCENTS : For the head of Ennerdale Water, reverse the route of ascent over Tongue End in preference to a more direct course alongside Silvercove Beck; for the foot of the lake follow the northwest ridge to Crag Fell and descend through the plantation; avoid an intermediate line down The Side, which is very rough. For Gosforth use the southwest ridge (the Hause) to reach Blengdale Lodge, but if, in mist, this route cannot be located, it is reassuring to know that all ways off down the western slopes are free from hazard.

RIDGE ROUTES

To HAYCOCK, 2618': 1 mile : E, then SE
  450 feet of ascent : Depression at 2210'
    An interesting move to rougher country
There is no danger of going astray, however bad the weather, the wall leading directly to the top of Haycock over ground at first grassy but becoming very stony. Little Gowder Crag is an interesting feature *en route.*

The boundary wall is interrupted by the low crags of Little Gowder Crag.

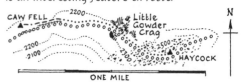

To CRAG FELL, 1716': 3½ miles : W, then NNW, NW and NNW
  550 feet of ascent : Depressions at 1900' and 1325'
    Too far unless heading thereafter for Ennerdale Bridge
This is a long walk over easy ground, as shown on the maps on Crag Fell 5 and 6. For much of its length the path runs parallel with the wall along the northwest ridge, of which Crag Fell is really a continuation. The path to Crag Fell from the old mine road is easily missed: look out for a cairn at the beginning of a clearing.

THE VIEW

Caw Fell is sufficiently removed from the dominant heights of the Pillar group to permit a fairly good all-round view; it is not, however, particularly attractive in any direction.

The wall across the top obstructs the panorama and those fells named in the diagram south of Scafell can only be seen by looking over it, all the others being visible from the cairn.

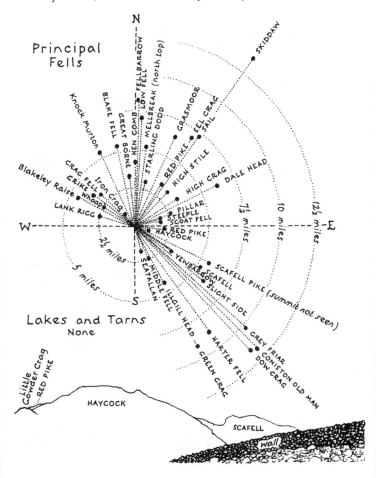

Principal Fells

Lakes and Tarns
None

Crag Fell

1716'

from Bowness Point

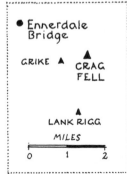

Ennerdale Bridge

GRIKE ▲   ▲ CRAG FELL

▲ LANK RIGG

MILES

0   1   2

from Ennerdale Bridge

NATURAL FEATURES

Crag Fell is a fine, abrupt height, prominently in view on the approach to Ennerdale from the west, its configuration being such that it may easily be, and often is, mistaken for Pillar by those who have not studied their maps sufficiently, the illusion being strengthened by the conspicuous excrescence of rock on its north slope, which, seen in profile, might, at a glance, be thought to be the famous Pillar Rock. This comparison is a compliment to Crag Fell because Pillar is in fact a greater mountain by far and its Rock much more impressive than anything Crag Fell can show. Yet the north face of Crag Fell, falling sheer into Ennerdale Water, is an arresting sight; it is the dull hinterland of smooth grassy slopes around the source of the River Calder that detracts from all round merit. In the rocky headland of Anglers' Crag, jutting into the lake; in the curious pinnacles of Revelin Crag, above; and not least in the tremendous ravine of Ben Gill, are centred the attractions of Crag Fell, and all face north. Elsewhere is moorland with nothing of interest but the few decayed remains of the former Cragfell Iron Ore Mines.

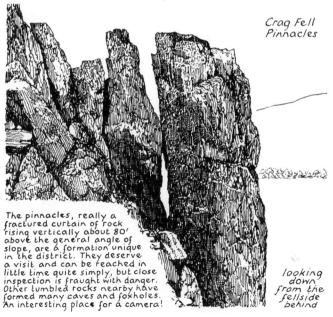

Crag Fell
Pinnacles

The pinnacles, really a fractured curtain of rock rising vertically about 80' above the general angle of slope, are a formation unique in the district. They deserve a visit and can be reached in little time quite simply, but close inspection is fraught with danger. Other tumbled rocks nearby have formed many caves and foxholes. An interesting place for a camera!

looking
down
from the
fellside
behind

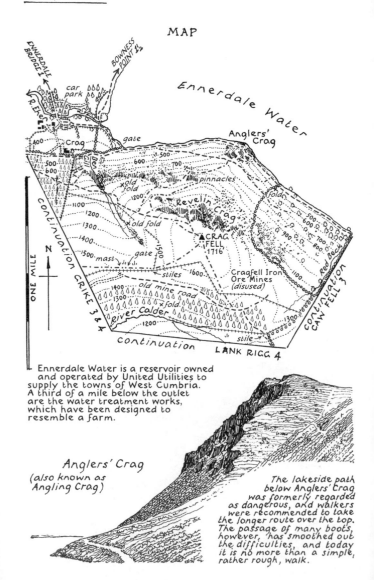

MAP

ENNERDALE BRIDGE

BOWNESS POINT 1½

car park

Ennerdale Water

R. Ehen

Crag

gate

Anglers' Crag

400

500
600

600

700

500

pinnacles

old fold

1200

Revelin Crag

CRAG FELL 1716

folds

600

700

800

900

1000

1100

Continuation GRIKE 3 & 4

1100

1200

1300

1400

1500 mast

gate

1500

old fold

stiles

1600

Cragfell Iron Ore Mines (disused)

Red Beck

ONE MILE

N

1400
1300
1200

old mine road

fold

1100

Continuation CAW FELL 3

River Calder

1200

continuation

stile

1300

LANK RIGG 4

Continuation

Ennerdale Water is a reservoir owned and operated by United Utilities to supply the towns of West Cumbria. A third of a mile below the outlet are the water treatment works, which have been designed to resemble a farm.

Anglers' Crag
(also known as Angling Crag)

The lakeside path below Anglers' Crag was formerly regarded as dangerous, and walkers were recommended to take the longer route over the top. The passage of many boots, however, has smoothed out the difficulties, and today it is no more than a simple, rather rough, walk.

ASCENT FROM ENNERDALE BRIDGE
1350 feet of ascent · 2½ miles

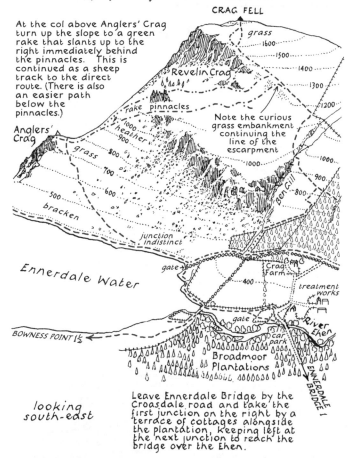

At the col above Anglers' Crag turn up the slope to a green rake that slants up to the right immediately behind the pinnacles. This is continued as a sheep track to the direct route. (There is also an easier path below the pinnacles.)

CRAG FELL

grass
1600
1500
1400
1300
1200

Revelin Crag

rake pinnacles

Note the curious grass embankment continuing the line of the escarpment

Anglers' Crag

grass
1000
heather
900
800
700
600
500
bracken

1000

1000
900
800

Ben Gill

junction indistinct

Ennerdale Water

gate

Crag Farm

400

treatment works

BOWNESS POINT 1½

gate

car park

River Ehen

ENNERDALE BRIDGE 1

Broadmoor Plantations

looking south-east

Leave Ennerdale Bridge by the Croasdale road and take the first junction on the right by a terrace of cottages alongside the plantation, keeping left at the next junction to reach the bridge over the Ehen.

All the routes shown here are difficult to follow. It is much better to use the path through the plantation, either *via* Crag Farm or over the footbridge. (See the diagram on Grike 5.)

If it is desired to visit the pinnacles, take the top route on the left of the diagram.

RIDGE ROUTES

ONE MILE

N

CRAG FELL ▲

1500 mast 1400 stile

▲ GRIKE

1500 1600

1300 old mine road

CRAG FELL

1500 1600 stile 1400

old mine road

1300

1300 1400 stile

1500 gate 1600 1700

To GRIKE, 1601': 1 mile:
SW, then W
Depression at 1450'
150 feet of ascent

The old mine road cannot be used because of the fence, and it is impossible to avoid marshy ground.

To LANK RIGG',
1775': 2 miles:
SSE, then SW
Depressions at
1325' & 1385'
750 feet
of ascent
Start as for Caw Fell but veer off over pathless grasslands to Whoap and Lank Rigg.

pool

1800

gate 1900

Whoap 1671'

1500 1600

1300 1400 1500

1400

LANK RIGG

1700 1400

To CAW FELL,
2288': 3½ miles:
SSE, then SE, SSE & E
Depressions at 1325' and 1900'
1200 feet of ascent
Head south-east, crossing the forest fence and the old mine road. Thereafter the wall is continuous to (and beyond) Caw Fell summit, but it is better to use the path that runs parallel with the wall to the south.

continuation on opposite page

THE SUMMIT

Sellafield complex
(Calder Hall)

The top is undulating and grassy, with a cairn crowning the highest of several mounds and nothing of interest nearby.

DESCENTS : The best way off is to the west-north-west and through the plantation, doubling back to the right for the car park or crossing the footbridge for Ennerdale Bridge. (See the diagram on Grike 5.) In mist, the old mine road gives a safe passage to the Cold Fell road. To reach it head south-west from the summit, using the gate shown on the map on page 3.

THE VIEW

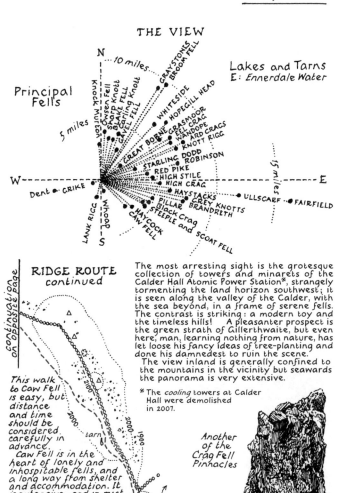

N
10 miles

Principal
Fells

5 miles

Lakes and Tarns
E: Ennerdale Water

GRAYSTONES
BROOK FELL
WHITESIDE
HOPEGILL HEAD
GRASMOOR
EEL CRAG
WANDOPE
YARD CRAGS
KNOTT RIGG
ROBINSON
STARLING DODD
RED PIKE
HIGH STILE
HIGH CRAG
HAYSTACKS
GREY KNOTTS
PILLAR
BRANDRETH
Black Crag
STEEPLE and SCOAT FELL
CAW FELL

KNOCK MURTON
OWSEN FELL
SHARP KNOTT
BLAKE FELL
GAVEL FELL
CARLING KNOTT
GREAT BORNE

W

15 miles

E

Dent ● GRIKE

LANK RIGG
WHOAP

ULLSCARF
FAIRFIELD

S

RIDGE ROUTE
continued

Continuation on opposite page

This walk
to Caw Fell
is easy, but
distance
and time
should be
considered
carefully in
advance.

Caw Fell is in the
heart of lonely and
inhospitable fells, and
a long way from shelter
and accommodation. It
is extensive, and in mist,
if sight of the wall is lost,
there may be difficulty
in taking bearings on
the indefinite top.

Before setting out for
Caw Fell there should
be a well-thought-out
plan for getting off it.

2000
tarn
1900
2000

CAW FELL ▲ 2200
stile
2200
2200

The most arresting sight is the grotesque
collection of towers and minarets of the
Calder Hall Atomic Power Station*, strangely
tormenting the land horizon southwest; it
is seen along the valley of the Calder, with
the sea beyond, in a frame of serene fells.
The contrast is striking: a modern toy and
the timeless hills!   A pleasanter prospect is
the green strath of Gillerthwaite, but even
here, man, learning nothing from nature, has
let loose his fancy ideas of tree-planting and
done his damnedest to ruin the scene.
   The view inland is generally confined to
the mountains in the vicinity but seawards
the panorama is very extensive.

* The *cooling* towers at Calder
  Hall were demolished
  in 2007.

*Another
of the
Crag Fell
Pinnacles*

Fellbarrow

1363'

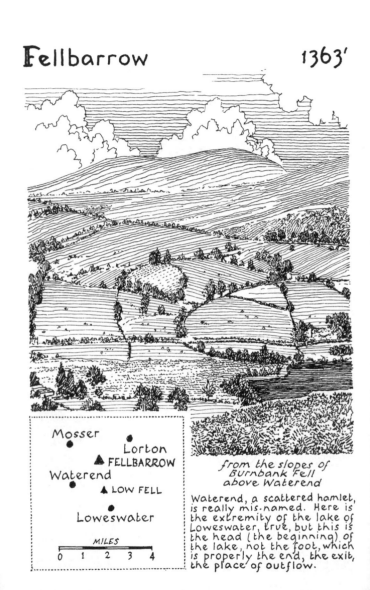

*from the slopes of
Burnbank Fell
above Waterend*

Mosser
Lorton
▲ FELLBARROW
Waterend
▲ LOW FELL
Loweswater

MILES
0 1 2 3 4

Waterend, a scattered hamlet, is really mis-named. Here is the extremity of the lake of Loweswater, true, but this is the head (the beginning) of the lake, not the foot, which is properly the end, the exit, the place of outflow.

NATURAL FEATURES

The Vale of Lorton is sheltered on the west by a low range of grassy rounded hills uncharacteristic of Lakeland and not really part of it, this despite having southern roots in Loweswater amid scenery that is wholly typical of the district.   The range has several tops of approximately the same height, none of them distinctive because the undulations are shallow, but the northern half builds up on all sides to the massive flattened dome of Fellbarrow.

The extensive slopes of grass, which serve as a vast sheep pasture, decline gradually westwards to quiet Mosser, northwards to Brandlingill and eastwards to the valley of the Cocker, all farming country.   The scenery is pleasant but unexciting. The underlying rock is slate, and rarely exposed to view below its smooth green covering. There are traces of an old plantation in a basin on the east, of which a few straggly trees remain, and a still-flourishing wood on the side of the abrupt headland of Dodd nearby.

Southwards, rounded humps succeed each other with little loss of height before a more distinctive shape resolves itself from the rolling acres. This is Low Fell and beyond is Loweswater.

The Fellbarrow range

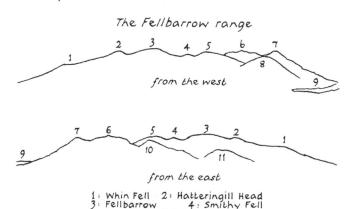

from the west

from the east

1: Whin Fell   2: Hatteringill Head
3: Fellbarrow   4: Smithy Fell
5: Sourfoot Fell   6: Low Fell, north top
7: Low Fell, main top 8: Darling Fell
9: Loweswater   10: Watching Crag 11: Dodd

The traverse of the Fellbarrow range on a clear sunny day is one of the most rewarding of the simpler fellwalks, although not often undertaken. Its particular merit, apart from the easy going, is the beautiful view of the Buttermere-Crummock valley, which is seen to perfection.

To enjoy it fully, walk the range from north to south.

MAP

Fellbarrow is extensive, its higher parts forming a vast sheep pasture and the lower slopes being cultivated for dairy farming. Woodlands and copses are a feature of the eastern flank.

There are many quiet and attractive hamlets just away from the main tourist routes in Lakeland that are seldom visited and remain unspoiled.

On the road between Mosser and Brandlingill, in a delightfully wooded setting, is Aikbank Mill, a neat and colourful group of buildings that arrests attention and cries aloud to be put on canvas.

Artists of Cockermouth, arise and go to Aikbank Mill!

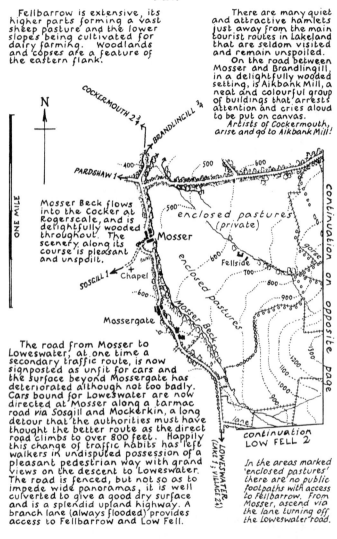

Mosser Beck flows into the Cocker at Rogerscale, and is delightfully wooded throughout. The scenery along its course is pleasant and unspoilt.

The road from Mosser to Loweswater, at one time a secondary traffic route, is now signposted as unfit for cars and the surface beyond Mossergate has deteriorated although not too badly. Cars bound for Loweswater are now directed at Mosser along a tarmac road via Sosgill and Mockerkin, a long detour that the authorities must have thought the better route as the direct road climbs to over 800 feet. Happily this change of traffic habits has left walkers in undisputed possession of a pleasant pedestrian way with grand views on the descent to Loweswater. The road is fenced, but not so as to impede wide panoramas, it is well culverted to give a good dry surface and is a splendid upland highway. A branch lane (always flooded) provides access to Fellbarrow and Low Fell.

In the areas marked 'enclosed pastures' there are no public footpaths with access to Fellbarrow. From Mosser, ascend via the lane turning off the Loweswater road.

MAP

The northern boundary of Fellbarrow may be regarded for fellwalking purposes as defined by the old road between Lorton and Mosser. Sometimes referred to as the Whinfell Road, this highway does not skirt the base of the fell but cuts across its shoulder at 700 feet. It is not signposted at either end, but, in spite of a rough surface, is negotiable by cars, a fact not generally known, and consequently it provides a first class terrace route for walkers with wide views northwards over the lower valley of the Cocker.

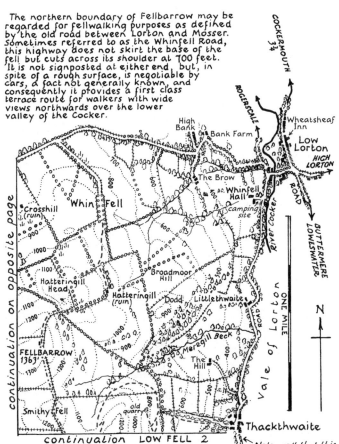

The Mosser-Loweswater old road, the Whinfell Road, and the Thackthwaite by-road can be linked to provide a good circular tour around Low Fell and Fellbarrow for walkers based anywhere on the perimeter, with very little traffic interference — a 9-mile exercise for the legs very suitable for a day when cloud or bad weather puts the tops out of bounds.

Note well that this is NOT the main road along the Vale of Lorton; it is the western by-road, and the bridge at Lorton is the only link.

ASCENT FROM THACKTHWAITE
ROUTE A : 1000 feet of ascent : 1¼ miles
ROUTE B : 1150 feet of ascent : 2 miles

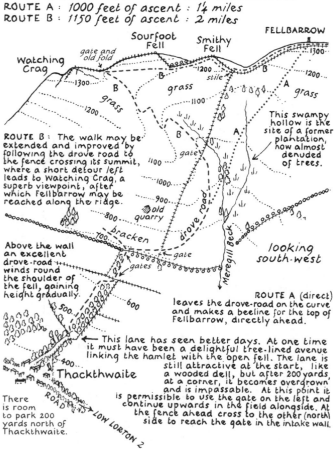

FELLBARROW

Sourfoot Fell

Smithy Fell

Watching Crag

gate and old fold

1300

1200

1300

1200

B

grass

1200

B

B

grass

stile

1200

A

1300

1200

grass

1100

ROUTE B: The walk may be extended and improved by following the drove road to the fence crossing its summit, where a short detour *left* leads to Watching Crag, a superb viewpoint, after which Fellbarrow may be reached along the ridge.

This swampy hollow is the site of a former plantation, now almost denuded of trees.

gate

A

1100

1000

900

800

old quarry

drove road

Above the wall an excellent drove-road winds round the shoulder of the fell, gaining height gradually.

bracken

700

gate

gates

looking south-west

Meregill Beck

ROUTE A (direct) leaves the drove-road on the curve and makes a beeline for the top of Fellbarrow, directly ahead.

500

600

← This lane has seen better days. At one time it must have been a delightful tree-lined avenue linking the hamlet with the open fell. The lane is still attractive at the start, like a wooded dell, but after 200 yards, at a corner, it becomes overgrown and is impassable. At this point it is permissible to use the gate on the left and continue upwards in the field alongside. At the fence ahead cross to the other (north) side to reach the gate in the intake wall.

400

Thackthwaite

ROAD TO LOW LORTON 2

There is room to park 200 yards north of Thackthwaite.

Thackthwaite, midway between Loweswater and Low Lorton on a quiet by-road and peacefully carrying on its rural activities virtually undisturbed by tourists, is a good place to leave the road for the ascent of Fellbarrow; in fact, with the former route from Low Lorton impracticable, this is now the only approach from the east. The climb is simple and the views excellent if Watching Crag is visited.

THE SUMMIT

Everything there is to see on the summit can be seen at a glance: a rounded swell of grass crossed by a fence, crowned with an Ordnance Survey column with a pile of large stones next to it. Note, 60 yards west, a collection of stones arranged in a ring. It has no special significance and no history.

THE VIEW

Fellbarrow stands on the fringe of the high country, and to north and west there is a wide and uninterrupted view over the coastal plain and across the Solway Firth to the Scottish hills. Southeast the best thing is the lofty ridge of the Hopegill Head range across the Vale of Lorton.

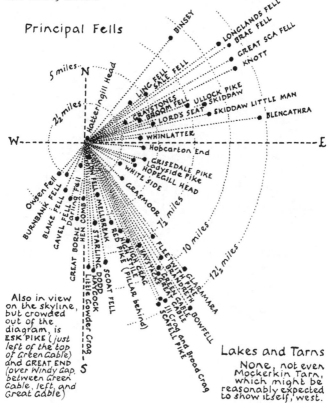

Principal Fells

Also in view on the skyline, but crowded out of the diagram, is ESK PIKE (just left of the top of Green Gable) and GREAT END (over Windy Gap, between Green Gable, left, and Great Gable)

Lakes and Tarns

None, not even Mockerkin Tarn, which might be reasonably expected to show itself, west.

Fleetwith Pike 2126'

from Gatesgarth

- Buttermere

Gatesgarth
●

▲ DALE HEAD

FLEETWITH ▲
PIKE

Seatoller
●

Honister Pass

MILES

0   1   2   3

NATURAL FEATURES

Honister Crag is a landmark of renown, wellknown to Lakeland's visitors and as familiar to those who journey on wheels as to those who travel on foot. This precipice towers dramatically above the road between Borrowdale and Buttermere, a savage wall of rock and heather strewn with natural debris and spoil from the quarry-workings high on the cliff, a place without beauty, a place to daunt the eye and creep the flesh. This huge barrier extends for two miles northwest from the top of Honister Pass, but becomes less intimidating as Gatesgarth is approached.

looking west

1 : The summit
2 : Honister Crag
3 : Honister Pass
4 : Gatesgarthdale Beck

The fell of which Honister Crag is so striking a part is Fleetwith, and its summit, overlooking Buttermere, is Fleetwith Pike, not so well known by name or shape as its illustrious subsidiary but nevertheless associated in the minds of many visitors with a conspicuous white memorial cross on its lower slopes. A smaller company of people, with better discrimination, relate the fell to a supremely beautiful view and a soaring ridge and a wild hollow rimmed by crags: the first is of the three lakes in the Buttermere valley, the second shoots into the sky like an arrow from the fields of Gatesgarth, and the third, Warnscale Bottom, is a natural amphitheatre of impressive proportions. These are the things that identify Fleetwith in the mind of the fellwalker.

looking south-east

1 : The summit
2 : Honister Crag
3 : Northwest ridge
4 : Gatesgarthdale Beck
5 : Warnscale Beck
6 : Warnscale Bottom

The downward slope of the summit, away from and behind the cliffs of Honister, is gently inclined to the upland marsh of Dubs Bottom, beyond which a broad moor rises gradually to Great Gable, the dominating influence hereabouts, of which Fleetwith Pike may be described, geographically, as the northern terminus.

All the Fleetwith streams are headwaters of the River Cocker and flow northwest into Buttermere, the green colour of the water of the lake being attributed to the slate dust carried down by them from the quarries.

Fleetwith Pike 3

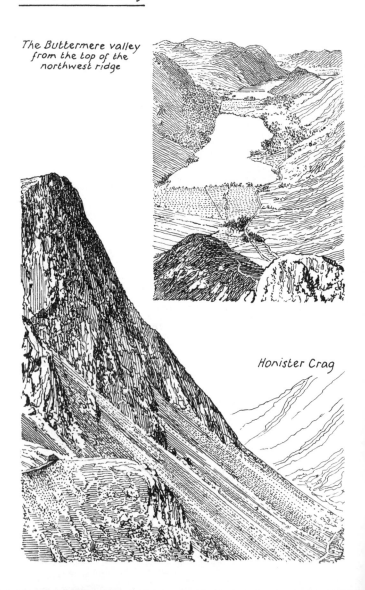

The Buttermere valley
from the top of the
northwest ridge

Honister Crag

MAP

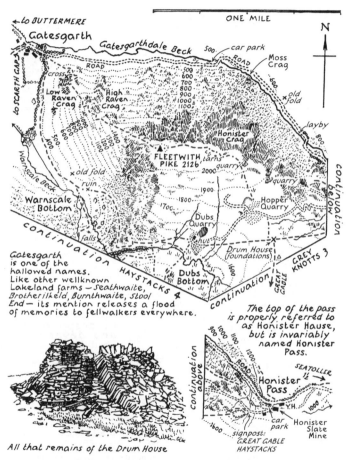

← to BUTTERMERE
Gatesgarth

Gatesgarthdale Beck

car park

ROAD

Moss Crag

cross

ROAD

Low Raven Crag

High Raven Crag

old fold

layby

Honister Crag

▲ FLEETWITH PIKE 2126

tarns

quarry

quarry

old fold

ruin

Hopper Quarry

Warnscale Bottom

Dubs Quarry

hut

Drum House (foundations)

GREAT GABLE

GREY KNOTTS 3

falls

continuation HAYSTACKS 4

Dubs Bottom

continuation below

to SCARTH GAP

Warnscale Beck

continuation above

N

ONE MILE

Gatesgarth
is one of the
hallowed names.
Like other wellknown
Lakeland farms — Seathwaite,
Brotherilkeld, Burnthwaite, Stool
End — its mention releases a flood
of memories to fellwalkers everywhere.

The top of the pass
is properly referred to
as Honister Hause,
but is invariably
named Honister
Pass.

ROAD

SEATOLLER ½

Honister Pass

Y.H.

car park

Honister Slate Mine

signpost: GREAT GABLE HAYSTACKS

All that remains of the Drum House

The path between the quarry buildings on Honister Pass and Dubs Quarry is the straightest mile in Lakeland. Originally it was the permanent way for trucks conveying stone, the winding gear being accommodated in the Drum House at the highest point on the line. Since abandonment of the tramway the track of the rails has been adopted as a path (the rails have been removed, but some sleepers remain) with the blessing of the quarry management, who have signposted it for walkers.

ASCENT FROM HONISTER PASS
1000 feet of ascent : 1¼ miles

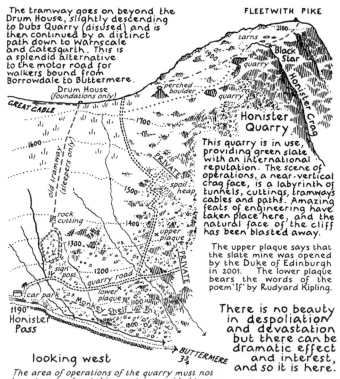

The tramway goes on beyond the Drum House, slightly descending to Dubs Quarry (disused) and is then continued by a distinct path down to Warnscale and Gatesgarth. This is a splendid alternative to the motor road for walkers bound from Borrowdale to Buttermere.

FLEETWITH PIKE

2100

tarns

1900

Black Star

quarry

Honister Crag

Drum House (foundations only)

perched boulder

quarry

GREAT GABLE

Honister Quarry

1700

This quarry is in use, providing green slate with an international reputation. The scene of operations, a near-vertical crag face, is a labyrinth of tunnels, cuttings, tramways cables and paths. Amazing feats of engineering have taken place here, and the natural face of the cliff has been blasted away.

1600

old tramway (sleepers only)

PRIVATE

spoil heap

1500

rock cutting

1400

upper plaque

1300

PRIVATE

sign post

1200

quarry road

lower plaque

car park

Monkey Shelf

1100

1190
Honister Pass

1000

The upper plaque says that the slate mine was opened by the Duke of Edinburgh in 2001. The lower plaque bears the words of the poem 'If' by Rudyard Kipling.

There is no beauty in despoliation and devastation but there can be dramatic effect and interest, and so it is here.

looking west

→ BUTTERMERE 3¾

The area of operations of the quarry must not be entered unless taking part in a guided tour.

The old tramway to the Drum House, long out of commission, has been adopted as a path and is in popular use. It leaves the quarry road beyond the second stream and is signposted to Great Gable and Haystacks. Farther along the quarry road a turning on the left follows the course of another abandoned tramway, but this is now unrecognisable as such. This is part of the public bridleway to Gatesgarth and may be followed across the shoulder of the fell to Dubs Quarry. When opposite the Drum House, note a perched boulder on a low crag and pass to the right of this. Follow the edge of the crags, skirting two quarries, and join a path for the final easy half-mile to the summit cairn. The top of Honister Crag (Black Star) occurs just beyond the second of these two quarries. The ledges of Honister Crag are so rich in wild flowers they have become known as the Hanging Gardens of Lakeland.

ASCENT FROM GATESGARTH

1750 feet of ascent
1⅛ mile

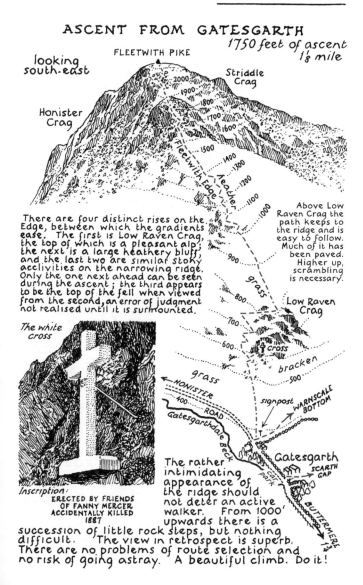

FLEETWITH PIKE

looking
south-east

Honister
Crag

Striddle
Crag

2000
1900
1800
1700
1600
1500
1400
1300
1200
1100
1000

Fleetwith Edge

Heather

There are four distinct rises on the Edge, between which the gradients ease. The first is Low Raven Crag, the top of which is a pleasant alp; the next is a large heathery bluff; and the last two are similar stony acclivities on the narrowing ridge. Only the one next ahead can be seen during the ascent; the third appears to be the top of the fell when viewed from the second, an error of judgment not realised until it is surmounted.

Above Low Raven Crag the path keeps to the ridge and is easy to follow. Much of it has been paved. Higher up, scrambling is necessary.

900

grass

800

Low Raven Crag

700

cross

600

bracken

500

grass

HONISTER
400
ROAD
Gatesgarthdale Beck

signpost

WARNSCALE BOTTOM

The white
cross

Inscription:
ERECTED BY FRIENDS
OF FANNY MERCER
ACCIDENTALLY KILLED
1887

Gatesgarth

car park

SCARTH GAP

BUTTERMERE 1¼

The rather intimidating appearance of the ridge should not deter an active walker. From 1000' upwards there is a succession of little rock steps, but nothing difficult. The view in retrospect is superb. There are no problems of route selection and no risk of going astray. A beautiful climb. Do it!

THE SUMMIT

HIGH CRAG   HIGH STILE   RED PIKE

Standing by the cairn, little is seen to suggest that there is a fearful downfall only a few score paces to the north, and the craggy southwest declivities contributing to Warnscale's barren and stony wilderness are similarly unsuspected although quite close. Indeed the environs are pleasant, with grass and heathery patches stretching into the distance amongst rocky outcrops and a fine company of greater hills all around. Eastwards along the top there is little change in altitude to an uprising a third of a mile away: this is the summit of Honister Crag.

DESCENTS: The northwest ridge is a splendid way down to the road at Gatesgarth, but it is necessary to proceed slowly in several places and to keep strictly to the track — there is a reason for every zigzag. The route is safe in mist, but care is then needed near the foot of the ridge, where the track is faint and Low Raven Crag forms a precipice. Remember the cause of the white cross and incline to the right (on grass) when the first rocks appear.

Under ice or snow the ridge is a different proposition, and it may be safer then to go down via Hopper Quarry and the road to Honister or the path to Gatesgarth.

For Honister Pass (top) the route of ascent may be reversed, but in bad weather wander southeast until the unmissable quarry road is struck, and follow it eastwards to the Pass.

A: to Gatesgarth
B: to Honister Pass (top) direct
C: to Drum House
D: to Dubs Quarry

PLAN OF SUMMIT

RIDGE ROUTES

The neighbouring heights on the same upland mass are Haystacks and Grey Knotts, but connecting ridges are absent, the journey to either being across open country. For Grey Knotts aim first for the Drum House (which is in sight) and for Haystacks aim first for Dubs Quarry (which is not), taking up the ascent from there as indicated in the chapters on those two fells.

THE VIEW

Most visitors to the cairn will consider the prospect along the Buttermere valley the best thing in view, and this is certainly remarkably fine, and exclusive to Fleetwith Pike (it is even better 100 yards down the north-west ridge).

Yet, predominantly, mountains occupy the scene. The Grasmoor fells, the High Stile and Dale Head groups, Great Gable and Pillar are all seen at close range, the latter two appearing as giants.

Principal Fells

N

10 miles

LONG SIDE
LONG SIDE
SKIDDAW

FELLBARROW
WHITELESS PIKE
LOW FELL
RANNERDALE KNOTTS
GRASMOOR
WANDOPE
EEL CRAGS
HIGH SNOCKRIGG
ROBINSON
SCAR CRAGS
CAUSEY PIKE
HINDSCARTH
BURNBANK FELL
MELLBREAK
BLAKE FELL
HEN COMB
GAVEL FELL
RED PIKE
DALE HEAD
HIGH STILE
HIGH CRAG

STYBARROW DODD
RAISE
WHITE SIDE
HELVELLYN LOWER MAN
HELVELLYN
NETHERMOST PIKE
DOLLYWAGGON PIKE
HIGH STREET
FAIRFIELD
ROSTHWAITE FELL
ULLSCARF
PILLAR
HAYSTACKS
KIRK FELL
GREY KNOTTS
CLARAMARA
HIGH RAISE
YEW BARROW
BRANDRETH
GREAT GABLE
GREAT GABLE
ESK PIKE
BOWFELL
SCAFELL
WHIN RIGG

W

7½ miles

5 miles

S

Lakes and Tarns
SSW: Blackbeck Tarn
SW: Innominate Tarn
NW: Loweswater
NW: Crummock Water (2 sections)
NW: Buttermere

GREAT END
GREEN GABLE
GREAT GABLE
LINGMELL
SCAFELL

BRANDRETH
Beck Head
KIRK FELL

Great Round How
Green Crag

looking south

Gavel Fell

1726'

from the terrace path below Carling Knott

Loweswater ●

▲ BLAKE FELL

▲ GAVEL FELL
● HEN COMB

● Croasdale

MILES
0 1 2 3

High Nook Farm

NATURAL FEATURES

Gavel Fell is the central and second highest of the five Loweswater fells south of the lake, having Blake Fell on the west and Hen Comb on the east. It rises as a well-defined ridge between Highnook Beck and Whiteoak Beck but becomes sprawling towards the summit, which is a wide grassy tableland of no particular interest and lacking a distinctive outline. Along the top is the Derwent-Ehen watershed; much of the rain that falls here, however, prefers to linger indefinitely in marshy ground and peaty pools by the side of the boundary fence, the remainder being taken down to the Loweswater valley in the two becks named above, or to Ennerdale by way of Croasdale Beck and Gill Beck. This latter watercourse rises near Floutern Tarn Pass, where there is a crossing between Ennerdale and Buttermere, and for two miles the path lies along the side of Banna Fell, a subsidiary of Gavel Fell south of the summit with some claim to independence. On this side, too, is the curious little crest of Floutern Cop overlooking Floutern Tarn.

All the Loweswater fells have a foundation of slate and the smooth grass slopes characteristic of the type. Less characteristic is the tarn nestling in a hollow of Gavel Fell's north flank, for tarns more usually favour the harder volcanic rock. Since Gavel Fell also has a stake in Floutern Tarn it is doubly distinguished and twice blessed.

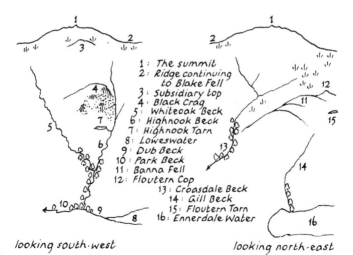

1 : The summit
2 : Ridge continuing to Blake Fell
3 : Subsidiary top
4 : Black Crag
5 : Whiteoak Beck
6 : Highnook Beck
7 : Highnook Tarn
8 : Loweswater
9 : Dub Beck
10 : Park Beck
11 : Banna Fell
12 : Floutern Cop
13 : Croasdale Beck
14 : Gill Beck
15 : Floutern Tarn
16 : Ennerdale Water

looking south-west

looking north-east

MAP

Gavel Fell is the only one of the five Loweswater fells that does not reach down to Loweswater (lake) or its issuing stream. Conversely, however, Gavel Fell is the only one of the five Loweswater fells that comes down to the shore of Ennerdale Water. Its territory above Loweswater terminates at High Nook, where its boundary streams meet.

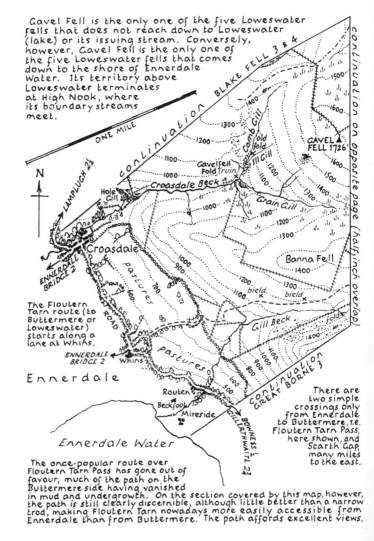

The Floutern Tarn route (to Buttermere or Loweswater) starts along a lane at Whins.

There are two simple crossings only from Ennerdale to Buttermere, i.e. Floutern Tarn Pass, here shown, and Scarth Gap, many miles to the east.

The once-popular route over Floutern Tarn Pass has gone out of favour, much of the path on the Buttermere side having vanished in mud and undergrowth. On the section covered by this map, however, the path is still clearly discernible, although little better than a narrow trod, making Floutern Tarn nowadays more easily accessible from Ennerdale than from Buttermere. The path affords excellent views.

MAP

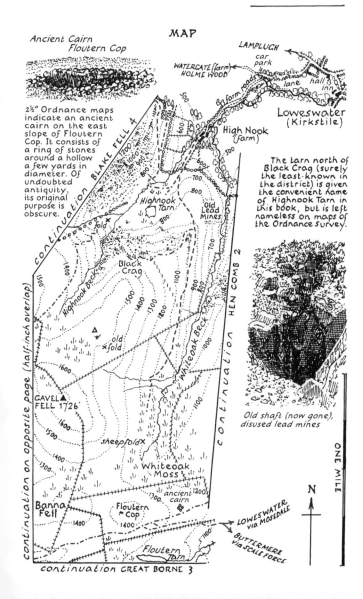

Ancient Cairn
Floutern Cop

2½" Ordnance maps indicate an ancient cairn on the east slope of Floutern Cop. It consists of a ring of stones around a hollow a few yards in diameter. Of undoubted antiquity, its original purpose is obscure.

LAMPLUGH
car park
WATERGATE (farm)
HOLME WOOD
farm road
lane
hall
inn
Loweswater
(Kirkstile)
High Nook (farm)

continuation BLAKE FELL 4

Highnook Tarn
fold
Old Lead Mines

The tarn north of Black Crag (surely the least-known in the district) is given the convenient name of Highnook Tarn in this book, but is left nameless on maps of the Ordnance Survey.

continuation on opposite page (half-inch overlap)

Highnook Beck

Black Crag

old fold

Whiteoak Beck

CONTINUATION HEN COMB 2

GAVEL FELL 1726'

sheepfold

Whiteoak Moss

Banna Fell

ancient cairn

Floutern Cop

LOWESWATER via MOSEDALE
BUTTERMERE via SCALE FORCE

Floutern Tarn

continuation GREAT BORNE 3

Old shaft (now gone), disused lead mines

ONE MILE

N

ASCENT FROM LOWESWATER
1400 feet of ascent : 3 miles

GAVEL FELL

BLAKE FELL →

Leave the drove road where it descends slightly and turns into the Whiteoak valley. A thin trod winds up to the top of Black Crag. Then the route is pathless. Pleasant dry walking leads over undulations to a cairn (which, in mist, might wrongly be thought to be the top). A marshy depression intervenes between this cairn and the summit.

stiles

1600
1500
1400
1300
1200
1100
1000

grass

stile

1400
1300

Alternative route (also suitable for descent)

groove

path disappears

fold

Highnook Beck

Black Crag

drove road

Whiteoak Beck

heather

Highnook Farm

bracken

800
700
600
900
1000

Gavel Fell, set well back and lacking in shapeliness, is not an obvious objective for a climb, yet it has clearly-defined boundaries, a direct ridge, and good views. This ascent is a fair example of the easy, unexciting climbing available from Loweswater.

disused lead mine

intake wall

gate

600

High Nook

500

High Nook is a farm enclosed by beautifully wooded becks and embowered in lovely trees. The situation is truly Arcadian. At the farm use the facing gate to gain a rising grass path to the intake wall.

looking south-west

MOSEDALE

In the shady hollow where Dub Beck is crossed, the lane divides into two farm roads and a car park is provided.

HIGHPARK

farm road

400

farm road

WATERGATE FARM
HOLME WOOD

Kirkstile Inn

Church

village hall

lane

car park

Dub Beck

(issuing from Loweswater lake)

kiosk

SCALE HILL

Loweswater

THACKTHWAITE

signpost

LAMPLUGH

This pleasant approach is typical of the shy charm of the Loweswater countryside. All is very rural and unspoilt. Here is an Old English scene of honeysuckle and wild roses.

THE SUMMIT

The summit is broad and gently undulating, but there is no difficulty in locating the highest point, which is decorated with a large cairn near a point where the fence is crossable. It is obvious that this cairn is the result of much labour (for loose stones are at a premium on the all-grassy top) by an ardent member of the ancient company of Cairnbuilders Anonymous.

DESCENTS: For Croasdale head south towards Floutern Tarn and follow the bridleway to the right. For Loweswater go down east to the drove-road near Whiteoak Beck, which leads pleasantly to High Nook.

THE VIEW

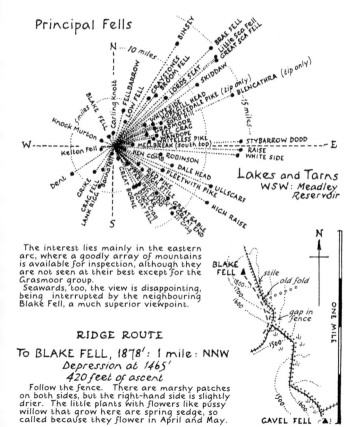

Principal Fells

Lakes and Tarns
WSW: Meadley Reservoir

The interest lies mainly in the eastern arc, where a goodly array of mountains is available for inspection, although they are not seen at their best except for the Grasmoor group.

Seawards, too, the view is disappointing, being interrupted by the neighbouring Blake Fell, a much superior viewpoint.

RIDGE ROUTE

To BLAKE FELL, 1878': 1 mile: NNW
Depression at 1465'
420 feet of ascent

Follow the fence. There are marshy patches on both sides, but the right-hand side is slightly drier. The little plants with flowers like pussy willow that grow here are spring sedge, so called because they flower in April and May.

Great Borne

also known as Herdus

from Mosedale

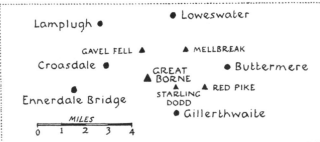

Loweswater •

Lamplugh •

GAVEL FELL ▲   ▲ MELLBREAK

Croasdale •

GREAT ▲ BORNE   • Buttermere

▲ STARLING DODD   ▲ RED PIKE

Ennerdale Bridge •

• Gillerthwaite

MILES

0   1   2   3   4

NATURAL FEATURES

Great Borne is the name of the summit of the fell locally and correctly known as Herdus, an abbreviated version of the former name of Herdhouse. The fell is a familiar sight to West Cumbrians: from Ennerdale Water it rises as a massive buttress to the High Stile ridge. It is not prominent in views from other directions, however, and is not frequented by walkers.

Along its northern base, where it towers imposingly above the shy Floutern Tarn, there is a crossing of the high ground between Buttermere and Ennerdale: this is the once-popular but no-longer-popular Floutern Pass, the route having been partly submerged in the quagmire of Mosedale Head.

Facing Ennerdale the slope is steep and rough, having the name of Herdus Scaw, or Scar, and has little appeal, but on this side there is a gem of mountain architecture on a small scale in Bowness Knott, which can be climbed by a short indirect scramble and commands a fine view of the valley but impresses most when the evening sun lights up its colourful rocks and screes. On the lower Ennerdale flanks the Forestry Commission's evergreens encroach rather patchily, there being areas of infertility.

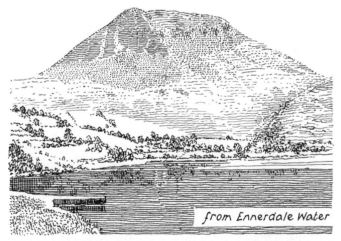

from Ennerdale Water

The viewpoint of this illustration is the lakeside path alongside the former Anglers Hotel, which was situated at the water's edge. The hotel was demolished because of a proposal by the South Cumberland Water Board to raise the level of the lake, but the plan never came to fruition and the demolition was unnecessary. If the level had been raised the pleasant lakeside path to Bowness would also have been sacrificed.

MAP

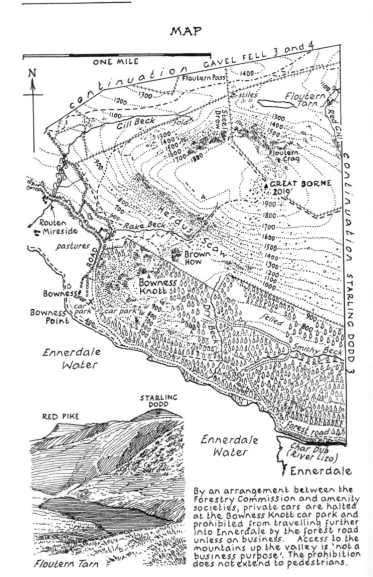

ONE MILE

N

continuation GAVEL FELL 3 and 4

Floutern Pass

stiles

Floutern Tarn

Gill Beck

fold

Steel Brow

Red Gill

1200
1300
1100
1400
1500
900
1300
1400
1500
1800
1700
1600
1500
1400

Floutern Crag

▲ **GREAT BORNE** 2019'

1900
1800
1700
1600
1500
1400
1300
1200
1100
1000

continuation STARLING DODD 3

Herdus Scaw

800
700
600

Routen Mireside

Rake Beck

pastures

Brown How

Bowness Knott

ROAD

Bowness

Bowness Point

car park

car park

900
800
700

Dry Beck

felled

Smithy Beck

900
800

400

Ennerdale Water

forest road

Char Dub (River Liza)

Ennerdale

RED PIKE

STARLING DODD

Ennerdale Water

Floutern Tarn

By an arrangement between the
Forestry Commission and amenity
societies, private cars are halted
at the Bowness Knott car park and
prohibited from travelling further
into Ennerdale by the forest road
unless on business. Access to the
mountains up the valley is 'not a
business purpose'. The prohibition
does not extend to pedestrians.

ASCENT FROM ENNERDALE BRIDGE
1600 feet of ascent
4 miles

looking east

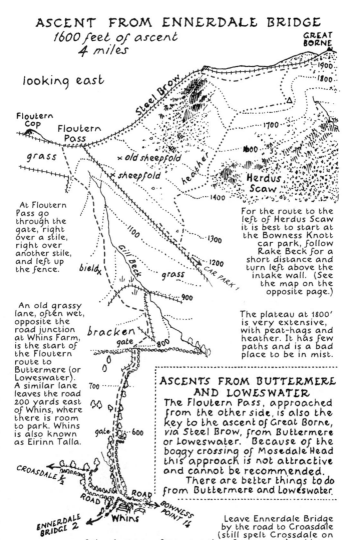

GREAT BORNE

Floutern Cop

Floutern Pass

Steel Brow

grass

1900
1800

1700

old sheepfold

sheepfold

heather

1600

Herdus Scaw

1400

1300

1200

900

CAR PARK 1

grass

1100

Gill Beck

bield

800

bracken

gate

700

600

gate

CROASDALE ½

ROAD

ROAD

ROAD

ENNERDALE BRIDGE 2

Whins

BOWNESS POINT 1½

At Floutern Pass go through the gate, right over a stile, right over another stile, and the left up the fence.

An old grassy lane, often wet, opposite the road junction at Whins Farm, is the start of the Floutern route to Buttermere (or Loweswater). A similar lane leaves the road 200 yards east of Whins, where there is room to park. Whins is also known as Eirinn Talla.

For the route to the left of Herdus Scaw it is best to start at the Bowness Knott car park, follow Rake Beck for a short distance and turn left above the intake wall. (See the map on the opposite page.)

The plateau at 1800' is very extensive, with peat-hags and heather. It has few paths and is a bad place to be in mist.

ASCENTS FROM BUTTERMERE AND LOWESWATER
The Floutern Pass, approached from the other side, is also the key to the ascent of Great Borne, via Steel Brow, from Buttermere or Loweswater. Because of the boggy crossing of Mosedale Head this approach is not attractive and cannot be recommended.
There are better things to do from Buttermere and Loweswater.

Leave Ennerdale Bridge by the road to Croasdale (still spelt Crossdale after more than forty years), taking a narrow byroad on the right (traffic warning sign) after 1¼ miles.

ASCENT FROM BOWNESS CAR PARK
via RAKE BECK
1550 feet of ascent : 1½ miles

This is shown on the map on page 3. At 1300 feet the route passes a curious circular structure. Higher up there is a short scramble which some people may find difficult.

THE SUMMIT

There are two separate tops, divided by a shallow 'valley', which is followed by a fence. The cairn illustrated above — a landmark for miles — was on the north top, but its stones have now been scattered. The south top, slightly higher, is the one chosen by the Ordnance Survey for the site of a triangulation column, and here too is a substantial wind-shelter.

above (left): the big cairn on the north top (now gone)
above: the column on the south top

DESCENTS : Leave by way of the shallow valley between the two tops. There should be no difficulty in clear weather, but if going down direct to Floutern Pass descend *exactly in line* with the fence seen crossing the pass below: it is easy to start down a false ridge and be stopped by crags. *In mist,* make a wide curve east to north on easy ground, descending into Mosedale Head beyond Red Gill. The Rake Beck path is difficult to find unless you came up this way.

Bowness Knott

From the public car park at Bowness the fell appears to be inaccessible, this western face being an untrodden chaos of steep crags and talus slopes above a fringe of roadside trees. But easy access to the top is provided by the bracken slope away to the left. At 900 feet the fence is crossed by a wobbly stile that comes into view as you leave the bracken. Remember where the stile is because it can't be seen from above.

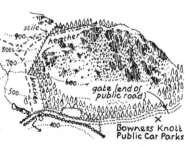

Bowness Knott
Public Car Parks

THE VIEW

Although not outstandingly good, the view has the merit of presenting old favourites from an unusual angle.

Principal Fells

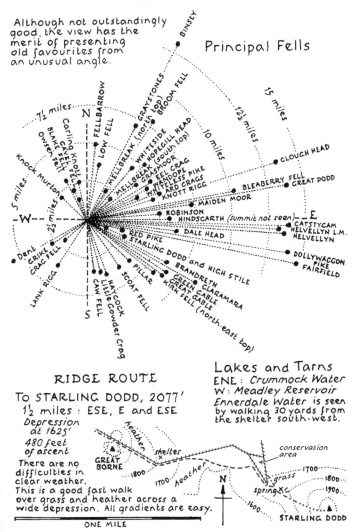

RIDGE ROUTE

To STARLING DODD, 2077'
1½ miles : ESE, E and ESE

Depression at 1625'

480 feet of ascent

There are no difficulties in clear weather. This is a good fast walk over grass and heather across a wide depression. All gradients are easy.

ONE MILE

Lakes and Tarns
ENE: Crummock Water
W: Meadley Reservoir
Ennerdale Water is seen by walking 30 yards from the shelter south-west.

Great Gable

2949'

from Wast Water

NATURAL FEATURES

Great Gable is a favourite of all fellwalkers, and first favourite with many. Right from the start of one's apprenticeship in the hills, the name appeals magically. It is a good name for a mountain, strong, challenging, compelling, starkly descriptive, suggesting the pyramid associated with the shape of mountains since early childhood.   People are attracted to it because of the name.   There is satisfaction in having achieved the ascent and satisfaction in announcing the fact to others.   The name has status, and confers status... Yes, the name is good, simple yet subtly clever. If Great Gable were known only as Wasdale Fell fewer persons would climb it.

continued

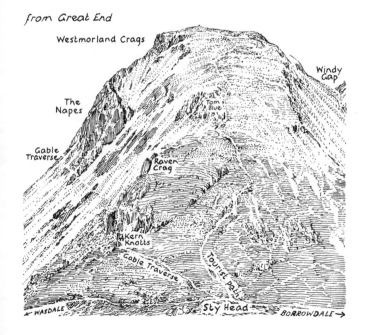

from Great End

Westmorland Crags

Windy Gap

The Napes

Tom Blue

Gable Traverse

Raven Crag

Kern Knotts

Gable Traverse

Tourist Path

← WASDALE

Sty Head

BORROWDALE →

NATURAL FEATURES

continued

In appearance, too, Great Gable has the same appealing attributes. The name fits well. This mountain is strong yet not sturdy, masculine yet graceful. It is the undisputed overlord of the group of hills to which it belongs, and its superior height is emphasised tremendously by the deep gulf separating it from the Scafells and allowing an impressive view that reveals the whole of its half-mile altitude as an unremitting and unbroken pyramid: this is the aspect of the fell that earned the name. From east and west the slender tapering of the summit as seen from the south is not in evidence, the top appearing as a massive square-cut dome. From the north, where the build-up of height is more gradual, the skyline is a symmetrical arc.

continued

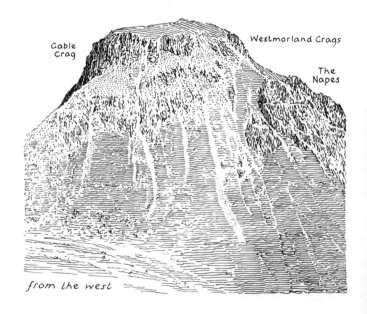

Gable Crag

Westmorland Crags

The Napes

from the west

NATURAL FEATURES

continued

Great Gable is a desert of stones. Vegetation is scanty, feeding few sheep. Petrified rivers of scree scar the southern slopes, from which stand out the bony ribs of the Napes ridges; the whole fell on this side is a sterile wilderness, dry and arid and dusty. The north face is a shadowed precipice, Gable Crag. Slopes to east and west are rough and stony. In some lights, especially in the afterglow of sunset, Great Gable is truly a beautiful mountain, but it is never a pretty one.

The view from the top is far-reaching, but not quite in balance because of the nearness of the Scafells, which, however, are seen magnificently. The aerial aspect of Wasdale is often described as the finest view in the district, a claim that more witnesses will accept than will dispute.

continued

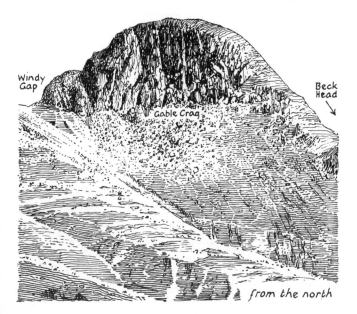

Windy Gap

Gable Crag

Beck Head

from the north

NATURAL FEATURES
continued

The failing of Great Gable is that it holds few mysteries, all its wares being openly displayed. The explorer, the man who likes to look around corners and discover secrets and intimacies, may be disappointed, not on a first visit, which cannot fail to be interesting, but on subsequent occasions. There are no cavernous recesses, no hidden tarns, no combes, no hanging valleys, no waterfalls, no streams other than those forming the boundaries.

Yet walkers tread its familiar tracks again and again, almost as a ritual, and climbers queue to scale its familiar rocks. The truth is, Great Gable casts a spell. It starts as an honourable adversary and becomes a friend. The choice of its summit as a war memorial is testimony to the affection and respect felt for this grand old mountain.

- ● Gatesgarth
  Honister
  Pass ≍
- Seatoller ●
-)(Scarth Gap Pass
- ▲ GREY KNOTTS
- ▲ BRANDRETH
- ● Seathwaite
- Black Sail // Pass
- ▲ BASE BROWN
- KIRK FELL ▲
- ▲ GREEN GABLE
- ▲ GREAT GABLE
- // Sty Head Pass
- ● Wasdale Head

MILES

0 1 2 3

Dry Tarn

This is a tarn that Nature fashioned and forgot. It is invariably bone-dry, but it is recognisable by dark plants that can stand temporary immersion. Dry Tarn is almost unknown, and yet it is close to the main path up Great Gable from Sty Head, being situated at 2100 feet on a grass shelf.
This is Great Gable's only tarn.

MAP

Crags and other features are shown in greater detail, and named, on the larger-scale maps and diagrams appearing elsewhere in this chapter.

A curious thing about Great Gable is that, although of commanding height and so far overtopping the supporting fells as to seem to rise in isolation, it is really a huge cone resting on a high land-mass. Great Gable overlooks many valleys and waters three, yet it has no roots in any except Wasdale; even here its foothold is ineffectual, being a mile beyond the true head of the valley in a side-opening. On all other flanks, it is a mountain hoisted on the shoulders of supporters that have direct valley links and take over the function of principal buttresses.

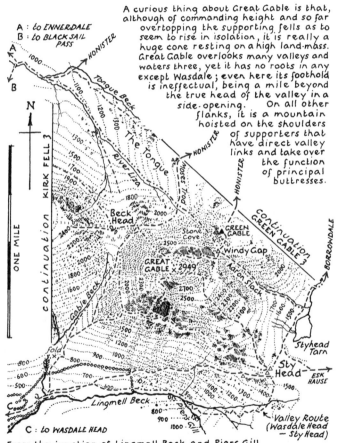

A : to ENNERDALE
B : to BLACK SAIL PASS
C : to WASDALE HEAD

From the junction of Lingmell Beck and Piers Gill the summit is two-thirds of a mile north in lateral distance and the difference in altitude is 2,200 feet, a gradient of 1 in 1½. This is the longest slope in the district of such continuous and concentrated steepness.

Moses' Trod

In the years before the construction of the gravitation tramways to convey slate from Dubs and the upper Honister quarries, when man-handled sledges were the only means of negotiating the steep slopes to the road below, it was more convenient to transport supplies destined for South Cumberland and the port of Ravenglass by packhorse directly across the high fells to Wasdale, a practice followed until the primitive highway through Honister Pass was improved for wheeled traffic. This high-level route, cleverly planned to avoid steep gradients and rough places, can still be traced almost entirely although it has had no commercial use since about 1850. Because of the past history and legend connected with it the early tourists in the district were well aware of its existence, and the path is kept in being today by discerning walkers who appreciate the easy contours, fast travel, glorious scenery and superb views.

In places, the original line of the path is in doubt. The earlier Ordnance Survey maps indicated a wide divergence from the present footpath in the vicinity of Dubs Beck, but this may have been a rare error of cartography, for there are now no signs of it and it would have involved an obviously unnecessary descent and re-ascent. Traces are also missing on both sides of the Brandreth fence, but beyond the way is clear to the west ridge of Great Gable above Beck Head, where again the path is indistinct for a short distance until it starts the descent to Wasdale Head.

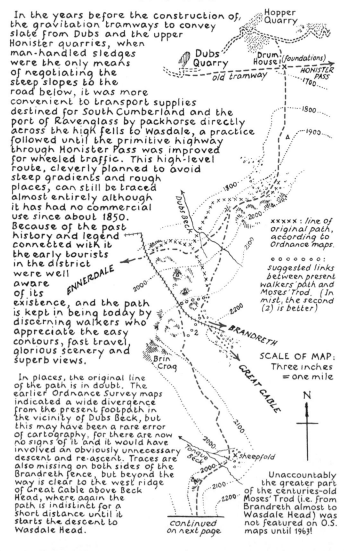

Hopper Quarry

Dubs Quarry

Drum House (foundations)

old tramway

HONISTER PASS
1700
1800
1900

Dubs Beck

ENNERDALE

2000

BRANDRETH

Brin Craq

GREAT GABLE

2000

2200

Tongue Beck

sheepfold

2100

2000

2100

2200

xxxxx : line of original path, according to Ordnance maps.

ooooooo : suggested links between present walkers' path and Moses' Trod. (In mist, the second (2) is better)

SCALE OF MAP: Three inches = one mile

N

continued on next page

Unaccountably the greater part of the centuries-old Moses' Trod (i.e. from Brandreth almost to Wasdale Head) was not featured on O.S. maps until 1963!

Moses' Trod

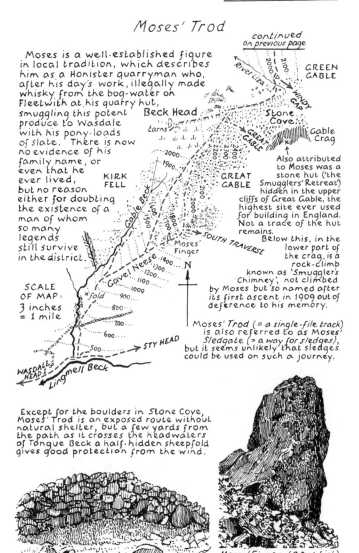

Moses is a well-established figure in local tradition, which describes him as a Honister quarryman who, after his day's work, illegally made whisky from the bog-water on Fleetwith at his quarry hut, smuggling this potent produce to Wasdale with his pony-loads of slate. There is now no evidence of his family name, or even that he ever lived, but no reason either for doubting the existence of a man of whom so many legends still survive in the district.

continued on previous page

GREEN GABLE

River Liza   2000 ft   2100   WINDY GAP

Stone Cove

Beck Head   tarns

GREAT GABLE   Gable Crag

KIRK FELL   GREAT GABLE

Cable Beck   2000   1900   2000

2400   2300   2200   2100

SOUTH TRAVERSE

Moses' Finger

Gavel Neese   1400   1300   1200   1100   1000   900   800   700   600   500

×fold

N

SCALE OF MAP: 3 inches = 1 mile

STY HEAD

WASDALE HEAD

Lingmell Beck

Also attributed to Moses was a stone hut ('the Smugglers' Retreat') hidden in the upper cliffs of Great Gable, the highest site ever used for building in England. Not a trace of the hut remains.

Below this, in the lower part of the crag, is a rock-climb known as 'Smuggler's Chimney', not climbed by Moses but so named after its first ascent in 1909 out of deference to his memory.

Moses' Trod (= a single-file track) is also referred to as Moses' Sledgate (= a way for sledges), but it seems unlikely that sledges could be used on such a journey.

Except for the boulders in Stone Cove, Moses' Trod is an exposed route without natural shelter, but a few yards from the path as it crosses the headwaters of Tongue Beck a half-hidden sheepfold gives good protection from the wind.

Moses' Finger (8 feet high)

The Gable Girdle
(linking the South Traverse and the North Traverse)

Originally a track for a privileged few (i.e. the early rock-climbers) the South Traverse, rising across the flank of Great Gable from Sty Head, has now become a much-fancied way for lesser fry (i.e. modern hikers). The North Traverse passes immediately below the base of Gable Crag, and although still largely the province of climbers is equally accessible to walkers. The two traverses can be linked on the west by tracks over the scree above Beck Head; to the east the North Traverse is continued by the regular path down Aaron Slack to Sty Head. It is thus possible for walkers to make a full circuit of the mountain through interesting territory with fairly distinct tracks underfoot the whole way.

This is the finest mountain walk in the district that does not aim to reach a summit.

It is not level going: the route lies between 1500' and 2500', with many ups and downs. There are rough places to negotiate and nasty scree to cross and climb, but no dangers or difficulties. It is a doddle compared with, say, Jack's Rake or even Lord's Rake. Here one never has the feeling that the end is nigh.

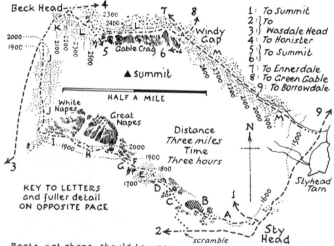

1: To Summit
2: } To
3: } Wasdale Head
4: To Honister
5: } To Summit
6: }
7: To Ennerdale
8: To Green Gable
9: To Borrowdale

Distance
Three miles
Time
Three hours

HALF A MILE

KEY TO LETTERS
and fuller detail
ON OPPOSITE PAGE

Boots, not shoes, should be worn, and they must have soles with a firm grip, or there will be trouble on the boulders. There are few sections where the splendid views may be admired while walking: always stop to look around. The route is almost sheep-free, and dogs may be taken. So may small children, who are natural scramblers, and well-behaved women — but nagging wives should be left to paddle their feet in Styhead Tarn. The journey demands and deserves concentration.

The Gable Circle

The South Traverse leaves Sty Head near the stretcher box, by an indistinct stony path slanting left of the direct route up the mountain. There has been a big change here in the last forty years. At one time the start of the traverse was clearer than the direct route, and many walkers entered upon it in the belief that it would lead them to the top of the mountain. It won't, not without a lot of effort. Nowadays the start of the direct route is much clearer, and the traverse can be difficult to find. The initial path peters out after about thirty yards, but it can be picked up again further to the right after another forty yards.

KEY TO THE MAP ON THE OPPOSITE PAGE

Sty Head to Kern Knotts :

A : Undulating path over grassy alps to bouldery depression and stony rise to the base of the crag.

B : Huge boulders to be negotiated along the base of the crag. [The best way to avoid these is to take the Wasdale path for a quarter of a mile and cut across from the top of the first scramble.]

Kern Knotts to Great Hell Gate :

C : Horizontal track over boulders leads to easier ground. A small hollow is skirted (boulders again) after which there is a short rise to a rocky corner.

D : A cave on the right may provide a trickle of water but it can't always be found. A short scramble up rocky slopes follows.

E : An easy rising path on scree.

F : The head of two gullies is crossed on rocky slabs.

G : Easy rising path to Great Hell Gate (a scree-shoot). Tophet Wall in view ahead.

Great Hell Gate to Little Hell Gate :

H : A section of some confusion, to be resolved by referring to page 11.

Little Hell Gate to Beck Head :

I : The scree-shoot of Little Hell Gate is crossed and a track picked up opposite : this trends downwards to the angle of the south and west faces. Here endeth the South Traverse. [A scree-path goes down to Wasdale Head at this point.]

J : Around the grassy corner a thin trod contours the west slope and joins a track rising to Beck Head.

Beck Head to Windy Gap :

K : Skirt the marshy ground ahead to a slanting scree-path rising to the angle of the north and west faces. [Moses' Trod goes off to the left here by a small pool.]

L : The steep loose scree of the north-west ridge is climbed for 100 yds. The two cairns illustrated on page 27 are no help in finding the path. Just aim for the foot of the crag. Here commenceth the North Traverse. A track runs along the base of Gable Crag, descending to round the lowest buttress and then rising across scree to Windy Gap.

Windy Gap to Sty Head :

M : A popular tourist path descends Aaron Slack to Styhead Tarn, where, if women are found paddling their feet, a greeting may be unwise.

High Kern Knotts

The water-hole (D)

The Great Napes

Rock climbers have played a much greater part than walkers in the selection of identifying names for natural features. All the names of the Great Napes are attributable to those who carried out the first exploration of the crags. Fortunately their choice was always appropriate, descriptive, and often inspired.

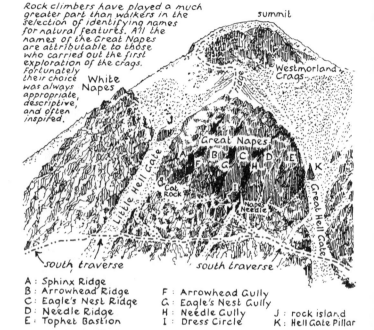

A : Sphinx Ridge
B : Arrowhead Ridge
C : Eagle's Nest Ridge
D : Needle Ridge
E : Tophet Bastion

F : Arrowhead Gully
G : Eagle's Nest Gully
H : Needle Gully
I : Dress Circle

J : rock island
K : Hell Gate Pillar

The Great Napes is a rocky excrescence high on the southern flank of Great Gable. Unlike most crags, which buttress and merge into the general slope of a mountain, the Great Napes rises like a castle above its surroundings so that there is not only a front wall of rock but side walls and a back wall too. This elevated mass is cut into by gullies to form four ridges, three of slender proportions and the fourth, and most easterly, broadly based and of substantial girth. The steepest rock occurs in the eastern part, the ground generally becoming more broken to the west. The front of the ridges, facing Wasdale, springs up almost vertically, but the gradient eases after the initial steepness to give grassy ledges in the higher reaches; the gullies, too, lose their sharp definition towards the top. Gradually the upper extremities of the Napes rise to a common apex, and here, at this point only, the Napes is undefended and a simple, grassy, and quite delightful ridge links with the main body of the fell. Here a climber may walk off the Napes and a walker may enter, with care, upon the easier upper heights. From the link ridge wide channels of scree pour down both sides of the Napes, thus defining the area clearly.

Across the westerly scree-channel the rocky tower of the White Napes emphasises the angle of the south and west faces of the mountain but has no notable crags and little of interest.

The Great Napes

continued

The South Traverse reaches its highest elevation in the section of about 250 yards between the two Hell Gates and beneath the Great Napes, but it does not venture to the base of the wall of crags, preferring an easier passage 50-80 yards lower down the slope, where it maintains a horizontal course on the 2000'contour. The intervening ground is steep and rocky, especially in the vicinity of the Needle, and its exploration calls for care. The Needle is in full view from the Traverse but does not seem its usual self (as usually seen in illustrations) and on a dull day is not easily distinguished from its background of rock. To visit it, take the rising branch-path from the Traverse into Needle Gully, and go up this to the base of the pinnacle; a scrambling track *opposite* climbs up to a ledge known as the Dress Circle, the traditional balcony for watching the ascent of the Needle. From this ledge a higher traverse can be made along the base of the crags, going below the Cat Rock into Little Hell Gate, but there is a tricky section initially and this is no walk for dogs, small children, well behaved women and the like.

Napes Needle

definitely not the author!

Midway between the two Hell Gates Needle Gully and a branch gully, full of scree, cut across the South Traverse, which otherwise hereabouts is mainly a matter of rounding little buttresses. Another bifurcation leads off to Little Hell Gate at a higher level, near the Cat Rock. If proceeding west (i.e. from Sty Head) the two rising branch-paths may be followed by mistake without realising that the Traverse has been left. (Walkers may find these instructions very difficult to follow, but it was not possible to improve on them.)

ROUTES TO THE SUMMIT FROM THE SOUTH TRAVERSE

It is no uncommon thing for walkers to venture upon the South Traverse, from Sty Head, in the fond hope that it will lead them in due course to the summit of Great Gable. This hope is dashed when the Napes is reached, for here the path becomes uncertain and the rocks are an impassable obstacle. The clue to further ascent is provided when it is remembered that 'gate' is a local word for 'way' and that the Napes is bounded by the two Hell Gates. Either of these will conduct the walker safely upwards, but both are chutes for loose stones and steep and arduous to climb. (In Little Hell Gate it is possible, with care, to scramble off the scree onto Sphinx Ridge at several points). The two routes converge at the little ridge below Westmorland Crags, which are rounded on the left by a good track that winds up to the summit plateau.

The Cat Rock

The Sphinx Rock

This is the same pinnacle, shown here from the two angles that have given the two names

The Great Napes

left:
Tophet Bastion, as seen from the South Traverse on the approach from Sty Head.
    The scree of Great Hell Gate runs down to the bottom left.

below:
    looking steeply down on Tophet Bastion and the upper wall of the Napes, with the scree of Great Hell Gate running down to the left, from Westmorland Cairn.

The Great Napes

Eagle's Nest Gully

Eagle's Nest Ridge
(lower part known as
Abbey Buttress)

*looking upwards
from just above
the South Traverse*

Needle Gully

Needle Ridge

Napes Needle

rock island

Westmorland Crags

looking up Little Hell Gate

Tophet Bastion

Hell Gate Pillar

looking up Great Hell Gate

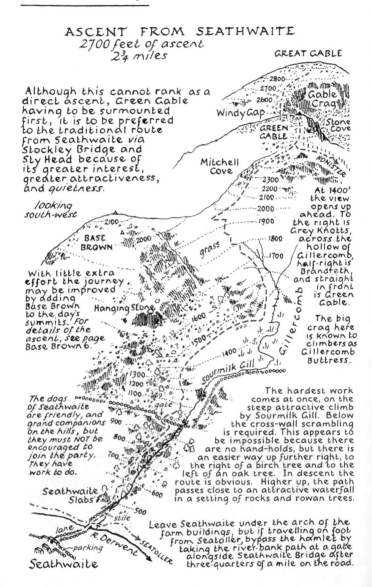

ASCENT FROM SEATHWAITE
2700 feet of ascent
2¾ miles

GREAT GABLE

2800
2700
2600
Gable Crag

Windy Gap

GREEN GABLE

Stone Cove

Mitchell Cove

HONISTER

2300
2200
2100
2000
1900
1800
1700

Although this cannot rank as a direct ascent, Green Gable having to be surmounted first, it is to be preferred to the traditional route from Seathwaite via Stockley Bridge and Sty Head because of its greater interest, greater attractiveness, and quietness.

At 1400' the view opens up ahead. To the right is Grey Knotts, across the hollow of Gillercomb, half-right is Brandreth, and straight in front is Green Gable.

looking south-west

2100

BASE BROWN

2000

grass

Gillercomb

The big crag here is known to climbers as Gillercomb Buttress.

With little extra effort the journey may be improved by adding Base Brown to the day's summits. For details of the ascent, see page Base Brown 6.

Hanging Stone

1600

1500

1400

Sourmilk Gill

1300
1200
1100

gate

900

800

700

600

500

stile

The dogs of Seathwaite are friendly, and grand companions on the hills, but they must NOT be encouraged to join the party. They have work to do.

Seathwaite Slabs

lane

parking

R. Derwent

SEATOLLER

Seathwaite

The hardest work comes at once, on the steep attractive climb by Sourmilk Gill. Below the cross-wall scrambling is required. This appears to be impossible because there are no hand-holds, but there is an easier way up further right, to the right of a birch tree and to the left of an oak tree. In descent the route is obvious. Higher up, the path passes close to an attractive waterfall in a setting of rocks and rowan trees.

Leave Seathwaite under the arch of the farm buildings, but if travelling on foot from Seatoller, bypass the hamlet by taking the river-bank path at a gate alongside Seathwaite Bridge after three-quarters of a mile on the road.

ASCENT FROM STY HEAD
1350 feet of ascent : 1 mile
(from Wasdale Head: 2750 feet : 3¼ miles
from Seathwaite: 2600 feet : 3¼ miles)

GREAT GABLE

Westmorland Crags

looking northwest

Cairns 2900
2800
2700
2600

GREEN GABLE

Windy Gap

Great Napes

grass   grass

MITCHELL GILL

2500
2400
2300
2200

Tom Blue

If approaching from Seathwaite consider, as an alternative, the Mitchell Gill route (quiet, pathless, no difficulties, on grass)
See Green Gable 6

South Traverse

Dry Tarn

2100

2000

Aaron Slack

Raven Crag

1900   grass

Kern Knotts

grass   1800

old fold

1700

WASDALE HEAD

1600   grass

grass

1500

BORROWDALE

Sty Head

Styhead Tarn

The usual line of ascent is the original tourist path (also known as the Breast Route) from Sty Head. This path has been restructured with every stone wedged in place so that it can't be dislodged, but in 1965 it was described as very bad underfoot (loose scree) on the steep rise by Tom Blue, where clumsy walkers had utterly ruined the path. This description inspired the following comments:

....

There are good walkers and bad walkers, and the difference between them has nothing to do with performances in mileage or speed. The difference lies in the way they put their feet down.

A good walker is a *tidy* walker. He moves quietly, places his feet where his eyes tell him to, on beaten tracks treads firmly, avoids loose stones on steep ground, disturbs nothing. He is, by habit, an improver of paths.

A bad walker is a *clumsy* walker. He moves noisily, disturbs the surface and even the foundations of paths by kicking up loose stones, tramples the verges until they disintegrate into debris. He is, by habit, a maker of bad tracks and a spoiler of good ones.

A good walker's special joy is zigzags, which he follows faithfully. A bad walker's special joy is in shortcutting and destroying zigzags.

All fellwalking accidents are the result of clumsiness.

....

The author lived to see the restructuring of the paths and to express his disapproval, but many who read his description of this path then and see it as it is now would agree that there has been an improvement.

ASCENT FROM HONISTER PASS
1950 feet of ascent : 3 miles

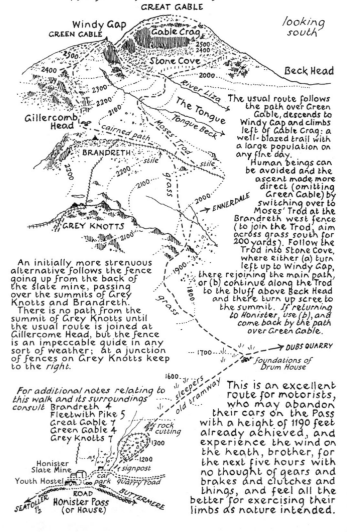

GREAT GABLE

looking south

Windy Gap
GREEN GABLE Gable Crag

2500
2400

Stone Cove

Beck Head

2500
2400
2300
2200
2180

River Liza

The Tongue

Tongue Beck

Moses' Trod

2000

Gillercomb Head

cairned path

BRANDRETH

2200

stile

stile

grass

ENNERDALE

2100

2000

GREY KNOTTS

2100

1900

grass

1800

... 1700 ...

DUBS QUARRY

foundations of Drum House

1600

sleepers
old tramway

rock cutting

1300

1200

signpost

car park   quarry road

Honister
Slate Mine

Youth Hostel

ROAD

SEATOLLER 1½

Honister Pass
(or Hause)

BUTTERMERE

The usual route follows the path over Green Gable, descends to Windy Gap and climbs left of Gable Crag: a well-blazed trail with a large population on any fine day.

Human beings can be avoided and the ascent made more direct (omitting Green Gable) by switching over to Moses' Trod at the Brandreth west fence (to join the Trod, aim across grass south for 200 yards). Follow the Trod into Stone Cove, where either (a) turn left up to Windy Gap, there rejoining the main path, or (b) continue along the Trod to the bluff above Beck Head and there turn up scree to the summit. If returning to Honister, use (b), and come back by the path over Green Gable.

An initially more strenuous alternative follows the fence going up from the back of the slate mine, passing over the summits of Grey Knotts and Brandreth.

There is no path from the summit of Grey Knotts until the usual route is joined at Gillercomb Head, but the fence is an impeccable guide in any sort of weather; at a junction of fences on Grey Knotts keep to the right.

For additional notes relating to this walk and its surroundings consult Brandreth 4
Fleetwith Pike 5
Great Gable 7
Green Gable 4
Grey Knotts 7

This is an excellent route for motorists, who may abandon their cars on the Pass with a height of 1190 feet already achieved, and experience the wind on the heath, brother, for the next five hours with no thought of gears and brakes and clutches and things, and feel all the better for exercising their limbs as nature intended.

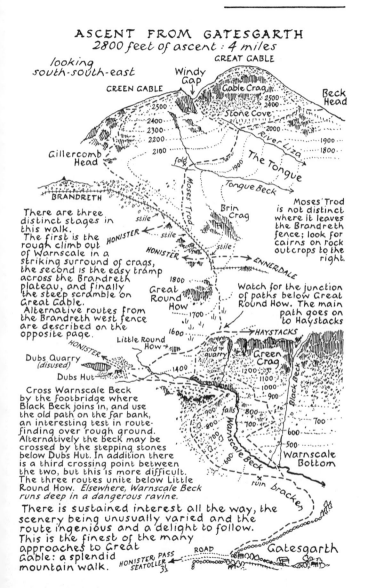

ASCENT FROM GATESGARTH
2800 feet of ascent : 4 miles

looking south-south-east

GREAT GABLE

CREEN GABLE   Windy Gap   Gable Crag

2500
2400   Stone Cove   2500
2400

2400
2300   2000
2200

Gillercomb Head   2100   fold   River Liza   1900
1800

BRANDRETH   1900   The Tongue

stile   Tongue Beck

Brin Crag   Moses' Trod is not distinct where it leaves the Brandreth fence; look for cairns on rock outcrops to the right.

There are three distinct stages in this walk.
The first is the rough climb out of Warnscale in a striking surround of crags, the second is the easy tramp across the Brandreth plateau, and finally the steep scramble on Great Gable.
Alternative routes from the Brandreth west fence are described on the opposite page.

HONISTER   stile
HONISTER   stile
HONISTER   ENNERDALE

1800
Great Round How   Watch for the junction of paths below Great Round How. The main path goes on to Haystacks.

1700
1600   HAYSTACKS

Little Round How   old quarry   Green Crag

HONISTER   1400   1200
1100
1000

Dubs Quarry (disused)   900   800   Black Beck
Dubs Hut

Cross Warnscale Beck by the footbridge where Black Beck joins in, and use the old path on the far bank, an interesting test in route-finding over rough ground. Alternatively the beck may be crossed by the stepping stones below Dubs Hut. In addition there is a third crossing point between the two, but this is more difficult. The three routes unite below Little Round How. Elsewhere, Warnscale Beck runs deep in a dangerous ravine.

900   falls   800
800   700   700   600
700   500
Warnscale Beck   Warnscale Bottom

ruin   bracken

There is sustained interest all the way, the scenery being unusually varied and the route ingenious and a delight to follow. This is the finest of the many approaches to Great Gable: a splendid mountain walk.

Beck Head

ROAD   Gatesgarth

HONISTER PASS SEATOLLER
3½

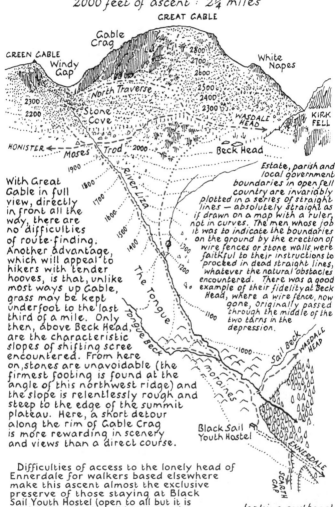

ASCENT FROM ENNERDALE
(BLACK SAIL YOUTH HOSTEL)
2000 feet of ascent : 2¼ miles

GREAT GABLE

GREEN GABLE

Gable Crag

Windy Gap

2800
2700
2600

White Napes

North Traverse

2300
2200

Stone Cove

2500
2400
2300

WASDALE HEAD

KIRK FELL

HONISTER ←—— Moses Trod 2000 ——→ Beck Head

1900
1800
1700
1600
1500
1400
1300
1200
1100
1000

River Liza

The Tongue

Tongue Beck

moraines

Sail Beck

WASDALE HEAD

With Great Gable in full view, directly in front all the way, there are no difficulties of route-finding. Another advantage, which will appeal to hikers with tender hooves, is that, unlike most ways up Gable, grass may be kept underfoot to the last third of a mile. Only then, above Beck Head, are the characteristic slopes of shifting scree encountered. From here on, stones are unavoidable (the firmest footing is found at the angle of this northwest ridge) and the slope is relentlessly rough and steep to the edge of the summit plateau. Here, a short detour along the rim of Gable Crag is more rewarding in scenery and views than a direct course.

Estate, parish and local government boundaries in open fell country are invariably plotted in a series of straight lines — absolutely straight as if drawn on a map with a ruler, not in curves. The men whose job it was to indicate the boundaries on the ground by the erection of wire fences or stone walls were faithful to their instructions to proceed in dead straight lines, whatever the natural obstacles encountered. There was a good example of their fidelity at Beck Head, where a wire fence, now gone, originally passed through the middle of the two tarns in the depression.

Black Sail Youth Hostel

ENNERDALE

SCARTH GAP

Difficulties of access to the lonely head of Ennerdale for walkers based elsewhere make this ascent almost the exclusive preserve of those staying at Black Sail Youth Hostel (open to all but it is advisable to book well in advance).

looking southeast

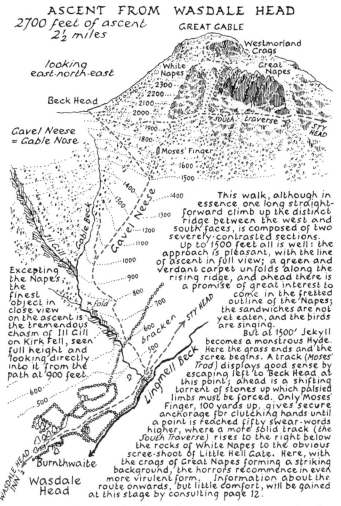

ASCENT FROM WASDALE HEAD

2700 feet of ascent
2½ miles

looking east-north-east

GREAT GABLE

GREAT GABLE

Westmorland Crags

White Napes

Great Napes

Beck Head

2300
2200
2100
2000
1900
1800

south traverse

STY HEAD

Gavel Neese
= Gable Nose

Moses' Finger

1600
1500

1400

Gavel Neese

1400
1300
1200
1100
1000
900
800
700

Gable Beck

Sil Gill

600
500

×fold

bracken

STY HEAD

Excepting the Napes, the finest object in close view on the ascent is the tremendous chasm of Ill Gill on Kirk Fell, seen full height and looking directly into it from the path at 900 feet.

600
500

Lingmell Beck

This walk, although in essence one long straight-forward climb up the distinct ridge between the west and south faces, is composed of two severely-contrasted sections.
Up to 1500 feet all is well: the approach is pleasant, with the line of ascent in full view; a green and verdant carpet unfolds along the rising ridge, and ahead there is a promise of great interest to come in the fretted outline of the Napes; the sandwiches are not yet eaten, and the birds are singing.
But at 1500' Jekyll becomes a monstrous Hyde. Here the grass ends and the scree begins. A track (Moses' Trod) displays good sense by escaping left to Beck Head at this point; ahead is a shifting torrent of stones up which palsied limbs must be forced. Only Moses' Finger, 100 yards up, gives secure anchorage for clutching hands until a point is reached fifty swear-words higher, where a more solid track (the South Traverse) rises to the right below the rocks of White Napes to the obvious scree-shoot of Little Hell Gate. Here, with the crags of Great Napes forming a striking background, the horrors recommence in even more virulent form. Information about the route onwards, but little comfort, will be gained at this stage by consulting page 12.

WASDALE HEAD INN ½

Burnthwaite

Wasdale Head

From Wasdale Head this route is clearly seen to be the most direct way to the summit. It is also the most strenuous. (Its conquest is more wisely announced at supper, afterwards, than at breakfast, in advance).

THE SUMMIT

Great Gable's summit is held in special respect by the older generation of fellwalkers, because here, set in the rocks that bore the top cairn, is the bronze War Memorial tablet of the Fell and Rock Climbing Club, dedicated in 1924, and ever since the inspiring scene of an annual Remembrance Service in November. It is a fitting place to pay homage to men who once loved to walk on these hills and gave their lives defending the right of others to enjoy the same happy freedom, for the ultimate crest of Gable is truly characteristic of the best of mountain Lakeland : a rugged crown of rock and boulders and stones in chaotic profusion, a desert without life, a harsh and desolate peak thrust high in the sky above the profound depths all around.

Gable, tough and strong all through its height, has here made a final gesture by providing an outcrop of rock even in its last inches, so that one must climb to reach the highest point. The cairn has gone, despite an entreaty by the author that no man tear it asunder lest a thousand curses accompany his guilty flight. On three sides the slopes fall away immediately, but to the north there extends a small plateau, with a little vegetation, before the summit collapses in the sheer plunge of Gable Crag. The rim of this precipice, and also the top of Westmorland Crags to the south, should be visited for their superlative views.

There are few days in the year when no visitors arrive on the summit. Snow and ice and severe gales may defy those who aspire to reach it in winter, but in the summer months there is a constant parade of perspiring pedestrians across the top from early morning to late evening.

To many fellwalkers this untidy bit of ground is Mecca.
continued

THE SUMMIT

continued

DESCENTS: Except for the improved path to Sty Head, all ways off the summit are paved with loose stones and continue so for most of the descent. Allied to roughness is steepness, particularly on the Wasdale side, and care is needed to avoid involuntary slips. In places, where scree-runners have bared the underlying ground, surfaces are slippery and unpleasant. Never descend Gable in a mad rush!

In fine weather there should be no trouble in distinguishing the various cairned routes; in mist their direction is identified by the memorial tablet, which faces north overlooking the path to Windy Gap. Not all cairns can be relied upon; some are not route-markers but indicators of viewpoints. Generally, however, the principal traffic routes are well blazed by boots.

In bad conditions the safest line is down the breast of the mountain to Sty Head. Care is needed in locating the descent to Beck Head, which keeps closely to the angle of the north and west faces and does not follow any of the inviting scree-runs on the west side, which end in fields of boulders. Caution is also advised in attempting direct descents of the Wasdale face if the topography of the Napes is not already familiar.

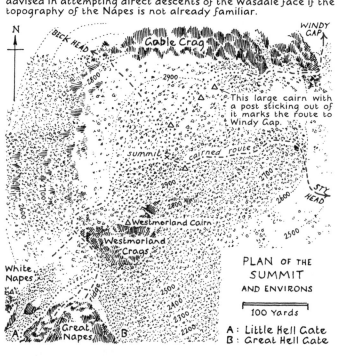

This large cairn with a post sticking out of it marks the route to Windy Gap.

PLAN OF THE
SUMMIT
AND ENVIRONS

|—————| 100 Yards

A : Little Hell Gate
B : Great Hell Gate

THE VIEW

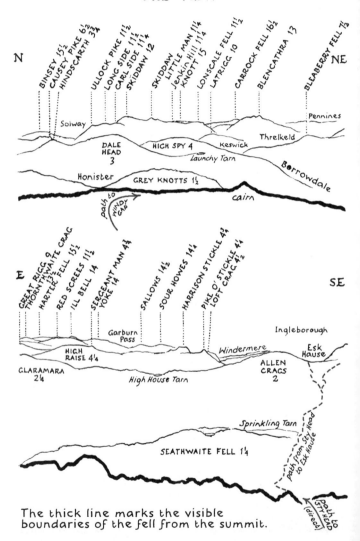

The thick line marks the visible boundaries of the fell from the summit.

THE VIEW

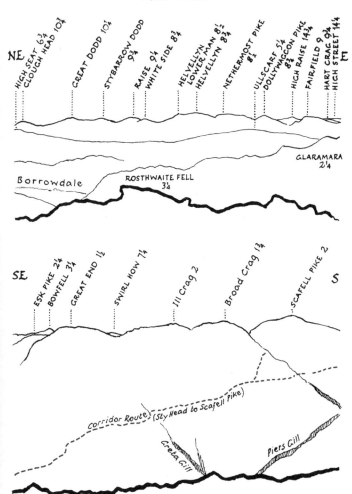

NE

HIGH SEAT 6¾
CLOUGH HEAD 10¾
GREAT DODD 10¼
STYBARROW DODD 9¾
RAISE 9¼
WHITE SIDE 8¾
HELVELLYN LOWER MAN 8½
HELVELLYN 8¾
NETHERMOST PIKE 8½
ULLSCARF 5¼
DOLLYWAGGON PIKE 8½
HIGH RAISE 14¾
FAIRFIELD 9
HART CRAG 9¼
HIGH STREET 14¼

E

GLARAMARA 2¼

Borrowdale

ROSTHWAITE FELL 3¼

SE

ESK PIKE 2¼
BOWFELL 3¼
GREAT END 1½
SWIRL HOW 7¼
Ill Crag 2
Broad Crag 1¾
Scafell Pike 2

S

Corridor Route (Sty Head to Scafell Pike)

Greta Gill

Piers Gill

The figures accompanying the names of fells indicate distances in miles

THE VIEW

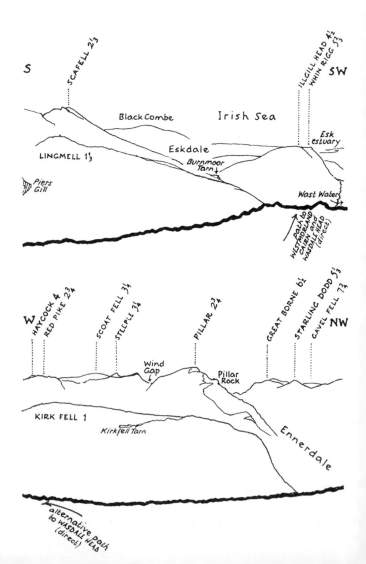

S

SCAFELL 2⅓

Black Combe   Irish Sea

ILLGILL HEAD 4½   WHIN RIGG 5⅔

SW

Eskdale

Esk estuary

LINGMELL 1⅓

Burnmoor Tarn ↓

Piers Gill

Wast Water

PATH TO WESTMORLAND CAIRN AND WASDALE HEAD (direct)

W

HAYCOCK 4   RED PIKE 2¾

SCOAT FELL 3¼   STEEPLE 3¼

PILLAR 2¾

GREAT BORNE 6½   STARLING DODD 5⅓   GAVEL FELL 7¼

NW

Wind Gap ↓

Pillar Rock

KIRK FELL 1

Kirkfell Tarn

Ennerdale

alternative path to WASDALE HEAD (direct)

THE VIEW

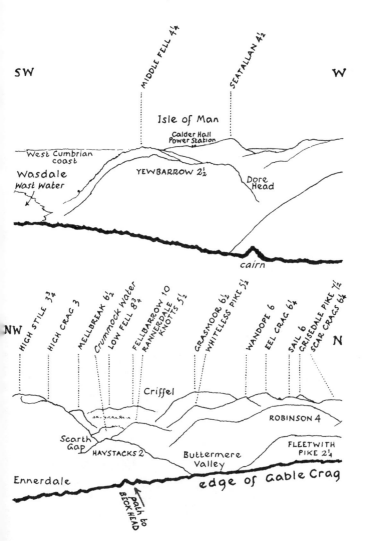

SW   W

MIDDLE FELL 4¼   SEATALLAN 4½

Isle of Man
Calder Hall
Power Station

West Cumbrian coast

Wasdale
Wast Water

YEWBARROW 2½   Dore Head

cairn

NW   N

HIGH STILE 3¾   HIGH CRAG 3   MELLBREAK 6½   Crummock Water   LOW FELL 8¾   FELLBARROW 10   RANNERDALE KNOTTS 5¼   GRASMOOR 6½   WHITELESS PIKE 5½   WANDOPE 6   EEL CRAG 6¼   SAIL 6   GRISEDALE PIKE ½   SCAR CRAGS 6¼

Criffel

ROBINSON 4

Scarth Gap
HAYSTACKS 2
Buttermere Valley

FLEETWITH PIKE 2¼

Ennerdale   edge of Gable Crag

path to BECK HEAD

RIDGE ROUTES

To GREEN GABLE, 2628': NNE, then E and NNE : ½ mile
Depression (Windy Gap) at 2460'
150 feet of ascent
Rough and stony all the way

The best that can be said for the path
is that it is clearly defined throughout,
which is as well, there being unseen
precipices in the vicinity. One section,
where Gable Crag is rounded to reach
Windy Gap, is particularly objectionable
and needs care on smooth rocky steps.

To KIRK FELL, 2630': NW, then W and SW : 1½ miles
Depression (Beck Head) at 2040'   700 feet of ascent.

A passing from the sublime to the less sublime, better done the other way.

Pick a way carefully down the north-west ridge, avoiding false
trails that lead only to boulder slopes and keeping generally near
the angle of the ridge, where the footing is firmest. When a line
of fence posts is joined, the remainder of the route is assured,
the posts leading across the depression of Beck Head, up the steep
facing slope of Rib End, and visiting first the lower and then the top
summit of Kirk Fell across a wide grassy plateau.

A place to remember.......

Some quite ordinary patches of fellside have
extraordinary significance when they indicate
important route junctions occurring in rough
terrain and not clearly defined by paths
on the ground. The best example is the
upper exit of Lords Rake on Scafell,
and there are many others.

Illustrated here is
the place where the
North Traverse leaves
the northwest ridge to
cross below Gable
Crag to Windy Gap.

Pass between the two cairns
and the track comes into view

Westmorland Cairn   Erected in 1876 by two brothers
of the name of Westmorland to
mark what they considered to be the finest mountain viewpoint
in the district, this soundly-built and tidy cairn is wellknown, to
climbers and walkers alike, and has always been respected. The
cairn has maintained its original form throughout the years quite
remarkably: apart from visitors who like to add a pebble, it has
suffered neither from the weather nor from human despoilers. It
stands on the extreme brink of the south face, above steep crags,
and overlooks Wasdale. Rocky platforms around make the place
ideal for a halt after climbing Great Gable. The cairn is not in
sight from the summit but is soon reached by walking 150 yards
across the stony top in the direction of Wast Water.

Green Gable 2628'

Gatesgarth
Seatoller
Honister Pass
Seathwaite
▲ GREEN GABLE
▲ GREAT GABLE
● Wasdale Head

MILES

from Great End

NATURAL FEATURES

A thousand people, or more, reach the summit-cairn of Green Gable every year, yet it is probably true to say that no visitor to Lakeland ever announced at breakfast that this fell was his day's objective; and, if he did, his listeners would assume a slip of the tongue: of course he must mean Great Gable. The two Gables are joined like Siamese twins, but they are not likenesses of each other. Great Gable is the mighty mountain that every walker wants to climb; Green Gable is a stepping stone to it but otherwise of no account. All eyes are fixed on Great Gable; Green Gable is merely something met en route. So think most folk who pass from one to the other.

But Green Gable is not at all insignificant. At 2628' its altitude, by Lakeland standards, is considerable. A sharp peaked summit, more delicately wrought than Great Gable's, adds distinction. Rock-climbers' crags adorn its western fringe. Important paths reach it on all sides. Unsought though the top may be, nevertheless it is much-used and well-known through the accident of its position. There are two main slopes, one going down to Styhead Gill, the other gaining a slender footing in Ennerdale.

It is a crowning misfortune for Green Gable, however, that the volcanic upheaval ages ago stopped upheaving at a moment when this fell was in a position completely subservient to a massive neighbour, and so fashioned the summit that it is forever destined to look up into the pillared crags of Great Gable as a suppliant before a temple. It is because of the inferiority induced by Big Brother that Green Gable cannot ever expect to be recognised as a fine mountain in its own right.

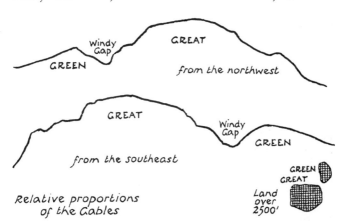

Windy Gap   GREAT

GREEN

from the northwest

GREAT

Windy Gap

GREEN

from the southeast

Relative proportions of the Gables

GREEN
GREAT

Land over 2500'

Green Gable 3

MAP

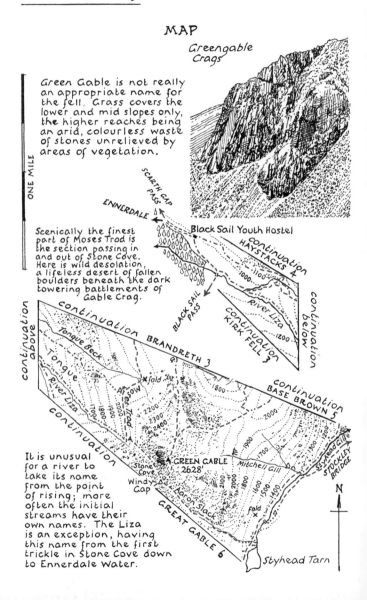

Greengable Crags

Green Gable is not really an appropriate name for the fell. Grass covers the lower and mid slopes only, the higher reaches being an arid, colourless waste of stones unrelieved by areas of vegetation.

ONE MILE

SCARTH GAP PASS

ENNERDALE

Black Sail Youth Hostel

continuation HAYSTACKS 4

continuation below

Scenically the finest part of Moses Trod is the section passing in and out of Stone Cove. Here is wild desolation, a lifeless desert of fallen boulders beneath the dark towering battlements of Gable Crag.

BLACK SAIL PASS

River Liza

continuation KIRK FELL 3

continuation above

continuation BRANDRETH 3

Tongue Beck

Tongue

River Liza

continuation

Moses Trod

fold

1000 1100

1200

1800

continuation BASE BROWN 5

2000

GREEN GABLE 2628'

Stone Cove

Windy Gap

Mitchell Gill

Stockley Gill

STOCKLEY BRIDGE

Aaron Slack

GREAT GABLE 6

fold

It is unusual for a river to take its name from the point of rising; more often the initial streams have their own names. The Liza is an exception, having this name from the first trickle in Stone Cove down to Ennerdale Water.

N

Styhead Tarn

ASCENT FROM HONISTER PASS
1550 feet of ascent : 2½ miles

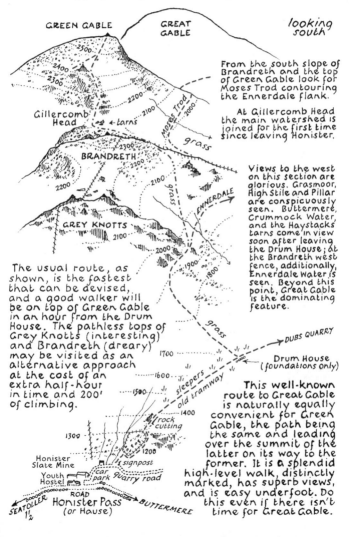

looking south

GREEN GABLE   GREAT GABLE

From the south slope of Brandreth and the top of Green Gable look for Moses Trod contouring the Ennerdale flank.

At Gillercomb Head the main watershed is joined for the first time since leaving Honister.

Views to the west on this section are glorious. Grasmoor, High Stile and Pillar are conspicuously seen. Buttermere, Crummock Water, and the Haystacks tarns come in view soon after leaving the Drum House; at the Brandreth west fence, additionally, Ennerdale Water is seen. Beyond this point, Great Gable is the dominating feature.

The usual route, as shown, is the fastest that can be devised, and a good walker will be on top of Green Gable in an hour from the Drum House. The pathless tops of Grey Knotts (interesting) and Brandreth (dreary) may be visited as an alternative approach at the cost of an extra half-hour in time and 200' of climbing.

This well-known route to Great Gable is naturally equally convenient for Green Gable, the path being the same and leading over the summit of the latter on its way to the former. It is a splendid high-level walk, distinctly marked, has superb views, and is easy underfoot. Do this even if there isn't time for Great Gable.

ASCENT FROM SEATHWAITE
2250 feet of ascent : 2¼ miles

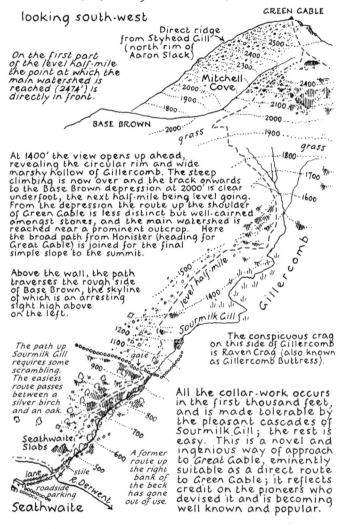

looking south-west

GREEN GABLE

Direct ridge from Styhead Gill (north rim of Aaron Slack)

2500

2400
2300

Mitchell Cove

2000
1900
1800

2400

2100

2000

BASE BROWN

2000

grass

1900

grass

1800

1700

1600

Gillercomb

On the first part of the level half-mile the point at which the main watershed is reached (2474') is directly in front.

At 1400' the view opens up ahead, revealing the circular rim and wide marshy hollow of Gillercomb. The steep climbing is now over and the track onwards to the Base Brown depression at 2000' is clear underfoot, the next half-mile being level going. From the depression the route up the shoulder of Green Gable is less distinct but well-cairned amongst stones, and the main watershed is reached near a prominent outcrop. Here the broad path from Honister (heading for Great Gable) is joined for the final simple slope to the summit.

Above the wall, the path traverses the rough side of Base Brown, the skyline of which is an arresting sight high above on the left.

1500

level half-mile

1400

Sourmilk Gill

1200
1100
gate
900

The path up Sourmilk Gill requires some scrambling. The easiest route passes between a silver birch and an oak.

800

The conspicuous crag on this side of Gillercomb is Raven Crag (also known as Gillercomb Buttress).

Seathwaite Slabs

700

600

lane   stile
roadside parking
R. Derwent
500

Seathwaite

A former route up the right bank of the beck has gone out of use.

All the collar-work occurs in the first thousand feet, and is made tolerable by the pleasant cascades of Sourmilk Gill; the rest is easy. This is a novel and ingenious way of approach to Great Gable, eminently suitable as a direct route to Green Gable; it reflects credit on the pioneers who devised it and is becoming well known and popular.

ASCENT FROM STYHEAD GILL
1200 feet of ascent : ¾ mile

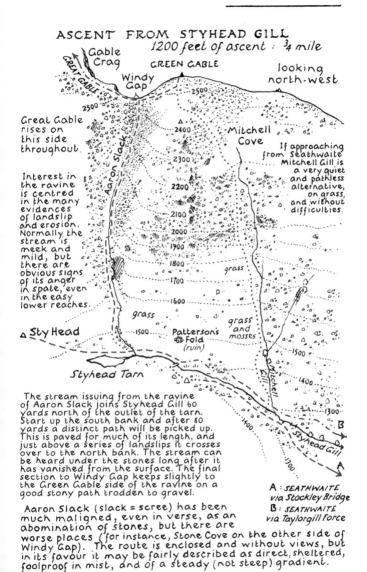

Gable Crag

GREAT GABLE

GREEN GABLE

Windy Gap

looking north-west

2500

2500

2500

2400

Mitchell Cove

Great Gable rises on this side throughout.

Interest in the ravine is centred in the many evidences of landslip and erosion. Normally the stream is meek and mild, but there are obvious signs of its anger in spate, even in the easy lower reaches.

If approaching from Seathwaite Mitchell Gill is a very quiet and pathless alternative, on grass, and without difficulties.

2300

2200

2100

2000

1900

1800

grass

1700

1600

Sty Head

grass

1500

Patterson's Fold (ruin)

grass and mosses

1500

1400

Styhead Tarn

1300

Mitchell

B

Styhead Gill

A

The stream issuing from the ravine of Aaron Slack joins Styhead Gill 60 yards north of the outlet of the tarn. Start up the south bank and after 80 yards a distinct path will be picked up. This is paved for much of its length, and just above a series of landslips it crosses over to the north bank. The stream can be heard under the stones long after it has vanished from the surface. The final section to Windy Gap keeps slightly to the Green Gable side of the ravine on a good stony path trodden to gravel.

A : SEATHWAITE
via Stockley Bridge

B : SEATHWAITE
via Taylorgill Force

Aaron Slack (slack = scree) has been much maligned, even in verse, as an abomination of stones, but there are worse places (for instance, Stone Cove on the other side of Windy Gap). The route is enclosed and without views, but in its favour it may be fairly described as direct, sheltered, foolproof in mist, and of a steady (not steep) gradient.

ASCENT FROM ENNERDALE
(BLACK SAIL YOUTH HOSTEL)
1650 feet of ascent : 2¼ miles

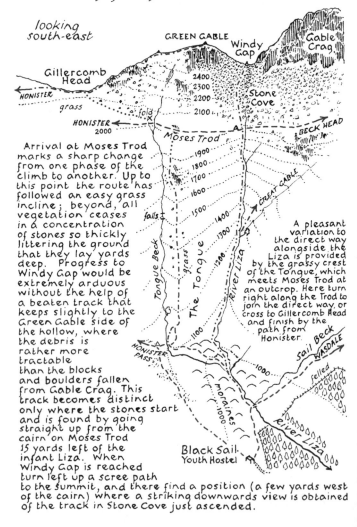

looking
south-east

GREEN GABLE

Windy Gap

Gable Crag

Gillercomb Head

2400
2300
2200
2100

Stone Cove

HONISTER

grass

fold

HONISTER ← 2000

BECK HEAD

Moses Trod

1900
1800
1700
1600
1500
1400
1300
1200
1100

GREAT GABLE

The Tongue

Tongue Beck

falls

grass

River Liza

HONISTER PASS

Sail Beck

WASDALE

felled

moraines

1000

River Liza

Black Sail Youth Hostel

Arrival at Moses Trod marks a sharp change from one phase of the climb to another. Up to this point the route has followed an easy grass incline; beyond, all vegetation ceases in a concentration of stones so thickly littering the ground that they lay yards deep. Progress to Windy Gap would be extremely arduous without the help of a beaten track that keeps slightly to the Green Gable side of the hollow, where the debris is rather more tractable than the blocks and boulders fallen from Gable Crag. This track becomes distinct only where the stones start and is found by going straight up from the cairn on Moses Trod 15 yards left of the infant Liza. When Windy Gap is reached turn left up a scree path to the summit, and there find a position (a few yards west of the cairn) where a striking downwards view is obtained of the track in Stone Cove just ascended.

A pleasant variation to the direct way alongside the Liza is provided by the grassy crest of the Tongue, which meets Moses Trod at an outcrop. Here turn right along the Trod to join the direct way, or cross to Gillercomb Head and finish by the path from Honister.

THE SUMMIT

It is a pity that most visitors to the summit are in a hurry to get off it, for the narrow strip of rough ground between the cairn and the rim of the western crags is a fine perch to study the massive architecture of Gable Crag and the deep pit of stones below it: this is a tremendous scene. A wide gravelly path crosses the top, which is uncomplicated, making a sharp angle at the cairn. There are windshelters.

DESCENTS: Honister can be reached at a fast exhilarating pace by the good cairned path northwards via the Drum House (where turn left for Buttermere, right for Borrowdale). The Gillercomb route to Seathwaite is the best direct way down to Borrowdale in clear weather. The Windy Gap and Aaron Slack descent for Sty Head is not recommended as a way down except in mist, when it is very safe; this route is the best for Wasdale, however. For Ennerdale it is palpably necessary first to go down to Windy Gap to avoid crags, there turning to the right on a scree path.

RIDGE ROUTES

TO BRANDRETH, 2344': NE, then N: 1 mile
Depression (Gillercomb Head) at 2160'
200 feet of ascent

On the descent from Green Gable it is easy to take the Seathwaite path by mistake, and it is necessary to bear left to stay on the ridge.

TO GREAT GABLE, 2949': SE, then SW: ½ mile
Depression (Windy Gap) at 2460'
500 feet of ascent
Follow everybody else.

HALF A MILE

THE VIEW

It might almost be thought that the summit had been expressly constructed for observing the northern crags of Great Gable, so convenient a platform is it for this purpose. The scene calls for first attention; wander west a few yards from the cairn (not too many!) to appreciate the full proportions of the cliff above Stone Cove. Elsewhere the view is very comprehensive, little of the district being hidden by Great Gable. The best picture, a beautiful one, is north-west, where four sheets of water nestle in the folds of rugged and colourful mountains: note how Blackbeck Tarn appears to spill into Buttermere, although in fact there is an unseen mile between.

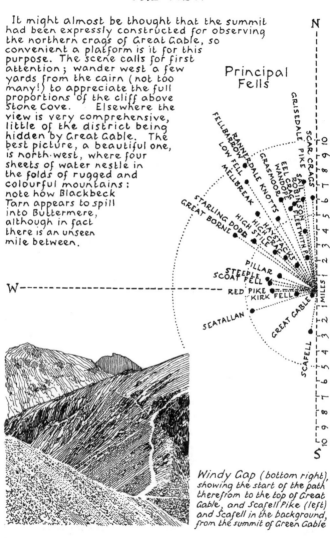

Principal Fells

N

RANNERDALE KNOTTS
FELLBARROW
LOW FELL
MELLBREAK
GRASMOOR
WANDOPE
EEL CRAG
ROBINSON
HINDSCARTH
DALE HEAD
FLEETWITH PK
GRISEDALE PIKE
SCAR CRAGS

STARLING DODD
GREAT BORNE
HIGH STILE
HIGH CRAG
HAYSTACKS

PILLAR
STEEPLE
SCOAT FELL
RED PIKE
KIRK FELL

SEATALLAN

GREAT GABLE

SCAFELL

W
S

Windy Gap (bottom right), showing the start of the path therefrom to the top of Great Gable, and Scafell Pike (left) and Scafell in the background, from the summit of Green Gable

THE VIEW

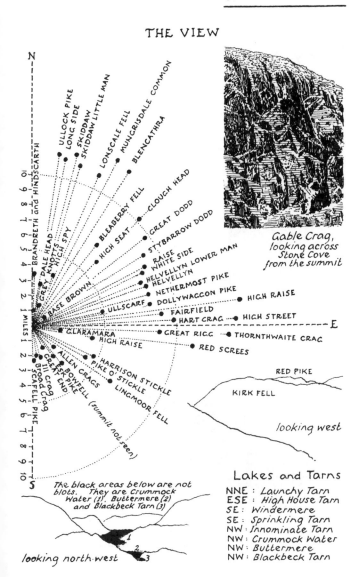

*Gable Crag,
looking across
Stone Cove
from the summit*

N

ULLOCK PIKE
LONG SIDE
SKIDDAW
SKIDDAW LITTLE MAN
LONSCALE FELL
MUNGRISDALE COMMON
BLENCATHRA

BRANDRETH and HINDSCARTH
NOTTS
HIGH SPY
BLEABERRY FELL
CLOUGH HEAD
GREY PALE HEAD
HIGH SEAT
GREAT DODD
STYBARROW DODD
RAISE
WHITE SIDE
HELVELLYN LOWER MAN
BASE BROWN
HELVELLYN
NETHERMOST PIKE
ULLSCARF
DOLLYWAGGON PIKE
HIGH RAISE
FAIRFIELD
HART CRAG
HIGH STREET

E

CLARAMARA
HIGH RAISE
GREAT RIGG
THORNTHWAITE CRAG
RED SCREES

HARRISON STICKLE
PIKE O' STICKLE
ALLEN CRAGS
BOWFELL
LINGMOOR FELL
TIL CRAG
GREAT END
BROAD CRAG
SCAFELL PIKE
SCAFELL (summit not seen)

0 9 8 7 6 5 4 3 2 1 MILES 1 2 3 4 5 6 7 8 9 10

S

*The black areas below are not
blots. They are Crummock
Water (1), Buttermere (2)
and Blackbeck Tarn (3).*

looking north-west

RED PIKE

KIRK FELL

looking west

Lakes and Tarns

NNE : Launchy Tarn
ESE : High House Tarn
SE : Windermere
SE : Sprinkling Tarn
NW : Innominate Tarn
NW : Crummock Water
NW : Buttermere
NW : Blackbeck Tarn

Grey Knotts

2277'

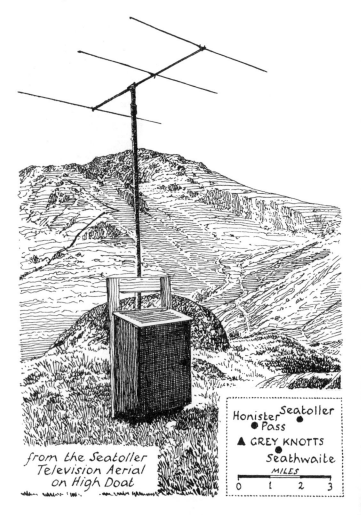

from the Seatoller
Television Aerial
on High Doat

Honister
● Pass
Seatoller
●
▲ GREY KNOTTS
Seathwaite
●

MILES

0   1   2   3

NATURAL FEATURES

Grey Knotts has an interesting situation, rising as a long narrow wedge between upper Borrowdale and an entrant valley half-concealed on the west that carries the motor-road over Honister to Buttermere. So thin is this wedge of high ground that, at the dreary and desolate summit of Honister Pass, sylvan Seathwaite in Borrowdale is still only a straight mile distant.

The ridge of Grey Knotts starts to rise at once, quite steeply, from the woods of Seatoller, levels out at mid height, and finally climbs roughly amongst crags to a broad summit decorated with rock-turrets and tarns. The Honister side of the ridge is plainly unattractive, the Borrowdale side pleasant and interesting, having several notable features: chiefly, high up, the massive buttress of Raven Crag and the scarped hanging valley of Gillercomb. Unique in Lakeland, a once-famous wad or plumbago mine pierces deeply into the Borrowdale flank above Seathwaite. Here, too, is yet another Sourmilk Gill, a leaping white cascade, and not far away is the location of the celebrated 'fraternal four', the Borrowdale Yews written of by Wordsworth and named on maps of Lakeland. One of them was blown down in 2005.

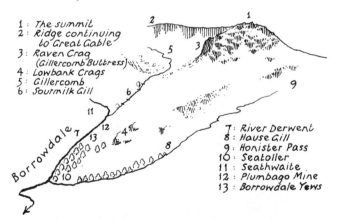

1 : The summit
2 : Ridge continuing to Great Gable
3 : Raven Crag (Gillercomb Buttress)
4 : Lowbank Crags
5 : Gillercomb
6 : Sourmilk Gill

7 : River Derwent
8 : Hause Gill
9 : Honister Pass
10 : Seatoller
11 : Seathwaite
12 : Plumbago Mine
13 : Borrowdale Yews

Grey Knotts is geographically the first stepping-stone to Great Gable from the north (although not commonly used as such), the connection being a high ridge that runs over the two intermediate summits of Brandreth and Green Gable. The western slope descends easily to halt in the marshes of Dubs Bottom and is redeemed from dreariness only by the fine views it commands.

MAP

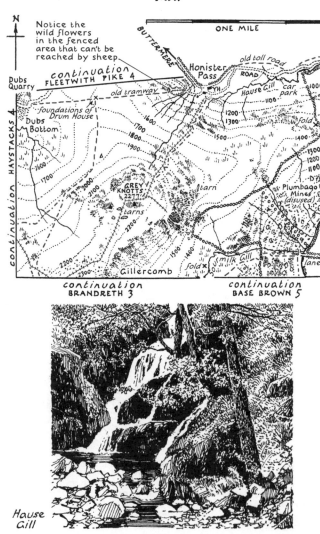

N

Notice the wild flowers in the fenced area that can't be reached by sheep

ONE MILE

BUTTERMERE

Dubs Quarry

continuation
FLEETWITH PIKE 4

Honister Pass

old toll road

ROAD

House Gill

car park

old tramway

foundations of Drum House

Dubs Bottom

Y H

1200
1300
1500
1100
1000

1600
1700
1800
1900

fold

1400

1300
1200
1100

continuation HAYSTACKS 4

1600
1700

2000
2100

GREY KNOTTS 2287

tarns

tarn

Plumbago Mines (disused)

continuation on opposite page

2200

2200
2300

Gillercomb

fold

milk Gill

lane

1500
1400

fold

continuation
BRANDRETH 3

continuation
BASE BROWN 5

Hause Gill

MAP

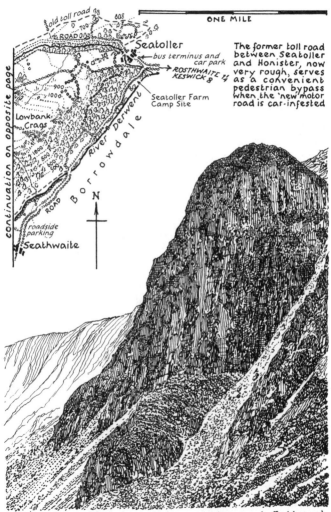

ONE MILE

old toll road

ROAD

Seatoller

← bus terminus and car park

→ ROSTHWAITE 1¼
KESWICK 8

Seatoller Farm Camp Site

continuation on opposite page

Lowbank Crags

River Derwent

Borrowdale

N

roadside parking

Seathwaite

ROAD

The former toll road between Seatoller and Honister, now very rough, serves as a convenient pedestrian bypass when the 'new' motor road is car-infested

Raven Crag (known to climbers as Gillercomb Buttress)

ASCENT FROM SEATHWAITE
1900 feet of ascent : 1½ miles

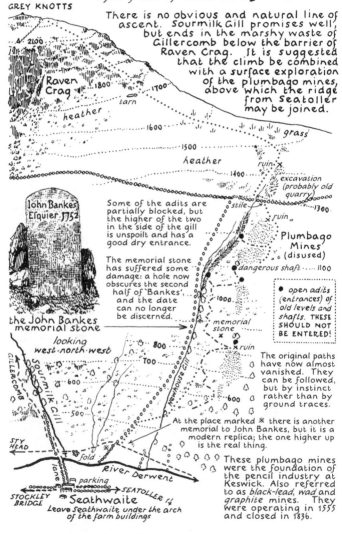

GREY KNOTTS

There is no obvious and natural line of ascent. Sourmilk Gill promises well, but ends in the marshy waste of Gillercomb below the barrier of Raven Crag. It is suggested that the climb be combined with a surface exploration of the plumbago mines, above which the ridge from Seatoller may be joined.

2100

Raven Crag 1800 1700

tarn

heather

1600 grass

1500

heather

1400 ruin ✕

excavation (probably old quarry)

stile ruin

1300

Plumbago Mines (disused)

dangerous shaft ···· 1100

● open adits (entrances) of old levels and shafts. THESE SHOULD NOT BE ENTERED!

Some of the adits are partially blocked, but the higher of the two in the side of the gill is unspoilt and has a good dry entrance.

The memorial stone has suffered some damage: a hole now obscures the second half of 'Bankes', and the date can no longer be discerned.

John Bankes Esquier 1752

the John Bankes memorial stone

looking west·north·west

1000

memorial stone ✕ ✕ ruin

800 700

600

GILLERCOMB

SOURMILK GILL

Newhouse Gill

600

The original paths have now almost vanished. They can be followed, but by instinct rather than by ground traces.

At the place marked ✕ there is another memorial to John Bankes, but it is a modern replica; the one higher up is the real thing.

STY HEAD

fold

River Derwent

lane

parking

STOCKLEY BRIDGE

Seathwaite ← SEATOLLER 1¼ →

Leave Seathwaite under the arch of the farm buildings

These plumbago mines were the foundation of the pencil industry at Keswick. Also referred to as black-lead, wad and graphite mines. They were operating in 1555 and closed in 1836.

ASCENT FROM SEATOLLER
1950 feet of ascent : 2½ miles

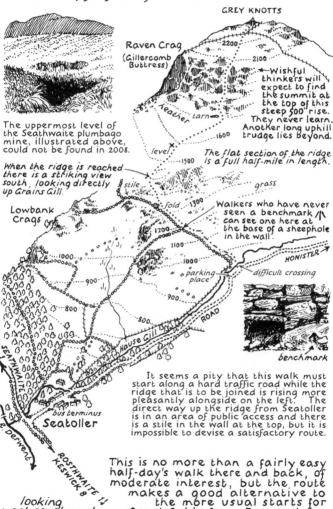

GREY KNOTTS

Raven Crag
(Gillercomb Buttress)

→ Wishful thinkers will expect to find the summit at the top of this steep 500' rise. They never learn. Another long uphill trudge lies beyond.

heather tarn

The uppermost level of the Seathwaite plumbago mine, illustrated above, could not be found in 2008.

level

The flat section of the ridge is a full half-mile in length.

When the ridge is reached there is a striking view south, looking directly up Grains Gill.

stile

grass

Lowbank Crags

fold

Walkers who have never seen a benchmark /|\ can see one here at the base of a sheephole in the wall.

HONISTER

parking place

difficult crossing

HOUSE GILL

ROAD

benchmark

It seems a pity that this walk must start along a hard traffic road while the ridge that is to be joined is rising more pleasantly alongside on the left. The direct way up the ridge from Seatoller is in an area of public access and there is a stile in the wall at the top, but it is impossible to devise a satisfactory route.

SEATHWAITE

bus terminus

Seatoller

to Derwent

ROSTHWAITE ¾
KESWICK 8 ¼

looking west-south-west

This is no more than a fairly easy half-day's walk there and back, of moderate interest, but the route makes a good alternative to the more usual starts for Great Gable from Borrowdale.

ASCENT FROM HONISTER PASS
1150 feet of ascent : 1 mile

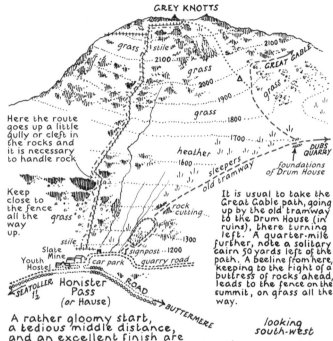

GREY KNOTTS

grass — 1 stile
2100
grass
2000 — GREAT GABLE
1900 — grass
grass — 1800

Here the route goes up a little gully or cleft in the rocks and it is necessary to handle rock

1700 — DUBS QUARRY
heather — 1600
sleepers — foundations of Drum House
old tramway

Keep close to the fence all the way up.

grass

rock cutting

stile
Slate Mine
Youth Hostel — signpost ..1200 — 1300
car park — quarry road

Honister Pass (or Hause)
SEATOLLER 1½ — ROAD — BUTTERMERE

It is usual to take the Great Gable path, going up by the old tramway to the Drum House (in ruins), there turning left. A quarter-mile further, note a solitary cairn 50 yards left of the path. A beeline from here, keeping to the right of a buttress of rocks ahead, leads to the fence on the summit, on grass all the way.

A rather gloomy start, a tedious middle distance, and an excellent finish are features of this mild exercise for the cramped legs of motorists who park their cars at the top of the Pass.

looking south-west

The rock cutting

The skyline of Grey Knotts from the Drum House

THE SUMMIT

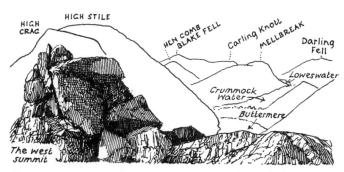

HIGH CRAG
HIGH STILE
HEN COMB
BLAKE FELL
Carling Knott
MELLBREAK
Darling Fell
Lowerswater
Crummock Water
Buttermere

The west summit

Five grey tors of rock, all looking much alike, and four small sheets of water make the top of the fell very attractive, but in mist this would be a most confusing place were it not crossed by a post-and-wire fence from which it is possible to take direction. Two tors compete for the distinction of being the highest: one within the angle of the fence and another 180 yards west and apparently at the same elevation or within inches of it. Only the west summit is given an altitude on the 2008 edition of the Ordnance Survey 2½" map.

DESCENTS: If the fence is being followed east from the angle, it is essential to watch for the junction of the Honister fence — the other branch, still going east, heads for sudden death over the edge of Gillercomb Buttress. For Seatoller, strike a course midway between the two fences, picking a way down among low crags to the level ridge below, and when a wall is reached it is preferable to follow it left to the Honister road. The easiest way off the summit is via the grass slope to the Gable-Honister path.

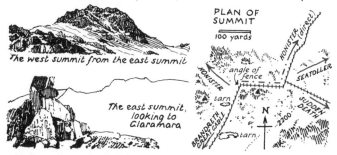

The west summit from the east summit

The east summit, looking to Glaramara

PLAN OF SUMMIT

100 yards

HONISTER (DIRECT)
angle of fence
HONISTER
SEATOLLER
tarn
SUDDEN DEATH
2200
N
BRANDRETH GREAT GABLE
tarn

The name 'Grey Knotts' is apt, and appropriate to the scenery of the top. But it clearly refers only to the summit, this being yet another example of a summit-name commonly but quite wrongly adopted for the whole fell from the roots up. Compare 'Great Gable', another descriptive name, which obviously applies to the mountain in its entirety, the summit having no separate name.

THE VIEW

The view is good on all sides, with a skyline of giants to the south. The finest prospect lies northwest, where the Buttermere district, seen over a foreground of rock, is of superlative beauty.

The diagram is based on the view from the west cairn.

Principal Fells

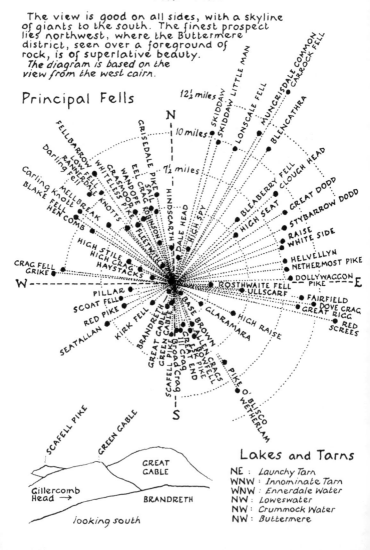

looking south

Lakes and Tarns

NE :	*Launchy Tarn*
WNW :	*Innominate Tarn*
WNW :	*Ennerdale Water*
NW :	*Loweswater*
NW :	*Crummock Water*
NW :	*Buttermere*

RIDGE ROUTE

To BRANDRETH, 2344': ½ mile: SW
Depression at 2250': 100 feet of ascent

Only those of unusual talent could go astray on this simple walk, the fence leading most of the way to the top of Brandreth. Some interest may be added by a detour leftwards to look down into Gillercomb.

ONE MILE

GREY KNOTTS

tarns

2200

stile

2200

2300

BRANDRETH

Gillercomb and Raven Crag

Grike

1601'

from Lanefoot

cows
sitting down
(explanatory note)

Ennerdale Bridge

Cleator Moor

CRAC FELL

GRIKE

MILES

0 1 2 3 4

from Kinniside Stone Circle

NATURAL FEATURES

Grike is the beginning of Lakeland from the west. Approaching from Whitehaven an industrial belt has first to be crossed to Cleator Moor, after which follows an attractive undulating countryside watered by the Ehen, until, quite sharply, Grike and Crag Fell dominate the view ahead, with a glimpse of greater fells beyond closing in the valley of Ennerdale.

Grike, with its smooth grass and forestry plantations, is not a typical forerunner, although the north side overlooking the valley is seamed and scarred with huge ravines, and only its position makes the fell interesting. It is a good viewpoint, and the summit boasts a large cairn and a wind-shelter, which can be seen for some distance around. The indefinite top forms a watershed, the southern slopes draining into the Calder, which, curiously, shares the same estuary near Sellafield as the Ehen, coming round from the north.

Over the past forty years Grike has undergone a transformation. The Forestry Commission, denied further activity in the central areas of the district after making such a mess of Ennerdale, acquired more land along the western fringe, where they were less subject to public outcry, and Grike, like Murton Fell and Blake Fell, was festooned with fences and decorated with little trees, that have now grown into big ones, all looking exactly the same, trees without character. This process of afforestation has turned Grike into another fox sanctuary, as the first edition of this guide predicted.

the Kinniside Stone Circle

looking north-east

Knock Murton BLAKE FELL   GAVEL FELL   HOPEGILL   GRASMOOR
                                             HEAD

It is a remarkable fact that the Kinniside Stone Circle, although a well-known local monument, was for many years omitted from Ordnance Survey maps. The popular explanation for this was that at the time of the first, and early subsequent, surveys, the Kinniside Stone Circle was non-existent, all twelve stones having long before been taken by local farmers for use as gateposts and building materials. Then in the 1920s a grand job of restoration was supposedly accomplished by an enterprising working party who located and recovered all twelve stones and completely restored the site. It eventually transpired, however, that the Kinniside Stone Circle is a modern creation, erected in 1925 by a local archaeologist. (See *A Coast to Coast Walk*, page 10.)

MAP

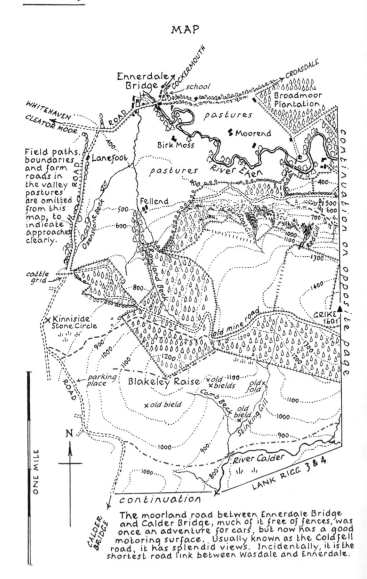

Field paths, boundaries and farm roads in the valley pastures are omitted from this map, to indicate approaches clearly.

WHITEHAVEN
CLEATOR MOOR

Ennerdale Bridge

COCKERMOUTH

school

CROASDALE

Broadmoor Plantation

pastures

Moorend

Lanefoot

Birk Moss

pastures

River Ehen

ROAD

Fellend

Stinking Gill

Red Gill

continuation on opposite page

cattle grid

Oxenside Beck

Coldfell road

× Kinniside Stone Circle

old mine road

GRIKE 1601

parking place

Blakeley Raise

× old bield

× old bields

Comb Beck

old × fold

ROAD

old bield

Stinking Gill

N

River Calder

LANK RIGG 3 & 4

continuation

ONE MILE

CALDER BRIDGE

The moorland road between Ennerdale Bridge and Calder Bridge, much of it free of fences, was once an adventure for cars, but now has a good motoring surface. Usually known as the Coldfell road, it has splendid views. Incidentally, it is the shortest road link between Wasdale and Ennerdale.

ASCENT FROM KINNISIDE STONE CIRCLE
850 feet of ascent : 2 miles

From the gate where the route leaves the forest road the stile is clearly visible ahead, and the summit is only a short distance further.

Part of the old mine road above the forest fence has been improved and is used as a forest road.

MAP

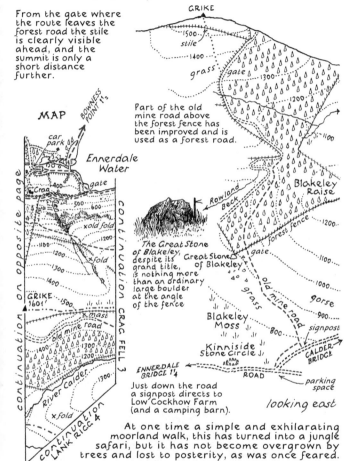

The Great Stone of Blakeley, despite its grand title, is nothing more than an ordinary large boulder at the angle of the fence

Just down the road a signpost directs to Low Cockhow Farm (and a camping barn).

looking east

At one time a simple and exhilarating moorland walk, this has turned into a jungle safari, but it has not become overgrown by trees and lost to posterity, as was once feared.

An alternative start (not shown on the diagram on this page, but shown on Caw Fell 9) leaves the Coldfell road at the cattle grid north of the stone circle and keeps to the forest road until it meets the route shown here at 1150 feet.   Features of note on the way up are a television or radio mast, and, close to it, a fenced area containing an anemometer and other equipment.

ASCENT FROM ENNERDALE BRIDGE
1250 feet of ascent : 2½ miles

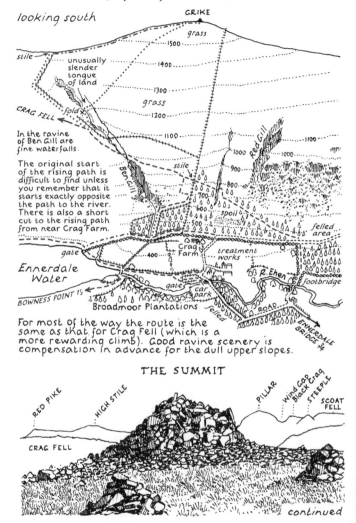

looking south

GRIKE

grass

1500

stile

1400

unusually
slender
tongue
of land

1300

grass

1200

CRAG FELL

fold

1100

In the ravine
of Ben Gill are
fine waterfalls.

The original start
of the rising path is
difficult to find unless
you remember that it
starts exactly opposite
the path to the river.
There is also a short
cut to the rising path
from near Crag Farm.

Ben Gill

stile

Red Gill

1100

1000

1000

900

800

700

600

500

spoil

felled
area

gate

400

Crag
Farm

treatment
works

Ennerdale
Water

gates

car
park

R. Ehen

footbridge

BOWNESS POINT 1½

Broadmoor Plantations

felled

ROAD

ENNERDALE BRIDGE ¾

For most of the way the route is the
same as that for Crag Fell (which is a
more rewarding climb). Good ravine scenery is
compensation in advance for the dull upper slopes.

THE SUMMIT

RED PIKE

HIGH STILE

PILLAR

Wind Gap
Black Crag
STEEPLE

SCOAT
FELL

CRAG FELL

continued

THE SUMMIT

continued

The summit is remarkable for its large cairn and even larger wind-shelter, cairn-building here being an easy task thanks to a rash of stones on the highest part of the fell, an eruption quite out of character: all around is uninterrupted grass. Diligent search will not reveal anything else of interest. A forest fence crosses the western shoulder very close to the summit, but a stile has been provided.

DESCENTS : Head east to a junction of fences, then left along the far side of the fence to the north to join the path from Crag Fell. This crosses Ben Gill and descends through the plantation to a forest road. Turn sharp right for the car park, or take the path directly opposite for Ennerdale Bridge. (See the diagram on page 5.) The descent by the mine road is a fast walk and the best way down in mist; head west to a stile and continue in the same direction to join the mine road at a gate. On reaching tarmac, turn right along it for Ennerdale Bridge.

THE VIEW

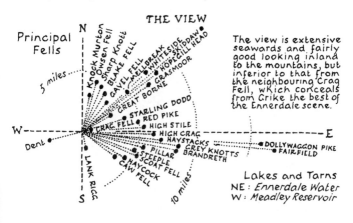

Principal Fells

N

5 miles....

Knock Murton
Sowsen Fell
Sharp Knott
Blake Fell
MELBREAK
WHITESIDE
SKIDDAW
HOPEGILL HEAD
GAVEL FELL
GRASMOOR
GREAT BORNE
STARLING DODD
RED PIKE
CRAC FELL
HIGH STILE
HIGH CRAG
HAYSTACKS
GREY KNOTTS
PILLAR
BRANDRETH
STEEPLE
SCOAT FELL
HAYCOCK
CAW FELL

W----

Dent

LANK RIGG

S

10 miles

E----

DOLLYWAGGON PIKE
FAIRFIELD

The view is extensive seawards and fairly good looking inland to the mountains, but inferior to that from the neighbouring Crag Fell, which conceals from Crike the best of the Ennerdale scene.

Lakes and Tarns
NE : *Ennerdale Water*
W : *Meadley Reservoir*

RIDGE ROUTE

To CRAG FELL, 1716':
1 mile : E, then NE
*Depression at 1450'
260 feet of ascent
An easy stroll*

The old mine road cannot be utilised because of the fence, and it is impossible to avoid marshy ground. Note the anemometer and other equipment in a fenced enclosure close to the mast.

CRAG FELL

-1500- mast -1400- stile

CRIKE

-1600-

-1500-

old mine road

-1300-

N

ONE MILE

Haycock

2618'

from Winscale Hows, Seatallan

NATURAL FEATURES

Haycock rises in a massive dome on the Wasdale and Ennerdale watershed, and its comparative neglect by walkers must be ascribed more to its remote position on the fringe of the dreary and unattractive moors of Kinniside and Copeland than to its own shortcomings, which are few. The fell, indeed, has all the qualities of ruggedness and cragginess characteristic of the Wasdale mountains, and the approaches to it have charm of surroundings not usually associated with such rough terrain. Despite its considerable height, however, Haycock is not rooted in valleys, being instead hoisted on the shoulders of supporting fells of lesser altitude but greater extensiveness. Pleasant streams flow north to Ennerdale and to Wasdale southwards, but the biggest waterway leaving the fell, a great natural channel, is that occupied by the River Bleng, southwest.   Seen from this latter direction, Haycock is a giant in stature, completely dominating the head of the valley and unchallenged by other peaks. Here, at least, it is supreme; it cannot be neglected.

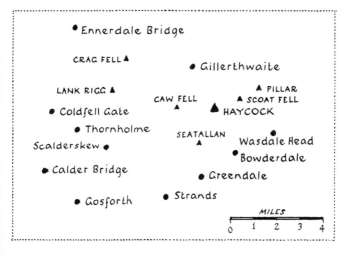

- Ennerdale Bridge
- CRAG FELL ▲
- Gillerthwaite
- LANK RIGG ▲
- ▲ PILLAR
- CAW FELL ▲
- ▲ SCOAT FELL
- ▲ HAYCOCK
- Coldfell Gate
- Thornholme
- SEATALLAN ▲
- Wasdale Head
- Scalderskew
- Bowderdale
- Calder Bridge
- Greendale
- Gosforth
- Strands

MILES
0 1 2 3 4

MAP

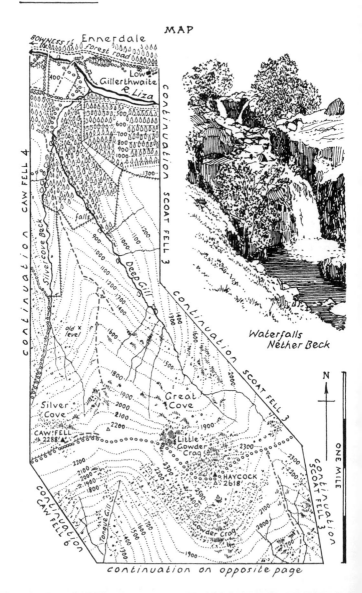

Waterfalls
Nether Beck

continuation on opposite page

MAP

continuation on opposite page

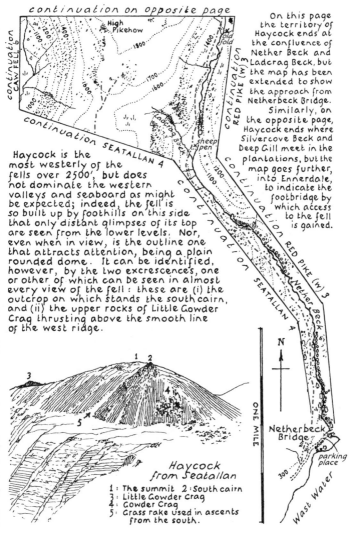

High Pikehow

continuation CAW FELL 6

continuation SEATALLAN 4

continuation RED PIKE (w) 3

Ladcrag Beck

sheep pen

old fold

continuation RED PIKE (w) 3

continuation SEATALLAN 4

Nether Beck

On this page the territory of Haycock ends at the confluence of Nether Beck and Ladcrag Beck, but the map has been extended to show the approach from Netherbeck Bridge. Similarly, on the opposite page, Haycock ends where Silvercove Beck and Deep Gill meet in the plantations, but the map goes further, into Ennerdale, to indicate the footbridge by which access to the fell is gained.

Haycock is the most westerly of the fells over 2500', but does not dominate the western valleys and seaboard as might be expected; indeed, the fell is so built up by foothills on this side that only distant glimpses of its top are seen from the lower levels. Nor, even when in view, is the outline one that attracts attention, being a plain rounded dome. It can be identified, however, by the two excrescences, one or other of which can be seen in almost every view of the fell: these are (i) the outcrop on which stands the south cairn, and (ii) the upper rocks of Little Gowder Crag thrusting above the smooth line of the west ridge.

N

ONE MILE

Netherbeck Bridge

parking place

300

Wast Water

Haycock from Seatallan

1: The summit   2: South cairn
3: Little Gowder Crag
4: Gowder Crag
5: Grass rake used in ascents from the south.

ASCENT FROM WASDALE
(GREENDALE)
2500 feet of ascent : 4¼ miles

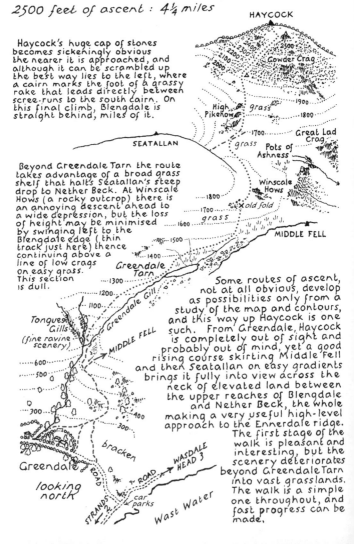

Haycock's huge cap of stones becomes sickeningly obvious the nearer it is approached, and although it can be scrambled up the best way lies to the left, where a cairn marks the foot of a grassy rake that leads directly between scree-runs to the south cairn. On this final climb, Blengdale is straight behind, miles of it.

Beyond Greendale Tarn the route takes advantage of a broad grass shelf that halts Seatallan's steep drop to Nether Beck. At Winscale Hows (a rocky outcrop) there is an annoying descent ahead to a wide depression, but the loss of height may be minimised by swinging left to the Blengdale edge (thin track just here) thence continuing above a line of low crags on easy grass. This section is dull.

Some routes of ascent, not at all obvious, develop as possibilities only from a study of the map and contours, and this way up Haycock is one such. From Greendale, Haycock is completely out of sight and probably out of mind, yet a good rising course skirting Middle Fell and then Seatallan on easy gradients brings it fully into view across the neck of elevated land between the upper reaches of Blengdale and Nether Beck, the whole making a very useful high-level approach to the Ennerdale ridge. The first stage of the walk is pleasant and interesting, but the scenery deteriorates beyond Greendale Tarn into vast grasslands. The walk is a simple one throughout, and fast progress can be made.

HAYCOCK

Cowder Crag

High Pikehow

SEATALLAN

grass

2500
2300
2200
2100
2000
1900
1800
1700
1600
1500
1400
1300
1200
1100

grass

Great Lad Crag

Pots of Ashness

Winscale Hows

old fold

MIDDLE FELL

Greendale Tarn

Greendale Gill

MIDDLE FELL

Tongues Gills (fine ravine scenery)

600
500

700

400

300

bracken

Greendale

looking north

ROAD

WASDALE HEAD 3

car parks

STRANDS 2

Wast Water

ASCENT FROM WASDALE
(NETHERBECK BRIDGE)
2400 feet of ascent : 4 miles

HAYCOCK

SCOAT FELL

2500

2400

2300

2200

Cowder Crag

2100

2000

grass

High Pikehow

grass

1800

1900

Little Lad Crag

SCOAT TARN

1500

1700

grass

B

Great Lad Crag

1500

old fold

Pots of Ashness

A

B

Ladcrag Beck

x sheep pen

1300

1200

1100

1000

900

Nether Beck

A fair path proceeds along the west side of Nether Beck. It leaves the road a quarter-mile from Netherbeck Bridge, but it is difficult to find. Cutting across from the bridge is not recommended because of thick bracken and marshy ground.

RED PIKE rises on this side

Two routes are shown beyond Ladcrag Beck. It is usual, and more simple, to continue up the valley and aim for the depression on the ridge ahead (to the *right* of Haycock), turning up alongside the wall to the summit. But if returning down the valley afterwards variety may be added to the later stages of the climb by going up instead by Ladcrag Beck to the plateau above and then finishing by the rake mentioned on the page opposite. If both routes are so employed, use B for ascent and A for coming down. In mist use A only, in both directions.

MIDDLE FELL

800

700

600

500

400

300

fall

fall

WASDALE HEAD 2

looking north·north·west

ROAD

parking place

Netherbeck Bridge

GOSFORTH 6½
STRANDS 2¾

Wast Water

ASCENT FROM ENNERDALE
(LOW GILLERTHWAITE)
2300 feet of ascent : 3 miles

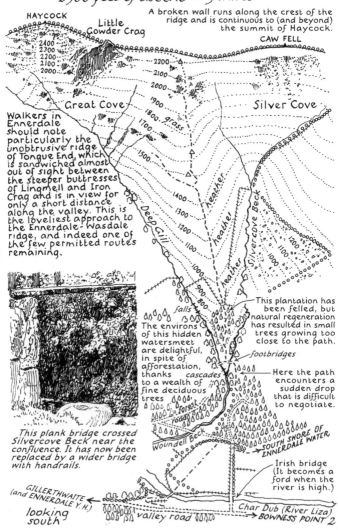

A broken wall runs along the crest of the ridge and is continuous to (and beyond) the summit of Haycock.

HAYCOCK

Little Cowder Crag

CAW FELL

2400
2300
2200
2100
2000

2200
2100
2000
1900. grass
1800
1700

Great Cove

Silver Cove

Walkers in Ennerdale should note particularly the unobtrusive ridge of Tongue End, which is sandwiched almost out of sight between the steeper buttresses of Lingmell and Iron Crag and is in view for only a short distance along the valley. This is the loveliest approach to the Ennerdale-Wasdale ridge, and indeed one of the few permitted routes remaining.

Deep Gill

1500
1400
1300
1200
1100
1000
900
800

heather

heather

heather

Silvercove Beck

1200
1100
1000

falls

This plantation has been felled, but natural regeneration has resulted in small trees growing too close to the path.

The environs of this hidden watersmeet are delightful, in spite of afforestation, thanks to a wealth of fine deciduous trees

cascades

footbridges

Here the path encounters a sudden drop that is difficult to negotiate.

forest road

Woundell Beck

SOUTH SHORE OF ENNERDALE WATER

This plank bridge crossed Silvercove Beck near the confluence. It has now been replaced by a wider bridge with handrails.

Irish bridge (It becomes a ford when the river is high.)

GILLERTHWAITE (and ENNERDALE Y.H.) ←

looking south

valley road

Char Dub (River Liza)
→ BOWNESS POINT 2

THE SUMMIT

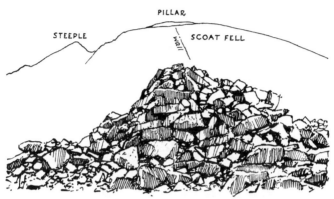

There are two summit cairns, one on each side of the ruined stone wall running over the top of the fell. That on the north side has slightly the greater elevation and has been made into a wind shelter with its entrance facing east. The top is stony everywhere and without paths: it is usual not to stray far from the wall. 150 yards south is another cairn, prominent on an outcrop of rock and commanding a better view of the Wasdale scene.

DESCENTS :

For Wasdale, the quickest route lies alongside the wall to the east depression, there turning right at a cairn onto an indistinct path down an easy grass slope. Keep to the right of an incipient stream. Nether Beck is joined on its way down from Scoat Tarn, and from here on the path, indistinct in places, can be followed down to the Wasdale road at Netherbeck Bridge. This is a simple and straightforward way off the fell, the best for a party that has already had enough for one day, and the safest route in mist, but the time required for it should not be under-estimated.

For Ennerdale, follow the north side of the wall north-west over Little Gowder Crag and on the grass beyond turn down an indefinite ridge that soon becomes more pronounced, and, when heather is reached, provides a good ridge path down Tongue End into the plantations, gaining the valley road across the footbridge a few fields east of the head of Ennerdale Water.

The second (slightly lower) summit cairn. Beyond the old wall is a wind shelter.

THE VIEW

Although the view of Lakeland tends to deteriorate on the long decline to the west from Pillar, that from the summit of Haycock is still remarkably good in all directions. The full length of the Scafell range is seen, but, curiously, only the uppermost feet of Pillar and Great Gable are visible above the intervening heights of Scoat Fell and Red Pike.

Principal Fells

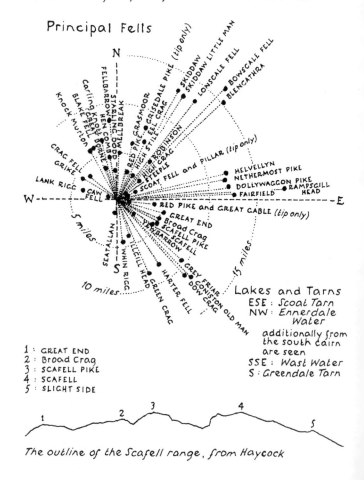

Lakes and Tarns
ESE: Scoat Tarn
NW: Ennerdale Water

additionally from the south cairn are seen
SSE: Wast Water
S: Greendale Tarn

1 : GREAT END
2 : Broad Crag
3 : SCAFELL PIKE
4 : SCAFELL
5 : SLIGHT SIDE

The outline of the Scafell range, from Haycock

RIDGE ROUTES

To SCOAT FELL, 2760': 1 mile : ENE
Depression at 2315': 450 feet of ascent
Just a matter of following the wall

The wall connects the two summits and there is no possibility of going astray. Starting east, the south side of the wall is rather less stony down to the depression, but here, with the remainder of the walk on grass, it is preferable to change sides to get the striking views into Mirklin Cove and across to Steeple.

To SEATALLAN, 2266': 2 miles
S, then SW, SE and SSW
Depression at 1610': 670 feet of ascent
Not recommended in mist

Haycock is defended to the south by a semi-circular barrier of broken rock and scree, but has one weakness — a grassy rake that leaves the top 10 yards short of the south cairn, on the right, in the direction of Blengdale. Go down this to the hummocky grassland, a mile of it, between the two fells. There is no difficulty in crossing over to Seatallan in clear weather, but the absence of paths and landmarks makes this a confusing area in mist.

To CAW FELL, 2288': 1 mile
NW, then W
Depression at 2210': 120 feet of ascent
The scenery deteriorates with every step

The wall leads over the top rocks of Little Gowder Crag.

Follow the wall north-west down a stony slope to a grassy saddle, where a slight ascent is made to the top rocks of Little Gowder Crag. Here, vertical steps, easily avoided, interrupt the continuity of the wall, which then resumes its aim for Caw Fell.

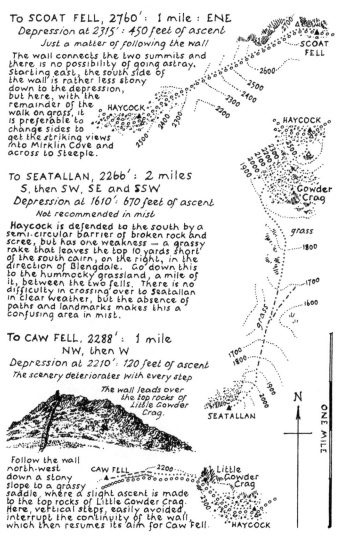

Haystacks

properly
Hay Stacks
(two words)
as on
Ordnance maps

from Gamlin End, High Crag

Gatesgarth
HIGH
▲CRAG ●
HAYSTACKS
▲
Black ●Sail Y.H.
MILES
0   1   2

NATURAL FEATURES

Haystacks stands unabashed and unashamed in the midst of a circle of much loftier fells, like a shaggy terrier in the company of foxhounds, some of them known internationally, but not one of this distinguished group of mountains around Ennerdale and Buttermere can show a greater variety and a more fascinating arrangement of interesting features. Here are sharp peaks in profusion, tarns with islands and tarns without islands, crags, screes, rocks for climbing and rocks not for climbing, heather tracts, marshes, serpentine trails, tarns with streams and tarns with no streams. All these, with a background of magnificent landscapes, await every visitor to Haystacks but they will be appreciated most by those who go there to linger and explore. It is a place of surprises around corners, and there are many corners. For a man trying to get a persistent worry out of his mind, the top of Haystacks is a wonderful cure.

The fell rises between the deep hollow of Warnscale Bottom near Gatesgarth, and Ennerdale: between a valley familiar to summer motorists and a valley reached only on foot. It is bounded on the west by Scarth Gap, a pass linking the two. The Buttermere aspect is the better known, although this side is often dark in shadow and seen only as a silhouette against the sky: here, above Warnscale, is a great wall of crags. The Ennerdale flank, open to the sun, is friendlier but steep and rough nevertheless.

Eastwards, beyond the tangle of tors and outcrops forming the boundary of Haystacks on this side, a broad grass slope rises easily and unattractively to Brandreth on the edge of the Borrowdale watershed; beyond is Derwent country.

The spelling of Haystacks as one word is a personal preference of the author (and others), and probably arises from a belief that the name originated from the resemblance of the scattered tors on the summit to stacks of hay in a field. If this were so, the one word *Haystacks* would be correct (as it is in *Haycock*).

But learned authorities state that the name derives from the Icelandic 'stack', meaning 'a columnar rock', and that the true interpretation is *High Rocks*. This is logical and appropriate. *High Rocks* is a name of two words and would be wrongly written as *Highrocks*.

The summit tarn

Haystacks 3

Big Stack,
looking east from a point
near the path to the
summit from
Scarth Gap.

In the picture below
Big Stack appears on
the extreme right.

The north crags,
looking west from the
slopes of Green Crag.

The path is seen
skirting the cliff
on the left.

MAP

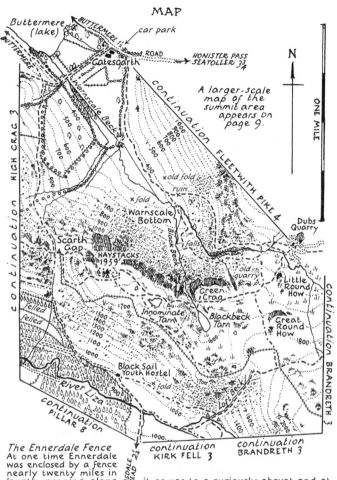

A larger-scale map of the summit area appears on page 9.

The Ennerdale Fence
At one time Ennerdale was enclosed by a fence nearly twenty miles in length, running along both watersheds and around the head of the valley. The fence was mainly of post and wire, and in most places only the posts survive. On Haystacks the fence has been restored, but it comes to a curiously abrupt end at Scarth Gap. In general, the line of the fence followed parish boundaries but on Haystacks there is considerable deviation. Here the series of iron stakes embedded in rock (erected to mark the boundary of the Lonsdale estate) coincides with the parish boundary, but the fence keeps well to the south of this line.

ASCENT FROM GATESGARTH
1550 feet of ascent : 1¼ miles

via SCARTH GAP

Big Stack

Stack Rake

HAYSTACKS

HIGH CRAG

Scarth Gap

From Scarth Gap a well-constructed path leads up to the summit, avoiding all scree, though in places it is necessary to handle rock.

1500

1400

1300

1200

1100

gap

High Wax Knott

Low Wax Knott

It is a test of iron discipline to pass without halting several large *comfortable* boulders athwart the path.

1000

gate

900

bracken

800

700

Scarth Gap is one of the pleasantest of the foot-passes. Apart from the steep section above the old sheepfold, the gradients are gentle and the views both ahead and behind are full of interest. The path is generally good, and the roughness formerly encountered on the early stages of the climb is buried underneath a new conifer plantation.

600

500

400

gap

Coupled with a return by the Warnscale route to make a full 'round' journey, the ascent of Haystacks via the pass of Scarth Gap is a prelude of much merit and beauty to a mountain walk of unique character, the whole distance being no more than five miles. Save it, however, for a fine clear day.

Leave Gatesgarth by the bridge, at a signpost to Ennerdale.

old sheepfold

Gatesgarth

BUTTERMERE via BURTNESS WOOD

ROAD

car park

Buttermere

looking south

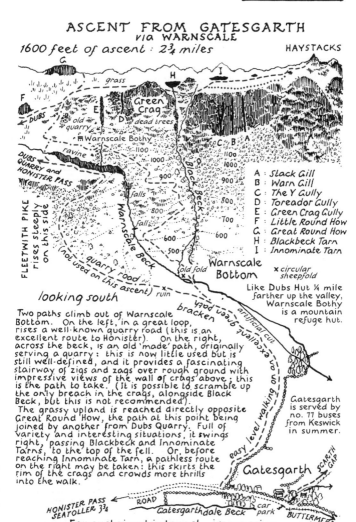

ASCENT FROM GATESGARTH
VIA WARNSCALE
1600 feet of ascent : 2¾ miles

HAYSTACKS

looking south

A : Slack Gill
B : Warn Gill
C : The Y Gully
D : Toreador Gully
E : Green Crag Gully
F : Little Round How
G : Great Round How
H : Blackbeck Tarn
I : Innominate Tarn

x *circular sheepfold*

Like Dubs Hut ¼ mile farther up the valley, Warnscale Bothy is a mountain refuge hut.

Two paths climb out of Warnscale Bottom. On the left, in a great loop, rises a well-known quarry road (this is an excellent route to Honister). On the right, across the beck, is an old 'made' path, originally serving a quarry: this is now little used but is still well-defined, and it provides a fascinating stairway of zigs and zags over rough ground with impressive views of the wall of crags above: this is the path to take. (It is possible to scramble up the only breach in the crags, alongside Black Beck, but this is not recommended).

The grassy upland is reached directly opposite Great Round How, the path at this point being joined by another from Dubs Quarry. Full of variety and interesting situations, it swings right, passing Blackbeck and Innominate Tarns, to the top of the fell. Or, before reaching Innominate Tarn, a pathless route on the right may be taken: this skirts the rim of the crags and crowds more thrills into the walk.

Gatesgarth is served by no. 77 buses from Keswick in summer.

Gatesgarth

HONISTER PASS
SEATOLLER 3¾   ROAD   Gatesgarthdale Beck   car park   BUTTERMERE 1¼

For sustained interest, impressive crag scenery, beautiful views, and a most delightful arrangement of tarns and rocky peaks, this short mountain excursion ranks with the very best.

ASCENT FROM HONISTER PASS
1050 feet of ascent : 2¼ miles

A note of explanation is required.   This ascent-route does not conform to the usual pattern, being more in the nature of an upland cross-country walk than a mountain climb : there are two pronounced descents before foot is set on Haystacks. The wide variety of scene and the fascinating intricacies of the path are justification for the inclusion of the route in this book.

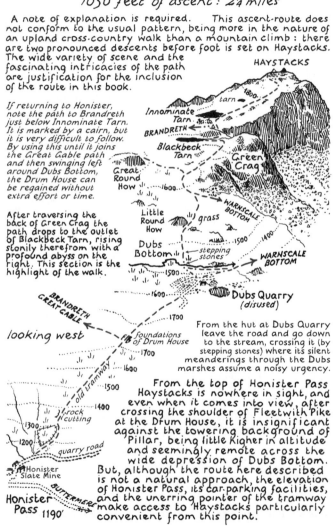

If returning to Honister, note the path to Brandreth just below Innominate Tarn. It is marked by a cairn, but it is very difficult to follow. By using this until it joins the Great Gable path and then swinging left around Dubs Bottom, the Drum House can be regained without extra effort or time.

After traversing the back of Green Crag the path drops to the outlet of Blackbeck Tarn, rising stonily therefrom with a profound abyss on the right. This section is the highlight of the walk.

HAYSTACKS

tarn 1800

Innominate Tarn

BRANDRETH

Blackbeck Tarn

Green Crag

Great Round How ... 1600 ...

Little Round How

grass

WARNSCALE BOTTOM

Dubs Bottom

stepping stones

1500 ... 1400 ...

WARNSCALE BOTTOM

1500

1600 ...

Dubs Quarry (disused)

BRANDRETH
GREAT GABLE

looking west

1700

foundations of Drum House

1700

old tramway ... 1600

1500

rock cutting

1400

1300

1200

quarry road

Honister Slate Mine

BUTTERMERE

Honister Pass 1190'

From the hut at Dubs Quarry leave the road and go down to the stream, crossing it (by stepping stones) where its silent meanderings through the Dubs marshes assume a noisy urgency.

From the top of Honister Pass Haystacks is nowhere in sight, and even when it comes into view, after crossing the shoulder of Fleetwith Pike at the Drum House, it is insignificant against the towering background of Pillar, being little higher in altitude and seemingly remote across the wide depression of Dubs Bottom. But, although the route here described is not a natural approach, the elevation of Honister Pass, its car-parking facilities, and the unerring pointer of the tramway make access to Haystacks particularly convenient from this point.

ASCENT FROM ENNERDALE
(BLACK SAIL YOUTH HOSTEL)

970 feet of ascent
1¼ miles

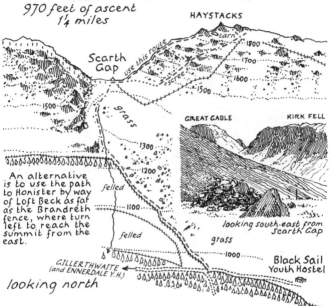

HAYSTACKS

use this route

Scarth Gap

scree

1800
1700
1600
1500

1500

grass

1300

GREAT GABLE   KIRK FELL

1200

felled

1100

An alternative
is to use the path
to Honister by way
of Loft Beck as far
as the Brandreth
fence, where turn
left to reach the
summit from the
east.

*looking south-east from
Scarth Gap*

felled

grass

1000

GILLERTHWAITE
(and ENNERDALE Y.H.)

Black Sail
Youth Hostel

looking north

This route is likely to be of interest only to those
staying at the magnificently situated Black Sail
Youth Hostel. This hostel is open to everyone, but those
intending to use it are advised to book well in advance.

*formerly a
shepherd's
hut......*

Black Sail Youth Hostel

THE SUMMIT

ONE MILE

PLAN OF THE TOP

The highest part of the fell is a small rocky ridge, fifty yards in length, with a cairn at each end and a tarn alongside to the west. The two cairns are at approximately the same elevation, but the north one, lying on the line of the path across the top of the fell, is usually regarded as the true summit. Its height is currently reckoned to be 1959 feet.

continued

THE SUMMIT

continued

Haystacks fails to qualify for inclusion in the author's "best half-dozen" only because of inferior height, a deficiency in vertical measurement. Another thousand feet would have made all the difference.

But for beauty, variety and interesting detail, for sheer fascination and unique individuality, the summit-area of Haystacks is supreme. This is in fact the best fell-top of all — a place of great charm and fairyland attractiveness. Seen from a distance, these qualities are not suspected: indeed, on the contrary, the appearance of Haystacks is almost repellent when viewed from the higher surrounding peaks: black are its bones and black is its flesh. With its thick covering of heather it is dark and sombre even when the sun sparkles the waters of its many tarns, gloomy and mysterious even under a blue sky: there are fierce crags and rough screes and outcrops that will be grittier still when the author's ashes are scattered here.✳

Yet the combination of features, of tarn and tor, of cliff and cove, the labyrinth of corners and recesses, the maze of old sheepwalks and paths, form a design, or a lack of design, of singular appeal and absorbing interest. One can forget even a raging toothache on Haystacks.

✳ *After his death in 1991,*
Wainwright's ashes were
duly scattered
on Haystacks.

perched boulder
on a rock platform

Note the profile
in shadow.
Some women
have faces
like that.

On a first visit, learn thoroughly the details of the mile-long main path across the top, a magnificent traverse, because this serves as the best introduction to the geography of the fell.

Having memorised this, several interesting deviations may be made: the parallel alternative above the rim of the north face, the scramble onto Big Stack, the 'cross-country' route around the basin of Blackbeck Tarn, the walk alongside the fence, and so on.

typical summit tors

DESCENTS: A well-made path starts just west of the summit and leads down to Scarth Gap. An alternative path farther south is marred by loose stones and should be avoided. It is advisable to regard the whole of the north edge as highly dangerous. The only advice that can be given to a novice lost on Haystacks *in mist* is that he should kneel down and pray for safe deliverance.

THE VIEW

This is not a case of distance lending enchantment to the view, because apart from a glimpse of Skiddaw above the Robinson-Hindscarth depression and a slice of the Helvellyn range over Honister, the scene is predominantly one of high mountains within a five-mile radius. And really good they look — the enchantment is close at hand. Set in a tight surround, they are seen in revealing detail: a rewarding study deserving leisurely appreciation.

Principal Fells

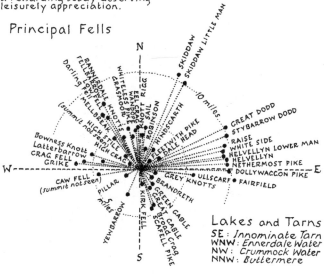

Lakes and Tarns

SE: *Innominate Tarn*
WNW: *Ennerdale Water*
NW: *Crummock Water*
NNW: *Buttermere*

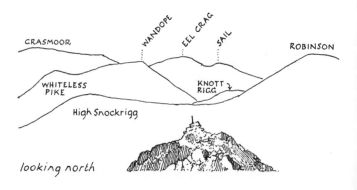

CRASMOOR   WANDOPE   EEL CRAG   SAIL   ROBINSON

WHITELESS PIKE   KNOTT RIGG

High Snockrigg

looking north

RIDGE ROUTES

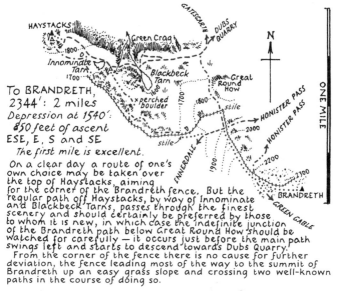

TO BRANDRETH, 2344': 2 miles
Depression at 1540':
850 feet of ascent
ESE, E, S and SE

The first mile is excellent.

On a clear day a route of one's own choice may be taken over the top of Haystacks, aiming for the corner of the Brandreth fence. But the regular path off Haystacks, by way of Innominate and Blackbeck Tarns, passes through the finest scenery and should certainly be preferred by those to whom it is new, in which case the indefinite junction of the Brandreth path below Great Round How should be watched for carefully — it occurs just before the main path swings left and starts to descend towards Dubs Quarry.

From the corner of the fence there is no cause for further deviation, the fence leading most of the way to the summit of Brandreth up an easy grass slope and crossing two well-known paths in the course of doing so.

TO HIGH CRAG, 2443'
1¼ miles : W, then NW
Depression at 1425' (Scarth Gap)
1100 feet of ascent
A fine walk in spite of scree

Follow faithfully the well-made path to the west from the summit, a delightful game of ins and outs and ups and downs. An alternative path south of the summit encounters an area of loose stones and should be avoided.

From Scarth Gap a beautiful path climbs through the heather to Seat; then a good ridge follows to the final tower of High Crag: this deteriorates badly into slippery scree on the later stages of the ascent.

High Crag, from Scarth Gap

HALF A MILE

Hen Comb

1670'

from Mosedale

Following the general pattern of the Loweswater Fells, Hen Comb rises as a long ridge from the valley to a round summit set well back. It is a grassy fell, almost entirely, with a rocky knuckle, Little Dodd, midway on the ridge, and there is very little of interest on the flanks apart from slight traces of former mining activity. The main mass of the fell rises on three sides from a desolate moorland with extensive tracts of marsh that serve as a moat and effectively discourage a close acquaintance. It is the sort of fell sometimes climbed, but rarely twice. It is unfortunate in having Mellbreak as a neighbour.

Loweswater ●

BLAKE FELL ▲

GAVEL FELL ▲

MELLBREAK ▲

HEN COMB ▲

GREAT BORNE ▲

Buttermere

MILES

0 1 2 3 4

MAP

The map shows Hen Comb's simple structure — a long ridge rising from a main valley (Loweswater) between side valleys that carry streams down from a wide upland morass, a desolate tract of marshland and bog encircling the extremity of the fell like a moat, out of which rise the summit slopes as an island from the sea.

The two becks, fed from such an unfailing source, bring down water in considerable volume, and, being without bridges above the intakes, make access to Hen Comb from the north difficult in wet weather.

In fact the only way up after heavy rain is from Ennerdale *via* the ancient cairn.

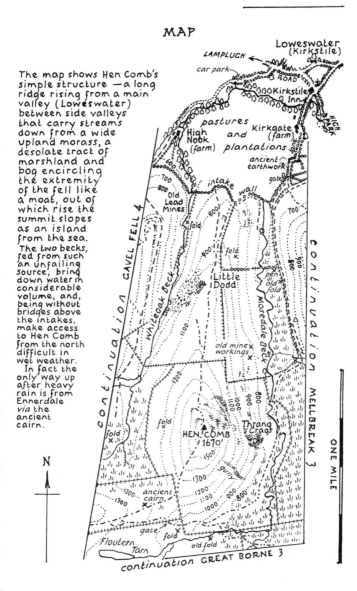

N

ONE MILE

continuation GAVEL FELL 4

continuation MELLBREAK 3

continuation GREAT BORNE 3

ASCENT FROM LOWESWATER
1300 feet of ascent : 2½ miles

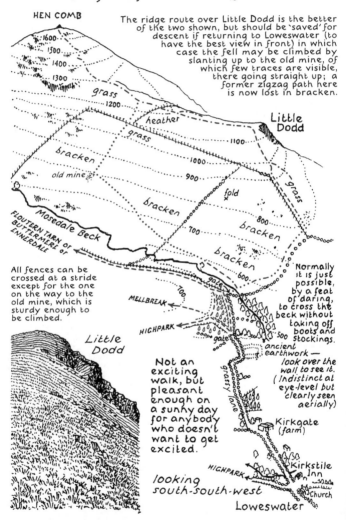

HEN COMB

The ridge route over Little Dodd is the better of the two shown, but should be 'saved' for descent if returning to Loweswater (to have the best view in front) in which case the fell may be climbed by slanting up to the old mine, of which few traces are visible, there going straight up; a former zigzag path here is now lost in bracken.

1600
1500
1400
1300

grass
1200
heather
grass
bracken
old mine
1000
900
fold
800
bracken
bracken
700
bracken

Little Dodd
1100
grass

Mosedale Beck
FLOUTERN TARN or
BUTTERMERE or
ENNERDALE

gate
100
MELLBREAK

600

HIGHPARK

All fences can be crossed at a stride except for the one on the way to the old mine, which is sturdy enough to be climbed.

Normally it is just possible, by a feat of daring, to cross the beck without taking off boots and stockings.

500

gate

ancient earthwork — look over the wall to see it. (Indistinct at eye-level but clearly seen aerially)

Little Dodd

Not an exciting walk, but pleasant enough on a sunny day for anybody who doesn't want to get excited.

grassy lane

Kirkgate (farm)

Kirkstile Inn

HIGHPARK

Church

looking
south-south-west

Loweswater

THE SUMMIT

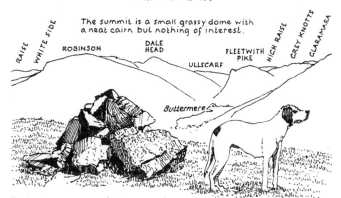

The summit is a small grassy dome with a neat cairn but nothing of interest.

RAISE — WHITE SIDE — ROBINSON — DALE HEAD — ULLSCARF — FLEETWITH PIKE — HIGH RAISE — GREY KNOTTS — GLARAMARA

Buttermere

The bystander, patiently waiting while details are noted but eager to be off, is Barmaid of the Melbreak Foxhounds.

THE VIEW

The view is better than anticipated, with one aspect in particular, that of Buttermere valley in a frame of fells, of classic beauty.

Principal Fells

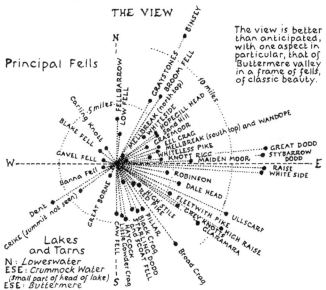

N

BINSEY

GRAYSTONES
BROOM FELL
FELLBARROW
LOW FELL
MELLBREAK (north top)
WHITESIDE
HOPEGILL HEAD
Sand Hill
GRASMOOR
EEL CRAG
MELLBREAK (south top) and WANDOPE
WHITELESS PIKE
KNOTT RIGG
MAIDEN MOOR

Carling Knott — 5 miles
BLAKE FELL
GAVEL FELL
Banna Fell
Dent
CRIKE (summit not seen)

10 miles

GREAT DODD
STYBARROW DODD
RAISE
WHITE SIDE

W — — — — — E

ROBINSON
DALE HEAD
FLEETWITH PIKE
ULLSCARF
HIGH STILE
HIGH RAISE
GREY KNOTTS
GLARAMARA
PILLAR
BLACK CRAG
STARLING DODD
SCARTH GAP
HAYCOCK
GREAT BORNE
RED PIKE
SELLING CRAG
LITTLE DODD
GAW FELL
Little Gowder Crag

Broad Crag

S

Lakes and Tarns
N : Loweswater
ESE : Crummock Water (small part of head of lake)
ESE : Buttermere

RIDGE ROUTES : There are no ridges connecting with other fells.

High Crag

from Haystacks

- Buttermere

HIGH STILE ▲   Gatesgarth •

▲ HIGH CRAG

Scarth)(HAYSTACKS
Gap ▲

Black Sail • Y.H.

MILES
0   1   2   3

NATURAL FEATURES

High Crag is the least known of the three linked peaks of the High Stile range towering above the Buttermere valley and is the lowest in elevation, but it concedes nothing in grandeur and ruggedness to the other two, High Stile and Red Pike, its formidable northern buttress being the finest object in the group. To the west of this buttress lies deeply inurned the stony rock-girt hollow of Burtness (or Birkness) Comb, a favourite climbing ground, with High Stile soaring beyond, the two summits being connected by a narrow ridge overlooking the Comb. Eastwards are vast scree runs, where few men venture; the continuation of the ridge on this side is at first unpleasantly stony until an easier slope of grass leads down to a depression beyond which the ridge re-asserts itself as a distinctive crest and then falls abruptly in crags and scree to the top of Scarth Gap Pass.   The fell's aspect from Buttermere is exceedingly impressive, giving an air of complete inaccessibility, but the opposite flank falling to Ennerdale's new forests lacks distinctive features although everywhere rough.   The summit commands a glorious view of mountainous country, a deserved reward for it is neither easily attained nor easily left, its defence of battlemented crags and hostile stones being breached only by the narrow ridge connecting with High Stile, a mountain with difficulties of its own. Indeed, if it were not for this ridge (which goes on to and beyond Red Pike) the summits of both would be almost unattainable by the ordinary pedestrian. With the help of the ridge they should certainly be visited, the scenery being of the highest order and the situations exciting.

High Crag
*from the north-east
ridge of High Stile*

MAP

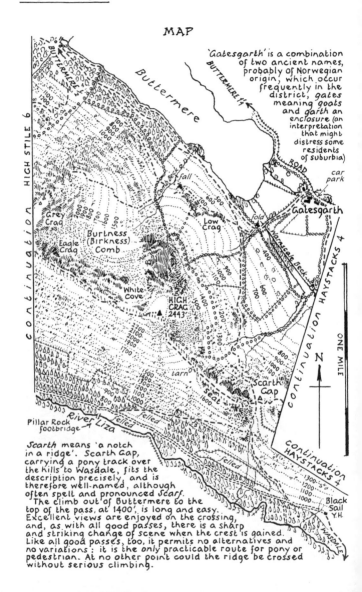

'Gatesgarth' is a combination of two ancient names, probably of Norwegian origin, which occur frequently in the district, *gates* meaning goats and *garth* an enclosure (an interpretation that might distress some residents of suburbia)

Scarth means 'a notch in a ridge'. Scarth Gap, carrying a pony track over the hills to Wasdale, fits the description precisely, and is therefore well-named, although often spelt and pronounced *Scarf*.

The climb out of Buttermere to the top of the pass, at 1400', is long and easy. Excellent views are enjoyed on the crossing, and, as with all good passes, there is a sharp and striking change of scene when the crest is gained. Like all good passes, too, it permits no alternatives and no variations: it is the only practicable route for pony or pedestrian. At no other point could the ridge be crossed without serious climbing.

ASCENT FROM ENNERDALE
(BLACK SAIL YOUTH HOSTEL)
1500 feet of ascent: 1¼ miles

Gamlin End looks unpromising when viewed from below and more so when one is engaged upon it. A path of miniature zigzags, with the posts now on the right, goes straight up the grass until no more grass can be found, but only loose slippery scree. Manoeuvres to avoid this nasty section are in vain, but it can be surmounted by frantic efforts and the firmer ground of the summit gained just above.

2300
2200
2100
Gamlin End
2000
grass
1900

big boulder is known as the Marble Stone (2½" O.S. map)

tarn

Seat

Scarth Gap

1700
1600
1500

Scarth Gap from the head of Ennerdale is the easiest of passes, the difference in altitude being only 400 feet, and the the path, at first skirting a felled area, is clear.

The stiff pull up from the top of the pass to the subsidiary ridge known as Seat, once consisting of loose scree and difficult to negotiate, has been improved out of all recognition. The crest of this ridge is pleasant, with a fair track that keeps mainly to the north side and soon reaches a grassy hollow containing a small tarn. The fence over Haystacks ends at Scarth Gap; from there to the top of High Crag only a few posts survive.

looking north

1300
felled
1200
felled
1100

GILLERTHWAITE
(and ENNERDALE Y.H.)

Ennerdale

Scarth Beck

1000

River Liza

Black Sail Youth Hostel

This route will be of use only to sojourners at the Youth Hostel, all other bases being too remote (although hardy travellers from Wasdale to Buttermere could include it as a variation finish from Scarth Gap).

It is the recognised (in fact, the only) way of gaining the High Stile ridge from the head of Ennerdale; and if this ridge is traversed throughout its length to Red Pike, finally descending to Buttermere, a splendid walk will have been enjoyed.

ASCENT FROM GATESGARTH
2100 feet of ascent : 1¼ miles

looking south-west

HIGH CRAG

Gamlin End

Seat

Scarth Gap

fence posts

2300
2200
2100
2000
1900
1800
1700
1600

old wall

1500

grass

1500

1400

1300

gap

High Wax Knott

1300

1200

Low Wax Knott
1000

1100

1000

900

bracken

The loose and nasty slope of scree leading up from Scarth Gap to the pleasant ridge of Seat has been transformed into a beautiful path winding up through rocks and heather. Before the improvements were made there was an alternative route that turned up by the last wall and reached the ridge at the foot of Gamlin End, but this has now gone out of use.

gate

800

700

600

500

400

old fold

There is a car park opposite Gatesgarth.

pastures

Gamlin End from Seat; line of path indicated

More often used for the purpose of gaining a foothold on the High Stile ridge, this popular route is well worth doing if the sole object is to climb High Crag only.

Gatesgarth

HONISTER PASS ←

ASCENT FROM BUTTERMERE
(DIRECT)

2100 feet of ascent
2½ miles

Leave the Comb at an outcrop on the left, go straight up through a rock gateway and descend to the left of the Buttress until the rock wall ceases and a scramble up a green slope leads to the summit plateau. Stones hidden by vegetation make the climb arduous.

Crossing the beck here is difficult unless the water is very low.

The route may be used with equal facility from Gatesgarth by direct path to the Comb (see High Stile 8)

HIGH CRAG

north top

2300
2200
2100
2000
Sheepbone 1900
Buttress 1800
1700
1600 Burtness
1500 (Birkness)
Comb

1400

This route is NOT advised for descent

This being a serious essay in mountaineering, it is appropriate to take the rock-climbers' route into the Comb (which is not generally known). It leaves the upper path in Burtness Wood as a green forest ride (not obvious) 120 yards beyond the wall in the wood and reaches a stile to gain the open fell.

1300
1200
1100
Comb Beck
1000

stile
1100
1000
gate 900
fall 700
600
500
stile
SCARTH GAP 400
Burtness Wood

RED PIKE

600

Buttermere

gravel lane
SCALE BRIDGE
Fish Hotel
Sail Beck

Buttermere

Ordinary pedestrians, having already been warned (page 2) that direct access to High Crag is virtually impossible, are here provided with a route that, if safely accomplished, will establish their right to be classed as better than ordinary.

The northern buttress is a thousand feet high, all of it craggy or of excessive steepness, but rising across it from the scree of the Comb is a curious slanting gangway free from obstacles that will lead an enterprising scrambler to the easier ground of the summit. This breach in the impregnability of the buttress is clearly in view from Buttermere village. The gangway is a safe route, but steep and sensational. Probably more than 50% of those who try it will live to tell a stirring tale of valour in high places. The casualties must accept the fact that they were only ordinary after all.

This surprising and uncharacteristic weakness in the mountain's defences must be given a name. The only topographical feature in the immediate vicinity of the gangway already named is Sheepbone Buttress, which forms part of the right wall. *Sheepbone Rake* is therefore suggested.

THE SUMMIT

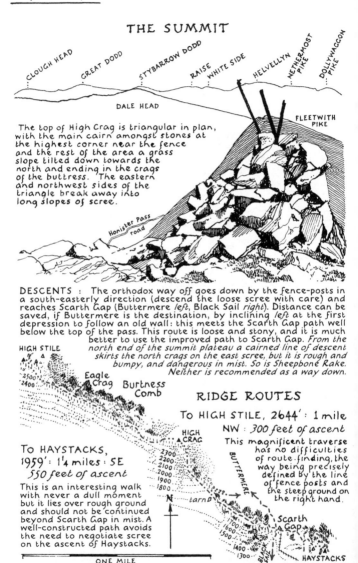

CLOUGH HEAD GREAT DODD STYBARROW DODD RAISE WHITE SIDE HELVELLYN NETHERMOST PIKE DOLLYWAGGON PIKE

DALE HEAD

FLEETWITH PIKE

The top of High Crag is triangular in plan, with the main cairn amongst stones at the highest corner near the fence and the rest of the area a grass slope tilted down towards the north and ending in the crags of the buttress. The eastern and northwest sides of the triangle break away into long slopes of scree.

Honister Pass road

DESCENTS : The orthodox way off goes down by the fence-posts in a south-easterly direction (descend the loose scree with care) and reaches Scarth Gap (Buttermere *left*, Black Sail *right*). Distance can be saved, if Buttermere is the destination, by inclining *left* at the first depression to follow an old wall: this meets the Scarth Gap path well below the top of the pass. This route is loose and stony, and it is much better to use the improved path to Scarth Gap. From the north end of the summit plateau a cairned line of descent skirts the north crags on the east scree, but it is rough and bumpy, and dangerous in mist. So is Sheepbone Rake. Neither is recommended as a way down.

HIGH STILE

2300'
2400'

Eagle Crag

Burtness Comb

HIGH CRAG

2300
2200
2100
2000
1900
1800

tarn

BUTTERMERE

RIDGE ROUTES

To HIGH STILE, 2644' : 1 mile
NW : 300 feet of ascent
This magnificent traverse has no difficulties of route-finding, the way being precisely defined by the line of fence posts and the steep ground on the right hand.

To HAYSTACKS, 1959' : 1¼ miles : SE
550 feet of ascent

This is an interesting walk with never a dull moment but it lies over rough ground and should not be continued beyond Scarth Gap in mist. A well-constructed path avoids the need to negotiate scree on the ascent of Haystacks.

N

1700
1600
1500
1400
1300

BLACK SAIL

Scarth Gap

HAYSTACKS

ONE MILE

THE VIEW

The view is less comprehensive than that from High Stile, but the outlook towards the heart of the district is even better. Wander north a little for some good camera shots not apparent from the top cairn.

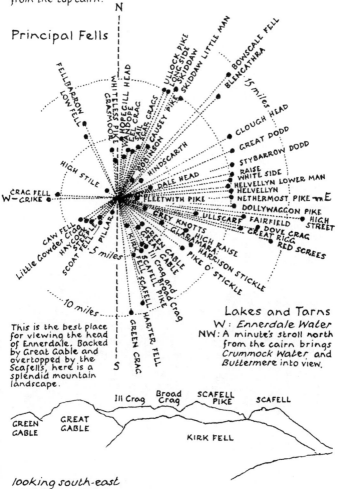

Principal Fells

This is the best place for viewing the head of Ennerdale. Backed by Great Gable and overtopped by the Scafells, here is a splendid mountain landscape.

Lakes and Tarns

W : *Ennerdale Water*
NW: A minute's stroll north from the cairn brings *Crummock Water* and *Buttermere* into view.

looking south-east

High Stile
2644′

from Buttermere

Buttermere

Gatesgarth

RED
PIKE ▲

HIGH
STILE ▲

HIGH
CRAG ▲

Gillerthwaite

Scarth
Gap

Black Sail Y.H.

MILES

0   1   2   3

from Gatesgarth

NATURAL FEATURES

The Buttermere valley is robbed of winter sunshine by a rugged mountain wall exceeding two thousand feet in height and of unusual steepness, its serrated skyline seeming almost to threaten the green fields and dark lake and homesteads far below in its shadow. No mountain range in Lakeland is more dramatically impressive than this, no other more spectacularly sculptured, no other more worth climbing and exploring. Here the scenery assumes truly Alpine characteristics, yet without sacrifice of the intimate charms, the romantic atmosphere, found in Lakeland and nowhere else. From the level strath of the valley the wall rises steeply at once, initially through forests, above which, without respite, buttresses spring upwards from the bare fellside to lose themselves high above in the battlemented crags of the long summit ridge. Three summits rise from this ridge, a trinity of challenging peaks, and of these the central one is the loftiest and grandest. This is High Stile.

1 : High Stile   2 : Red Pike
3 : High Crag
4 : Burtness Comb
5 : Bleaberry Comb
6 : Ling Comb
7 : Burtness Wood
8 : Buttermere
9 : Crummock Water

looking south

The range is magnificently carved to a simple design on a massive scale. Each of the three summits sends down to the valley a broad buttress, steep, rough, untrodden. To the north of each buttress natural forces ages ago eroded a great hollow, leaving a rim of broken crags. A stream cascades from each hollow.   A tarn lies in the central recess like a jewel.

This is superb architecture.

NATURAL FEATURES

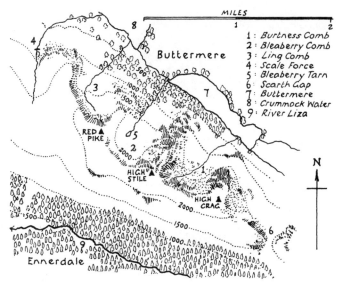

MILES

1 : Burtness Comb
2 : Bleaberry Comb
3 : Ling Comb
4 : Scale Force
5 : Bleaberry Tarn
6 : Scarth Gap
7 : Buttermere
8 : Crummock Water
9 : River Liza

Buttermere

RED PIKE

HIGH STILE

HIGH CRAG

Ennerdale

N

Most mountains have a good side and a not-so-good side, and High Stile and its lesser companions, Red Pike and High Crag, conform to the rule. The Buttermere side of the ridge is tremendously exciting and darkly mysterious, compelling attention, but the other flank, by comparison, is plain and dull, without secrets, falling to the new forests of Ennerdale steeply but lacking attractive adornment; for here the contours do not twist and leap about, they run evenly in straight lines. Ennerdale, repeating the Buttermere design, concentrates its finest features on the southern wall of the valley.

North-flowing streams from the High Stile range contribute to the Cocker river system, so reaching the sea at Workington, but the sparser drainage southwards joins the River Ehen* on its remarkable journey from Great Gable to the sea at Sellafield — remarkable because of its obvious hesitation before taking the final plunge.

* nee Liza

Chapel Crags
from
Bleaberry Tarn

Dale Head
and
Fleetwith Pike
from
Grey Crag,
northeast spur

MAP

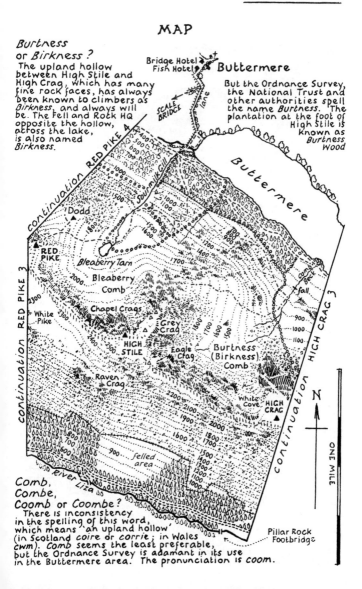

Burtness or Birkness?
The upland hollow between High Stile and High Crag, which has many fine rock faces, has always been known to climbers as *Birkness*, and always will be. The Fell and Rock HQ opposite the hollow, across the lake, is also named *Birkness*.

But the Ordnance Survey, the National Trust and other authorities spell the name *Burtness*. The plantation at the foot of High Stile is known as *Burtness Wood*

Comb, Combe, Coomb or Coombe?
There is inconsistency in the spelling of this word, which means 'an upland hollow' (in Scotland *coire* or *corrie*; in Wales *cwm*). *Comb* seems the least preferable, but the Ordnance Survey is adamant in its use in the Buttermere area. The pronunciation is *coom*.

Bridge Hotel
Fish Hotel
Buttermere

SCALE BRIDGE

lane

Buttermere

continuation RED PIKE 4

Dodd

▲ RED PIKE

Bleaberry Tarn

Bleaberry Comb

White Pike

Chapel Crags

Grey Crag

HIGH STILE

Eagle Crag

Burtness (Birkness) Comb

Raven Crag

White Cove

HIGH CRAG ▲

continuation RED PIKE 3

Sourmilk Gill

fall

Comb Beck

felled area

river Liza

Pillar Rock Footbridge

continuation HIGH CRAG 3

N

ONE MILE

ASCENT FROM BUTTERMERE
2350 feet of ascent : 2¼ miles

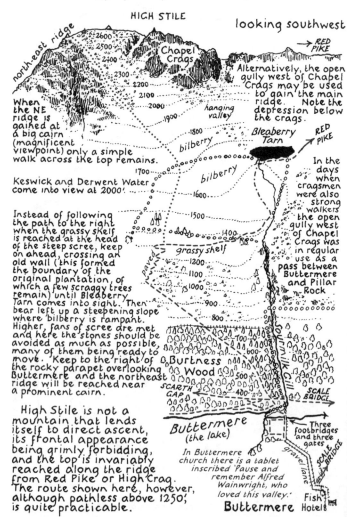

HIGH STILE

looking southwest

north-east ridge

2600
2500
2400
2300
2200
2100
2000
1900

Chapel Crags

→ RED PIKE

Alternatively, the open gully west of Chapel Crags may be used to gain the main ridge. Note the depression below the crags.

hanging valley

Bleaberry Tarn

RED PIKE →

bilberry

1800

When the NE ridge is gained at a big cairn (magnificent viewpoint) only a simple walk across the top remains.

Keswick and Derwent Water come into view at 2000'.

bilberry

1700

1600

In the days when cragsmen were also strong walkers the open gully west of Chapel Crags was in regular use as a pass between Buttermere and Pillar Rock.

Instead of following the path to the right when the grassy shelf is reached at the head of the steep scree, keep on ahead, crossing an old wall (this formed the boundary of the original plantation, of which a few scraggy trees remain) until Bleaberry Tarn comes into sight. Then bear left up a steepening slope where bilberry is rampant. Higher, fans of scree are met and here the stones should be avoided as much as possible, many of them being ready to move. Keep to the right of the rocky parapet overlooking Buttermere and the northeast ridge will be reached near a prominent cairn.

1500

grassy shelf

1400

1300

1200

1100

1000

900

800

700

600

500

400

paved

Sourmilk Gill

Burtness Wood

SCARTH GAP ←

SCALE BRIDGE →

High Stile is not a mountain that lends itself to direct ascent, its frontal appearance being grimly forbidding, and the top is invariably reached along the ridge from Red Pike or High Crag. The route shown here, however, although pathless above 1250', is quite practicable.

Buttermere (the lake)

In Buttermere church there is a tablet inscribed 'Pause and remember Alfred Wainwright, who loved this valley.'

Three footbridges and three gates

gravel lane

SCALE BRIDGE

Fish Hotels

Buttermere

ASCENT FROM GATESGARTH
2300 feet of ascent · 2 miles

looking west

HIGH STILE

HIGH CRAG

Grey Crag

north-east ridge

2300 2400 2300 2200 2100 2000

2300

1800

The north-east ridge is decidedly rough, consisting of successive turrets of rock surrounded by boulders, which cannot be avoided (some are balanced precariously: handle with care). There are no insuperable barriers, however, and an agile scrambler will have no difficulty in reaching the top.

Burtness (Birkness) Comb

The crossing of Comb Beck is difficult at 700'. This may be avoided by keeping left of the stream, but paths in this area are hard to follow. Above the wall a long incline leads to the foot of the north-east ridge, where the fun starts.

heather

1600 1700

1300

grass

1200

1100

stiles

1000

bracken

grass

1100

1000

900

800

700

gate

fall

500

600

bracken

400

Comb Beck

Low Crag

SCARTH GAP

The north-east ridge does not start to look really impressive until one sets foot on it. Quite the most imposing object on the walk thus far is the tremendous buttress of High Crag on the other side of the Comb.

A

stile

BUTTERMERE

This line of ascent may be used conveniently from Buttermere village. Take the broad rising path through Burtness Wood to reach the junction (point A on the edge of the diagram) 120 yards beyond a cross-wall and a stream.

Buttermere

fold

Gatesgarth

HONISTER

car park

BUTTERMERE (VILLAGE) 1½

This is the only feasible *direct* route (it is usual to proceed *via* High Crag). Expect some moments of unhappiness on the steep north-east ridge

ASCENT FROM ENNERDALE
(HIGH GILLERTHWAITE)
2200 feet of ascent : 2½ miles

Access to the Ennerdale slopes of High Stile is completely barred by fenced forests, and the only public right of way up the fellside is a narrow strip of unplanted ground further to the west provided for the ascent of Red Pike. This route may also be adopted for High Stile, following the ridge path south-east when it is reached at 2400'; up to this point the route is identical with that for Red Pike and suffers from the same demerits and disabilities. A diagram is given on page Red Pike **9**, and there is no point in repeating it.

Let's have some pictures of Burtness Comb instead.

Two scenes in Burtness Comb

left : looking across the Comb to Eagle Crag from Sheepbone Rake.
right : looking up the Comb to Eagle Crag.

Burtness Comb has no tarn, and cannot compete with Bleaberry Comb in popular favour. Yet it is the finer of the two, as cragsmen have long realised, and is a grand place to spend a quiet day.

Unlike most mountain hollows its floor is bone-dry and even the beck is partly subterranean; it is notable for a rich July harvest of bilberries, which grow in lush carpets among the tumbled boulders.

THE SUMMIT

The location of the highest point is in doubt. The main ridge (that followed by the fence) rises sharply on the Red Pike side, gradually on the High Crag side, to a rocky eminence crowned with two cairns immediately over the abrupt fall to Chapel Crags, and it is customary to consider the climb ended when this point is reached. The cairns are only a few yards apart. The more northerly of the two is in a magnificent situation with a dramatic view downwards to Bleaberry Tarn. Away to the east, however, a large cairn indicates the Ordnance Survey station, the height of which, 2644', is accepted as the altitude of the fell, but this cairn, situated where the northeast spur takes shape before narrowing to the northeast ridge, does not seem to be quite so elevated as the two first mentioned, perhaps because the latter occupy a more pronounced rise, nor are the environs so attractive. Just north of this large cairn, a smaller one marks the highest point of the northeast spur. Without measuring instruments it is not possible to say definitely where the highest inches are, and better not to worry about it but to enjoy the sublime surroundings instead.

Stones and boulders litter the top everywhere, and, as all visitors prefer to pick their own way amongst these obstacles, no clear path has been formed.

DESCENTS : A woe-begone series of fence-posts, shorn of all connecting strands, pursues an erratic course across the stony top. The posts are too far apart to guide woe-begone walkers to zones of safety, but the ridge is easy enough to follow. To the east, it leads over High Crag to Scarth Gap; west, to Red Pike, and these are the best ways off. The routes of ascent (pages 7 and 8) from Buttermere and Gatesgarth are not recommended for descent, but Ennerdale (page 9) is a good, fast route.

In emergency, the gully between the ridge-top and the northeast spur may be resorted to — it is a rough and steep but safe descent to Bleaberry Tarn, for Buttermere

N

BLEABERRY TARN

100 YARDS

2700 2400

Chapel Crags

2500

Northeast spur

← RED PIKE

fence posts

△ 2644

HIGH CRAG

2600

PLAN OF SUMMIT

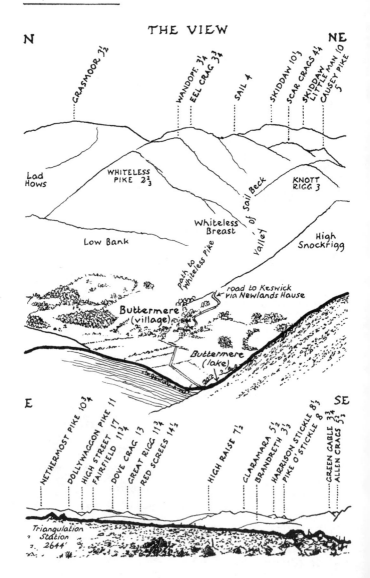

THE VIEW

THE VIEW

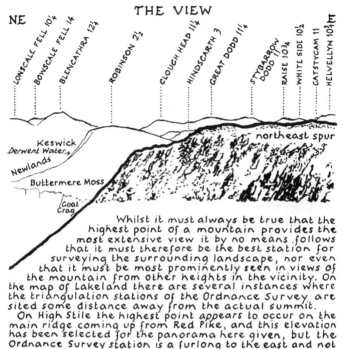

NE

LONSCALE FELL 10¼
BOWSCALE FELL 14
BLENCATHRA 12¼
ROBINSON 2½
CLOUGH HEAD 11¼
HINDSCARTH 3
GREAT DODD 11¼
STYBARROW DODD 11¾
RAISE 10¾
WHITE SIDE 10½
CATSTYCAM 11
HELVELLYN 10¾ E

Keswick
Derwent Water
Newlands
Buttermere Moss
Goat Crag
northeast spur

Whilst it must always be true that the
highest point of a mountain provides the
most extensive view it by no means follows
that it must therefore be the best station for
surveying the surrounding landscape, nor even
that it must be most prominently seen in views of
the mountain from other heights in the vicinity. On
the map of Lakeland there are several instances where
the triangulation stations of the Ordnance Survey are
sited some distance away from the actual summit.
On High Stile the highest point appears to occur on the
main ridge coming up from Red Pike, and this elevation
has been selected for the panorama here given, but the
Ordnance Survey station is a furlong to the east and not
quite on the highest point of the northeast spur, which,
in the view above, cuts into the horizon between White
Side and Catstycam.

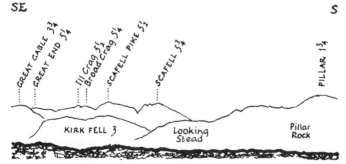

SE   S

GREAT GABLE 3¾
GREAT END 5¼
ILL CRAG 5½
BROAD CRAG 5¼
SCAFELL PIKE 5½
SCAFELL 5¾
PILLAR 1¾

KIRK FELL 3
Looking Stead
Pillar Rock

THE VIEW

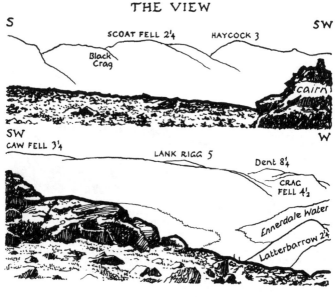

S   SW

SCOAT FELL 2¼   HAYCOCK 3

Black Crag

cairn

SW   W

CAW FELL 3¼

LANK RIGG 5

Dent 8¼

CRAG FELL 4½

Ennerdale Water

Latterbarrow 2¼

W   NW

Knock Murton 5⅓   GAVEL FELL 4   BLAKE FELL 4¾

GREAT BORNE 3

Bowness Knott 3½

STARLING DODD 1¾

RED PIKE ⅔

White Pike

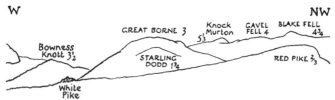

The figures accompanying the names of fells are distances in miles

The thick line marks the visible boundaries of the fell from the viewpoint

In clear weather, the Isle of Man appears over Lank Rigg, Scotland and the Solway Firth above Crummock Water, and the Irish Sea extends across the western horizon.

THE VIEW

NW N

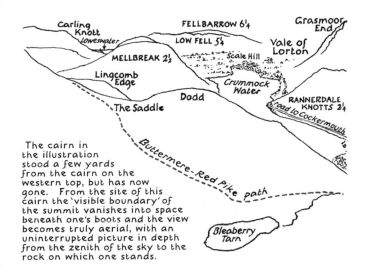

Carling Knott
Loweswater
FELLBARROW 6¼
Grasmoor End
LOW FELL 5¼
Vale of Lorton
MELLBREAK 2½
Scale Hill
Lingcomb Edge
Crummock Water
The Saddle
Dodd
RANNERDALE KNOTTS 2¼
Road to Cockermouth
Buttermere-Red Pike path
Bleaberry Tarn

The cairn in the illustration stood a few yards from the cairn on the western top, but has now gone. From the site of this cairn the 'visible boundary' of the summit vanishes into space beneath one's boots and the view becomes truly aerial, with an uninterrupted picture in depth from the zenith of the sky to the rock on which one stands.

RIDGE ROUTE

TO RED PIKE, 2479' : ¾ mile : NW
Depression at 2300' : 200 feet of ascent
Very easy walking after initial roughness.

RED PIKE

Bleaberry
Comb

Chapel
Crags

2300'

N

200

2100

2400

2500

2200

HIGH STILE

ONE MILE

The line of fence posts that follows
the ridge and skirts the summit of
Red Pike survives only in places.
Elsewhere the posts are too far
apart to be followed in mist, but
there is a path for most of the
way, and the last part of the
route is cairned. The route
passes the gaping mouth of
the Chapel Crags gully.

*Red Pike
from High Stile*

RIDGE ROUTE

To HIGH CRAG, 2443′ : 1 mile : SE

80 feet of ascent.

Minor depressions only.

Simple, but grand.

There is no path at first, but one forms when the ridge narrows. The line of fence posts is continuous to High Crag, and it is important to keep them in sight in bad weather.

ONE MILE

Looking back to High Stile from the ridge, a view of Eagle Crag in profile, and Grey Crag, more distant across the depths of the Comb, is seen. The escarpment here falls away suddenly and vertically; this danger, fortunately, lurks some distance below the path used by walkers along the ridge.

Kirk Fell

2630'

from Green Gable

NATURAL FEATURES

Kirk Fell is the patron fell of Wasdale Head, a distinction little recognised. To most visitors in this grandest of all daleheads, Great Gable so catches the eye that Kirk Fell, next to it, is hardly looked at; and even the other two fells enclosing the valley, Lingmell and Yewbarrow, win more glances. Kirk Fell, although bulking large in the scene, is in fact plain and unattractive, a vast wall of bracken and grass, every yard of it much like the rest. Everybody's camera points to Great Gable, nobody's to Kirk Fell. But look at the map. The streams coming down each side of Kirk Fell, Lingmell Beck and Mosedale Beck, are long in meeting: for a mile or more at valley level they enclose a flat tongue of land at the foot of Kirk Fell. Every building in the little hamlet of Wasdale Head — cottages, farmhouses, church and inn, and all the valley pastures, lie in the lap of Kirk Fell on this flat extension between the two streams. The fell takes its name from the church. Kirk Fell accommodates the community of Wasdale Head, but the footings in the valley of Great Gable and Lingmell and Yewbarrow are barren.

Bland the southern aspect may be, but the dark north face is very different. Here, shadowed cliffs seam the upper slopes in a long escarpment, a playground for climbers, above rough declivities that go down to the Liza in Ennerdale. Linking with Great Gable is the depression of Beck Head to the east; westwards is a counterpart in Black Sail Pass, linking with Pillar. And between is a broad undulating top, with tarns, the ruins of a wire fence, and twin summits: on the whole a rather disappointing ornamentation, a poor crown for so massive a plinth.

- Gatesgarth
- Seatoller
- Black Sail Y.H
- ▲ PILLAR
- Seathwaite
- ▲ KIRK FELL
- ▲ GREAT GABLE
- Wasdale Head

MILES
0   1   2   3

MAP

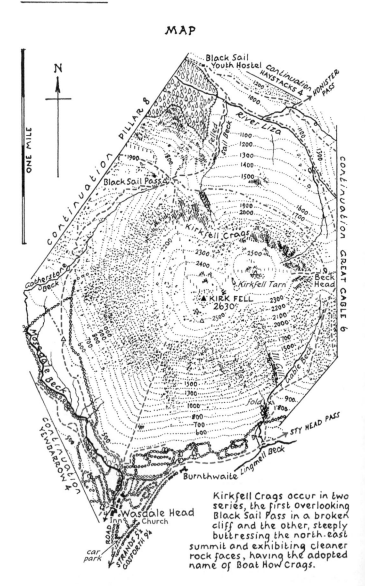

Kirkfell Crags occur in two series, the first overlooking Black Sail Pass in a broken cliff and the other, steeply buttressing the north-east summit and exhibiting cleaner rock faces, having the adopted name of Boat How Crags.

ASCENT FROM WASDALE HEAD
2330 feet of ascent : 1¼ miles

KIRK FELL

A straight line is the shortest distance between two points. This route is the straightest and therefore the most direct ascent in Lakeland. It is also the steepest — a relentless and unremitting treadmill, a turf-clutching crawl, not a walk. There are only three opportunities of standing upright, three heaven-sent bits of horizontal, before the slope eases into the summit plateau. Apart from steepness, there are no difficulties or hazards of any sort.

natural dykes

2500
2400

third halting place (small delectable grass ridge at the top of the scree)

2300
2200
2100
2000
1900
1800
1700
grass
1600

Highnose Head

second halting place (crest of steep grass slope)

1500
1400
grass
1300
1200

Back buttons cannot stand the strain, and wearers of braces are well advised to profit from a sad experience of the author on this climb and take a belt as reserve support.

1100
1000
grass
900

first halting place (top of small crag)

800
700

Looking backwards (between one's legs) there is a superb upside-down view of Wasdale Head

600
500

bracken

BLACK SAIL PASS

looking north

Wasdale Head

Inn

Row Head

Two alternative routes are available and more generally used. Either (a) proceed to the top of Black Sail Pass, thence climbing the north ridge, or (b) go up to Beck Head and ascend Rib End. In both cases the top of the fell is reached after an interesting scramble on a stony track alongside the watershed fence.

Leave Wasdale Head by the Black Sail path, passing through the yard of the Wasdale Head Inn and following Mosedale Beck upstream.

ASCENT FROM ENNERDALE
(BLACK SAIL YOUTH HOSTEL)

1700 feet of ascent
1½ miles (direct)

looking south

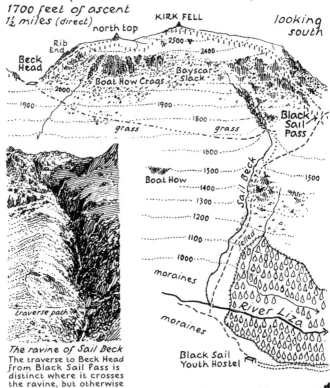

KIRK FELL

north top

Rib End

Beck Head

Boat How Crags

Bayscar Slack

2500

2400

Black Sail Pass

2000

1900

1900

1800

grass   grass

1600

1500   1500

Boat How   1400

Sail Beck

1300

1200

1100

felled

1000

moraines

River Liza

moraines

Black Sail Youth Hostel

The ravine of Sail Beck
The traverse to Beck Head from Black Sail Pass is distinct where it crosses the ravine, but otherwise it is difficult to follow.

traverse path

The *best* route is via Black Sail Pass and the fenced ridge going up therefrom. The *easiest* route, free of crags, is by Bayscar Slack (avoid the boulder-fields). The *most interesting* route, passing beneath Boat How Crags, is along the traverse and up from Beck Head via Rib End.

Boat How Crags

THE SUMMIT

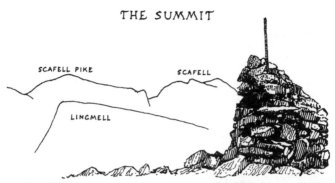

Kirk Fell has two separate tops, the higher being at the head of the Wasdale slope in an area of stones. Here is the main cairn, which takes the form of a windshelter, and there is a second windshelter 30 yards further north. The fence, which otherwise follows the water-shed strictly, rather oddly does not quite visit the highest point at 2630'. The other top, north east, is appreciably lower, the cairn here surmounting a rocky outcrop. In a hollow between the two summits are two unattractive tarns, named as one, Kirkfell Tarn. (One of the tarns has dried up.)

DESCENTS: The top of the fell is usually left with the guidance of the fence, which, after a long crossing of the summit plateau, goes down northwards to Black Sail Pass; or, eastwards, over the lesser summit and down Rib End to Beck Head. Either route may be used for Wasdale Head or Ennerdale and both descend roughly on distinct stony tracks amongst crags although the top of the fell is pathless. For Wasdale Head direct, wander south, where a line of cairns leads down to a small and dainty grass ridge (it is important to find this). Below starts the very steep and straight descent, stony at first. Grass is reached at 2000', and from this point onwards a badly-shod walker will suffer many slips and spills, none fatal, and it is not a bad plan to continue in bare or stockinged feet, which give a better grip than boots.

The north east summit

THE VIEW

Great Gable dominates the scene but does not rob the view of detail, which is well distributed over all sectors. The Scafells look magnificent, and the path up to the Pike from the Lingmell col is clearly seen. Criffel appears over High Crag.

Principal Fells

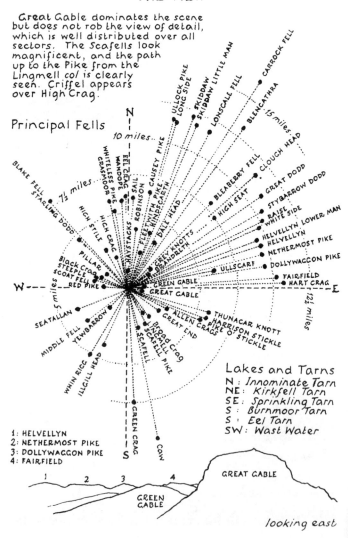

Lakes and Tarns
N: Innominate Tarn
NE: Kirkfell Tarn
SE: Sprinkling Tarn
S: Burnmoor Tarn
S: Eel Tarn
SW: Wast Water

1: HELVELLYN
2: NETHERMOST PIKE
3: DOLLYWAGGON PIKE
4: FAIRFIELD

looking east

RIDGE ROUTES

To PILLAR, 2927': 2½ miles : NW, then N and WNW
Depression at 1800' (Black Sail Pass)
1150 feet of ascent

A walk full of interest, but a long one.
Check there is sufficient time to do it.

PILLAR

ONE MILE

N

2800
2700
2600
2500
2400
2300
2200
2100
2000
1900
1800

△ Looking Stead

tarn

WASDALE
HEAD

Black Sail
Pass

Kirkfell
Crags

1800
1900
2000
2100
2200
2300
2400
2500

KIRK
FELL

Very easy walking
by the fence leads to a
steepening slope, and here
a track materialises amongst the
stones. When crags are reached the
fence does a bit of rock-climbing, but
prefer to keep the track underfoot, and,
after one awkward step, Black Sail Pass
will be duly reached. An opportunity of
changing one's mind and beating a quick
retreat to Wasdale Head or into Ennerdale
here arises. In front there is a splendid walk
across Looking Stead (detour to the cairn for
the view) before the first of the three stony
rises on the ridge is tackled. The whole climb
from Black Sail Pass is quite easy.

To GREAT GABLE, 2949': 1⅓ miles : NE, then E and SE
Depression at 2040' (Beck Head) : 990 feet of ascent.
Rough going, but well worth the effort.

Beck Head

2500
2500
Kirkfell Tarn
Rib End
2200
2100
2000
2100
2800

KIRK FELL

△ GREAT GABLE

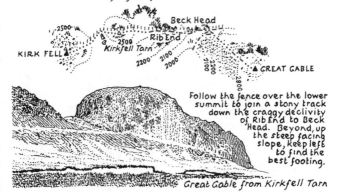

Follow the fence over the lower
summit to join a stony track
down the craggy declivity
of Rib End to Beck
Head. Beyond, up
the steep facing
slope, keep left
to find the
best footing.

Great Gable from Kirkfell Tarn

Lank Rigg

1775'

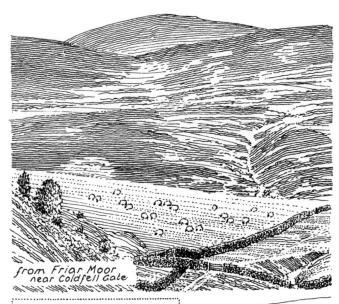

*from Friar Moor
near Coldfell Gate*

● Ennerdale Bridge

GRIKE ▲   ▲ CRAG FELL

▲ LANK RIGG
CAW FELL ▲
● Coldfell Gate
● Thornholme
● Scalderskew

● Calder Bridge

MILES
0   1   2   3   4

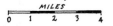

*Water Intake Works
Worm Gill*

NATURAL FEATURES

Ridgewalkers on the more frequented western fells will occasionally notice the isolated summit of Lank Rigg appearing on the skyline and almost certainly will need to refer to a map to determine its identity, for this is a fell most visitors have never heard of and few know sufficiently well to recognise on sight. The map will confirm further that Lank Rigg is an outsider, beyond the accepted limits of Lakeland, too remote to bother about. If Pillar and High Stile haven't yet been climbed, there is admittedly no case to be made out for this humble fell, but walkers already familiar with the district might well devote a day to this lonely outpost of Kinniside; they will do so with especial advantage if of an enquiring turn of mind for things ancient. A column on the summit shows that the Ordnance men have a regard for the place. And Lank Rigg is, after all, within the Lake District National Park boundary.

The fell has wide sprawling slopes and is extensive. It calls for a full day's expedition even if the problem of reaching its environs can be overcome by car or helicopter, for it is distant from tourist centres. To walk all round it, having got there, is a rough tramp of ten miles. Meeting another human is outside the realms of possibility. Die here, unaccompanied, and your disappearance from society is likely to remain an unsolved mystery.

Lank Rigg is bounded by two streams that quickly assume the proportions of rivers. One of them, the Calder, has the name of river from birth; the other, Worm Gill, at one time tapped for water supplies, is a fast-flowing torrent that has carved a wide course through the hills.

Some prehistoric remains suggest that the fell was probably better known in ages past. More recent, but still many centuries old, is a pack-horse bridge spanning a ravine of the Calder, a thing of beauty.

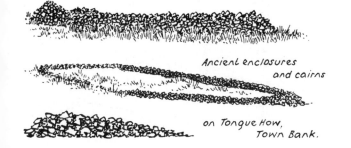

Ancient enclosures
and cairns

on Tongue How,
Town Bank.

MAP

In conversation Lank Rigg becomes one word, pronounced *Lan-krigg*.

Matty Benn's Bridge, although known thus locally, is named Monks Bridge on maps of the Ordnance Survey.

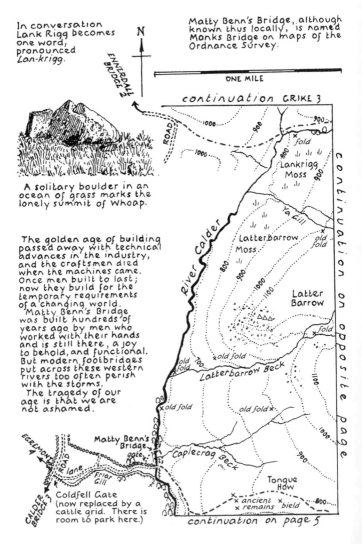

A solitary boulder in an ocean of grass marks the lonely summit of Whoap.

The golden age of building passed away with technical advances in the industry, and the craftsmen died when the machines came. Once men built to last; now they build for the temporary requirements of a changing world.

Matty Benn's Bridge was built hundreds of years ago by men who worked with their hands and is still there, a joy to behold, and functional. But modern footbridges put across these western rivers too often perish with the storms.

The tragedy of our age is that we are not ashamed.

Coldfell Gate (now replaced by a cattle grid. There is room to park here.)

continuation CRIKE 3

continuation on opposite page

continuation on page 5

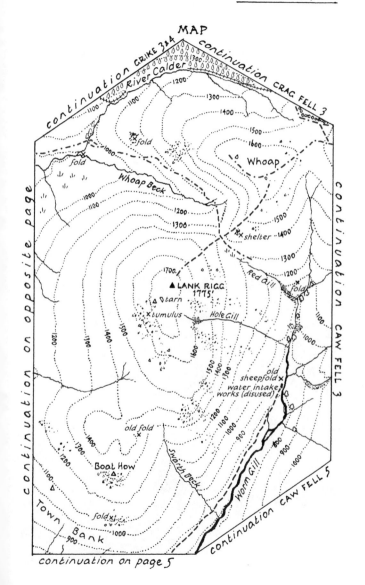

MAP

continuation CRIKE 3&4

continuation CRAG FELL 3

River Calder

1300
1200
1100
1400
1000
1500
1600

×fold

fold

Whoap

Whoap Beck

1000
1100
1200
1300

1500

×shelter 1400

1300

1200

1700

▲ LANK RIGG
1775'

△ tarn

×tumulus

Hole Gill

Red Gill

×fold

1200
1100
1000

1400
1500
1200

1500
1300
1400

old
sheepfold ×

water intake
works (disused)

old fold
×

1400
1300
1200

1100
1000
900

800
900
1000

Boal How

fold ×

Swarth Beck

Worm Gill

continuation on opposite page

continuation CAW FELL 3

continuation CAW FELL 5

Town
Bank

1000
900

continuation on page 5

continuation CAW FELL 5

MAP

continuation on pages 3 and 4

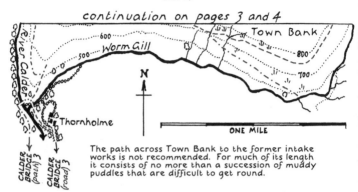

The path across Town Bank to the former intake works is not recommended. For much of its length it consists of no more than a succession of muddy puddles that are difficult to get round.

Matty Benn's Bridge

The valley of
the River Calder
near Thornholme

ASCENT FROM THE COLDFELL ROAD
1400 feet of ascent : 2½ miles

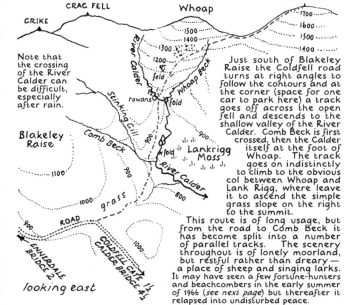

Note that the crossing of the River Calder can be difficult, especially after rain.

looking east

Just south of Blakeley Raise the Coldfell road turns at right angles to follow the contours and at the corner (space for one car to park here) a track goes off across the open fell and descends to the shallow valley of the River Calder. Comb Beck is first crossed, then the Calder itself at the foot of Whoap. The track goes on indistinctly to climb to the obvious col between Whoap and Lank Rigg, where leave it to ascend the simple grass slope on the right to the summit.

This route is of long usage, but from the road to Comb Beck it has become split into a number of parallel tracks. The scenery throughout is of lonely moorland, but restful rather than dreary — a place of sheep and singing larks. It may have seen a few fortune-hunters and beachcombers in the early summer of 1966 (*see next page*) but thereafter it relapsed into undisturbed peace.

For the man who wants to get away from it all, alone.

ASCENT FROM COLDFELL GATE

Rather less conveniently, a footing may be gained on Lank Rigg from Coldfell Gate (3 miles from Calder Bridge; 4¼ from Ennerdale Bridge, on the Coldfell road). Here a lane goes down to ford the Calder, and upstream 120 yards from this point, reached from a gate in the field-wall, is Matty Benn's Bridge, which *must* be visited even though its function has been taken over by a modern footbridge alongside the ford. Across the river rise the long gentle slopes of Lank Rigg and they may be tackled anywhere, but the most interesting plan is to go *via* Tongue How and Boat How, both of which have many ancient remains in the vicinity. The summit is a mile north of Boat How.

ASCENT FROM CALDER BRIDGE

Now that there is a footbridge across Worm Gill just short of its confluence with the Calder at Thornholme, a very pleasant approach can be made from Calder Bridge, visiting the Abbey on the way. In fact, there is also a footbridge over the Calder at Thornholme, which means that the public footpath from Stakes Bridge can be used. The route is practicable and pleasant, but there is no continuous path.

THE SUMMIT

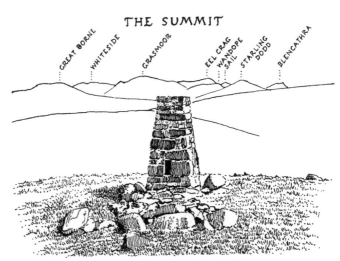

GREAT BORNE · WHITESIDE · GRASMOOR · EEL CRAG · WANDOPE · SAIL · STARLING DODD · BLENCATHRA

The highest point on the grassy summit is indicated by a column of the Ordnance Survey, S 5647. Southwest across the flat top is a small tarn and beyond this a rough outcrop and cairn from which is seen, further southwest, a large tumulus of antiquarian interest.

DESCENTS : In dry weather the best way down is by way of Whoap Beck, but after rain it is better to head south to Tongue How.

Buried Treasure on Lank Rigg
The only exciting experience in the lonely life of the Ordnance column occurred on a gloriously sunny day in April 1965, when it was a mute and astonished witness to an unparalleled act of generosity. In an uncharacteristic mood of magnanimity which he subsequently regretted, the author decided on this summit to share his hard-won royalties with one of his faithful readers and placed a two-shilling piece under a flat stone four feet from the column : it awaited the first person to read this note and act upon it. The finder was invited to write in c/o the publishers and confirm his claim by stating the year of the coin's issue. If nobody had done so by the end of 1966 the author intended to go back and retrieve it for the purchase of fish and chips. It is reported that the coin was recovered the day after publication, and it has become a tradition for visitors to the summit to leave a coin here for others to find.

Ancient and Modern —
Tumulus on Lank Rigg
and atomic power
station at
Calder Hall
(cooling towers
demolished
in 2007)

THE VIEW

Except for an unexpected appearance by Blencathra, the scene inland to the mountains is unremarkable, and it is the villages and towns of West Cumbria, seen as on a map, that provide most interest.

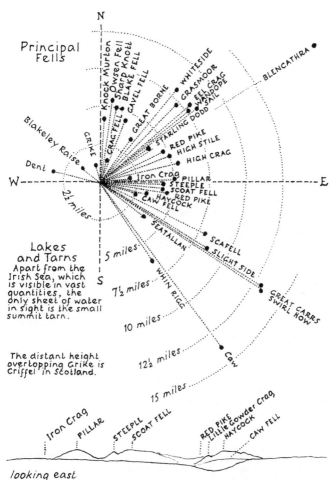

Principal Fells

N

Knock Murton
Owsen Fell
Sharp Knott
BLAKE FELL
GAVEL FELL
CRAG FELL
GREAT BORNE
WHITESIDE
GRASMOOR
EEL CRAG
WANDOPE
SAIL
STARLING DODD
RED PIKE
HIGH STILE
HIGH CRAG
BLENCATHRA

Blakeley Raise
GRIKE
Dent

W — — — — — — — — E

2½ miles

Iron Crag
PILLAR
STEEPLE
SCOAT FELL
RED PIKE
HAYCOCK
CAW FELL

Lakes and Tarns
Apart from the Irish Sea, which is visible in vast quantities, the only sheet of water in sight is the small summit tarn.

SEATALLAN
SCAFELL
SLIGHT SIDE
WHIN RIGG

5 miles

S

7½ miles

10 miles

GREAT CARRS
SWIRL HOW

12½ miles

Caw

The distant height overtopping Grike is Criffel in Scotland.

15 miles

Iron Crag
PILLAR
STEEPLE
SCOAT FELL
RED PIKE
Lillie Gowder Crag
HAYCOCK
CAW FELL

looking east

Low Fell

from Lanthwaite Hill

The lesser heights and foothills of Lakeland, especially those on the fringe, are too much neglected in favour of the greater mountains, yet many of these unsought and unfashionable little hills are completely charming. In this category is Low Fell, north of Loweswater and west of the Vale of Lorton. It has many tops, uniformly around 1350 feet, rising from a ridge. The most southerly eminence has the main cairn and a perfectly composed view of mountain and lake scenery, a connoisseur's piece.

Low Fell and Fellbarrow together form a separate range, a final upthrust of land between Lakeland and the sea. The underlying rock is slate, and the hills exhibit smooth rounded slopes in conformity to pattern; but they deny conformity to the lake of Loweswater, forcing its issuing stream, by a freak of contours, to flow inland, away from the sea, in compliance with the inexorable natural law that water always obeys.

▲ FELLBARROW

● Thackthwaite

▲ LOW FELL

Loweswater

●

MILES

0   1   2

MAP

continuation FELLBARROW 3·4

MOSSER

This lane is permanently flooded to a depth of 12".

Smithy Fell

old quarry

Thackthwaite

Sourfoot Fell

Watching Crag

ROAD

Wilderness Wood

Red How

Loftbarrow

Thackthwaite Leys Wood

Latterhead

Askill Knott

LAMPLUGH MOCKERKIN

stile

Darling Fell

old fold

stile

Crabtree Beck

LOW FELL 1352

stile

Oak Bank

River Cocker

Loweswater

700

Scale Hill

car park

Foulsyke

Crabtreebeck

Thrushbank

Highcross

Dub Beck

ROAD

ROAD

Loweswater (also known as Kirkstile)

Hall Church

Inn

N

ONE MILE

Fellwalkers in Lakeland are privileged by complete freedom to wander on the hills (by the grace of owners and tenants until 2005, and now as of right) and rarely meet obstructions to progress other than natural obstacles. The stone walls and wire fences above the intakes are not generally maintained and often ruinous.

This is not the position, however, on Low Fell and the neighbouring Fellbarrow, and it is surprising to find here that, although some fences have gone most of them are kept in tight repair. Unusual, too, is the neat parcelling of the upland pastures into enclosed allotments. Sheep normally live their lives on the heaf they were brought up on, convinced there's no place like home, and need no fences to persuade them to stay. It seems that the fences must therefore define the individual grazing rights of several farmers. It is not unusual for farmers to have rights in common, but it is unusual to separate their holdings so distinctly on the felltops.

ASCENT FROM LOWESWATER
1050 feet of ascent : 2 miles (direct route)
1350 feet of ascent : 3 miles (via Darling Fell)

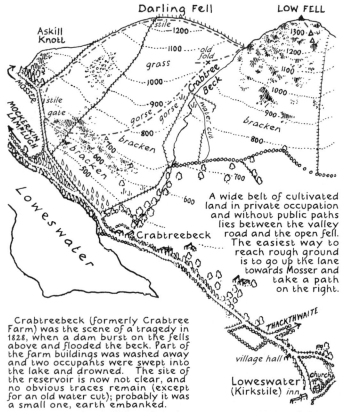

A wide belt of cultivated land in private occupation and without public paths lies between the valley road and the open fell. The easiest way to reach rough ground is to go up the lane towards Mosser and take a path on the right.

Crabtreebeck (formerly Crabtree Farm) was the scene of a tragedy in 1828, when a dam burst on the fells above and flooded the beck. Part of the farm buildings was washed away and two occupants were swept into the lake and drowned. The site of the reservoir is now not clear, and no obvious traces remain (except for an old water cut); probably it was a small one, earth embanked.

Follow the Mosser lane for a third of a mile, leaving at a gate recessed on the right. The path from here to the old fold is very difficult to follow, particularly where it passes through gorse bushes. If the path is lost aim for the fold.

To include Darling Fell in the walk continue up the Mosser lane beyond the gate for a hundred yards and turn right at a stile and signpost. This route is easy to follow, but there is a considerable depression between Darling Fell and Low Fell.

Wait for a bright clear day.   Don't forget the camera.

ASCENT FROM THACKTHWAITE
1250 feet of ascent : 2 miles

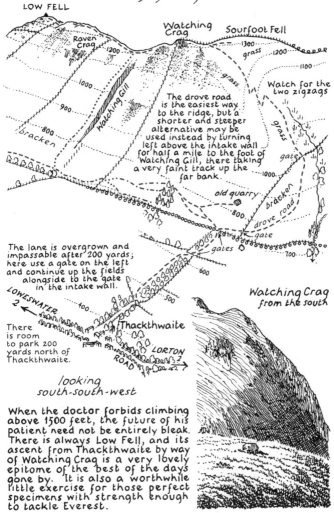

LOW FELL

Raven Crag

Watching Crag

Sourfoot Fell

1200

1300

grass

1200

1100

1000

900

800

bracken

Watching Gill

The drove road is the easiest way to the ridge, but a shorter and steeper alternative may be used instead by turning left above the intake wall for half a mile to the foot of Watching Gill, there taking a very faint track up the far bank.

Watch for the two zigzags

grass

gate

1000

old quarry

800

bracken

drove road

gate

The lane is overgrown and impassable after 200 yards; here use a gate on the left and continue up the fields alongside the gate in the intake wall.

gates

700

600

LOWESWATER 2

400

There is room to park 200 yards north of Thackthwaite.

500

Thackthwaite

LORTON ROAD 2

looking south-south-west

Watching Crag from the south

When the doctor forbids climbing above 1500 feet, the future of his patient need not be entirely bleak. There is always Low Fell, and its ascent from Thackthwaite by way of Watching Crag is a very lovely epitome of the best of the days gone by. It is also a worthwhile little exercise for those perfect specimens with strength enough to tackle Everest.

THE SUMMIT

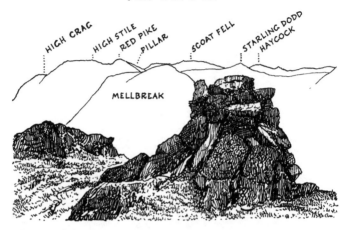

The biggest cairn is on the southern eminence, which is treated as the summit in this book, but the smooth north top appears to be slightly higher. This is confirmed by the 2008 edition of the 2½" map, which gives the altitudes as 1352' and 1388' respectively. This means that the column at 1363' on the more massive Fellbarrow is not the highest point on the range, as was once thought. Two cairns 100 and 120 yards southeast of the main cairn indicate better viewpoints for the Loweswater valley.

DESCENTS : For Foulsyke head north and follow the fence steeply down to a horizontal path leading to a stile in the intake wall. The steepness may be avoided by taking the longer route to Thackthwaite. For Crabtreebeck follow the ridge to the north and look for a path on the left leading to a fence. Follow the fence down to Crabtree Beck and turn left to a sheepfold. Beyond here the route becomes confusing, and it is easier to use the longer route over Darling How.

Cairn on the north top (now just a pile of stones)

GRASMOOR

LOW FELL (south top)

Cairn on Darling Fell

The cairn on Darling Fell marks the end of the ridge and not the highest point. The highest point is situated forty yards east of the fence coming up from the Mosser lane.

THE VIEW

Southeast the view is of classical beauty, an inspired and inspiring vision of loveliness that has escaped the publicity of picture postcards and poets' sonnets, a scene of lakes and mountains arranged to perfection.   The grouping of fells above Mosedale is also attractively presented, with Pillar an unexpected absentee, only a small section of its western shoulder being seen behind Red Pike.   Grasmoor is a tremendous object.
Westwards is the sea.

Principal Fells

The diagram is based on the view from the south top.

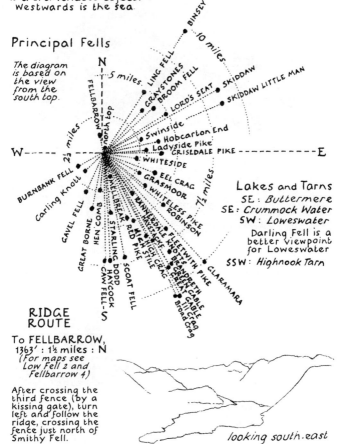

Lakes and Tarns

SE: *Buttermere*
SE: *Crummock Water*
SW: *Loweswater*
     Darling Fell is a better viewpoint for Loweswater
SSW: *Highnook Tarn*

RIDGE ROUTE

To FELLBARROW, 1363′ : 1½ miles : N
(For maps see Low Fell 2 and Fellbarrow 4)

After crossing the third fence (by a kissing gate), turn left and follow the ridge, crossing the fence just north of Smithy Fell.

looking south-east

Mellbreak

1676'

from Kirkhead

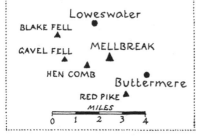

BLAKE FELL ▲

Loweswater ●

GAVEL FELL ▲

MELLBREAK ▲

HEN COMB ▲

Buttermere ●

RED PIKE ▲

MILES

0   1   2   3   4

In West Cumbria, where Mellbreak is a household word (largely through long association with the Mellbreak Foxhounds (spelt with one 'l')) the fell is highly esteemed, and there have always been people ready to assert that it is the finest of all. This is carrying local patriotism too far, but nevertheless it is a grand hill in a beautiful situation with a character all its own and an arresting outline not repeated in the district.

There is only one Mellbreak.

NATURAL FEATURES

There is, of course, a natural affinity between mountains and lakes; they have developed side by side in the making of the earth. Often there is a special association between a particular mountain and a particular lake, so that, in calling the one to mind the other comes inevitably to mind also: they belong together. The best example of this is provided by Wast Water and the Screes, and perhaps next best is the combination of Mellbreak and Crummock Water, essential partners in a successful scenery enterprise, depending on each other for effectiveness. Crummock Water's eastern shore, below Grasmoor, is gay with life and colour — trees, pastures, farms, cattle, traffic, tents and people — but it is the view across the lake, where the water laps the sterile base of Mellbreak far beneath the mountain's dark escarpment, where loneliness, solitude and silence prevail, that makes the scene unforgettable.

Mellbreak, seen thus, is a grim sight, the austere effect often heightened by shadow, and a much closer examination is needed to reveal the intimate detail of crag and gully and scree, the steep declivities cushioned in heather, the hidden corners and recesses, the soaring ravens of Raven Crag. From Kirkstile, at the northern foot, the gable of the fell assumes the arresting outline of a towering pyramid, suggesting a narrow crest, but the top widens into a considerable plateau having two summits of almost equal height separated by a broad saddle. Symmetry and simplicity are the architectural *motifs*, and the steep flank above Crummock Water has its counterpart to the west descending to the dreariest and wettest of Lakeland's many Mosedales. Thus the severance from other fells is complete. Mellbreak is isolated, independent of other high ground, aloof.

Its one allegiance is to Crummock Water.

from Scalehill Bridge

MAP

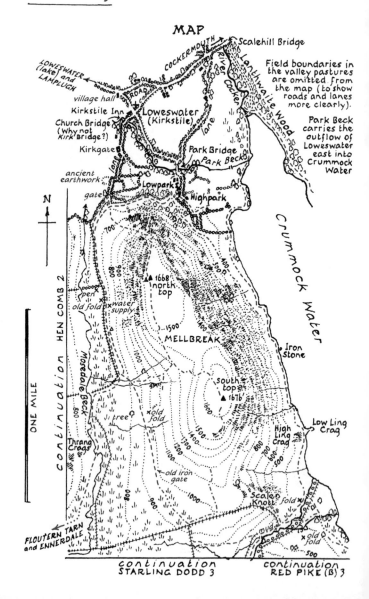

Field boundaries in the valley pastures are omitted from the map (to show roads and lanes more clearly).

Park Beck carries the outflow of Loweswater east into Crummock Water

COCKERMOUTH

Scalehill Bridge

LOWESWATER (lake) and LAMPLUGH

ROAD

Cocker

Lanthwaite Wood

village hall

Kirkstile Inn

Loweswater (Kirkstile)

lane

Church Bridge (Why not 'Kirk' Bridge?)

Kirkgate

Park Bridge

Park Beck

ancient earthwork

gate

Lowpark

Highpark

Crummock Water

N

700

1668 north top

800

pen

old fold

water supply

900

1500

400

MELLBREAK

1000

500

Iron Stone

Moredale Beck

800

tree?

old fold

south top

1676

600

1400

High Ling Crag

Low Ling Crag

ONE MILE

CONTINUATION HEN COMB 2

Thrang Crags

1200

1100

old iron gate

800

1000

900

700

900

800

500

600

Scale Knott

fold

old fold

500

FLOUTERN TARN and ENNERDALE

continuation STARLING DODD 3

continuation RED PIKE (B) 3

" .... a lovely peep around a corner..."
(direct ascent from Loweswater)

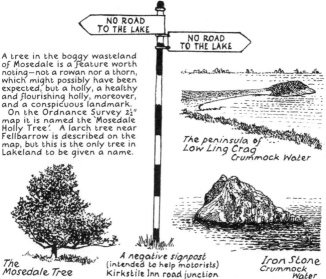

NO ROAD
TO THE LAKE

NO ROAD
TO THE LAKE

A tree in the boggy wasteland
of Mosedale is a feature worth
noting—not a rowan nor a thorn,
which might possibly have been
expected, but a holly, a healthy
and flourishing holly, moreover,
and a conspicuous landmark.
   On the Ordnance Survey 2½"
map it is named the 'Mosedale
Holly Tree'.   A larch tree near
Fellbarrow is described on the
map, but this is the only tree in
Lakeland to be given a name.

The peninsula of
Low Ling Crag
Crummock Water

The Mosedale Tree

A negative signpost
(intended to help motorists)
Kirkstile Inn road junction

Iron Stone
Crummock
Water

ASCENT (to the north top) FROM LOWESWATER
1300 feet of ascent : 1¼ miles

looking south

MELLBREAK
(north top)

MELLBREAK
(south top)

At the second promontory
go on a few paces for
a lovely peep, around
a corner, of Crummock
Water and Buttermere

depression

1500

1400

A : the direct route,
and the best.

B : a straight-up
track to the
depression
from the
valley.

second
promontory

Heather

1300

1200

first
promontory

A

Heather

Heather

big gully

heather

1100

1000

900

800

B

1000

900

800

700

bracken

valley path

Mosedale Beck

Mosedale

tongue
of small
scree

bracken

The tongue of light-coloured scree
is conspicuously seen on the approach.
Reach it from the corner of the fence.
The scree is loose and laborious
to climb. The ascent is steep
but after passing through
a rock gateway soon reaches
the first promontory: a delightful
spot on the brink of the big gully
splitting the crags. A path now
winds up a heathery slope to a
second promontory and then
continues pleasantly in
curves up a narrowing
ridge to reach the
cairn after a final
easy walk, still in
heather, of 250
yards along the
Mosedale edge.

600

500

gate

There is room
to park beside
the Kirkgate
road just past
the bridge.

ancient earthwork
— look over the wall to see
this scanty ruin. Then try
to remember, when high up
on Mellbreak, to look down
at it: the aerial view gives
a clearly distinct outline.

stony lane

400

HIGHPARK

400

SCALE HILL

Church

Kirkgate
(farm)

Kirkstile Inn

Loveswater

HIGHLY RECOMMENDED.
This short climb (by the
direct route) is a grand
way to the top — except
for the initial scree. It
is especially beautiful
when the heather is in
bloom. The upper part of
the path is a joy to follow.
Steep, but no difficulties.

ASCENT FROM CRUMMOCK WATER
1350 feet of ascent : ¾ mile (to the north top).
1450 feet of ascent : 1 mile
(to the south top)

MELLBREAK
south top

MELLBREAK
north top

The only merit in
this steep line of ascent
is the remarkable
rock scenery of the
short section of the
route below the upper
crag. A rising grass
rake at the base of
the crag provides a
narrow passage and
from this gangway
four rocky pillars
form a broken
parapet and fall
as aretes towards
the lake.
In *descent* the
Rake is very
difficult to
find: it starts
just north of
a narrow
promontory.

Pillar Rake

Do NOT attempt
a slanting route to the
Rake from Green Wood: deep
heather and steepness make it a
bad crossing. Go up the scree slope
further along, keeping left of the
outcrop with bushes. At the top
of the longest scree run bear
right and a faint path to
the Rake will be found.

heather

Green
Wood

grass

bracken

gate

Crummock Water

gate

SCALEHILL BRIDGE

Pillar Rake,
lower section,
from the north.
(route indicated)

looking
southwest

SCREE
SLOPE

Pillar Rake, looking back
at the first two pillars
(route indicated)

ASCENT (to the south top) FROM BUTTERMERE
1300 feet of ascent : 2½ miles

looking north-west

The popular path to Scale Force is taken until it starts to climb leftwards in bracken after crossing Far Ruddy Beck; leave it here and continue on the same contour (this is the line of the former path to Scale Force, and the way to the lakeside walk by Crummock Water). When the path peters out aim for a bridge over the first of two branches of Scale Beck. The second branch is usually dry, but it can also be crossed by a bridge if necessary. Now tackle Scale Knott, where a fence goes up to the right of a series of little outcrops forming a short steep ridge. From the corner of the fence follow the ridge to Mellbreak's south top. This section is dreary, and it is hard to feel enthusiasm for the climb because of the distraction of the backward view, which is superlatively lovely.

It is a good rule, when planning a walk, to arrange as far as possible, to proceed *towards* the finest scenery on the route, not away from it, so as to have the best views in front, not behind. Often this means no more than doing the walk the other way round.

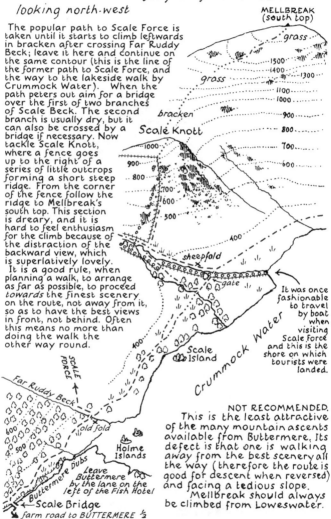

MELLBREAK
(south top)

grass

grass

bracken

Scale Knott

sheepfold

gate

It was once fashionable to travel by boat when visiting Scale Force and this is the shore on which tourists were landed.

Crummock Water

SCALE FORCE

Far Ruddy Beck

old fold

Scale Island

Holme Islands

Leave Buttermere by the lane on the left of the Fish Hotel

Buttermere Dubs

←Scale Bridge
farm road to BUTTERMERE ½

NOT RECOMMENDED. This is the least attractive of the many mountain ascents available from Buttermere. Its defect is that one is walking away from the best scenery all the way (therefore the route is good for descent when reversed) and facing a tedious slope.

Mellbreak should always be climbed from Loweswater.

THE SUMMIT

2 5 6
1 3 4 7
HIGH STILE   RED PIKE   PILLAR

south top

Buttermere

1: FLEETWITH PIKE
2: GLARAMARA
3: GREY KNOTTS
4: BRANDRETH
5: GREEN GABLE
6: GREAT GABLE
7: HAYSTACKS

south-east
from the
north top

Mellbreak has two distinct summits, two-thirds of a mile apart and separated by a pronounced depression. The more attractive of the two is the heathery north top, measured by the Ordnance Survey as 1668 feet above sea level; the duller grassy south top is credited with 1676 feet. Nobody would have complained if the measurements had been reversed, by some rare error, for it is the lower north top, crowning a splendid tower of rock, that captures the fancy, not the other. The width and extent of the top of the fell between the two summits comes as a surprise — the narrow ridge promised by distant views of the fell is an illusion.

DESCENTS : It is usual to descend into Mosedale from the west edge of the depression. From the south top, for Buttermere, follow the ridge to the south until you come to a fence. Turn right to avoid the steep descent from Scale Knott, or turn left to avoid the mud along Scale Beck. For Loweswater, from the north top, the route from the depression into Mosedale is safest unless the direct route is already familiar and the weather clear: in mist, there is a very bad trap at the head of the big gully where a path along the promontory suggests a way down that can only lead to disaster; in fact the true path turns down left a few paces short of this point. On no account should a descent down the eastern flank to Crummock Water be attempted, except by Pillar Rake, and then only if the route is already known and the weather is clear. The start of the Rake, very difficult to find in descent, lies just north of a narrow promontory.

Dent Floutern Cop
HEN COMB   GAVEL FELL

west
from the
south top

RIDGE ROUTES

Mellbreak is itself a ridge, like the keel of an overturned boat (collapsed in the middle). It has no links with other fells.

THE VIEW

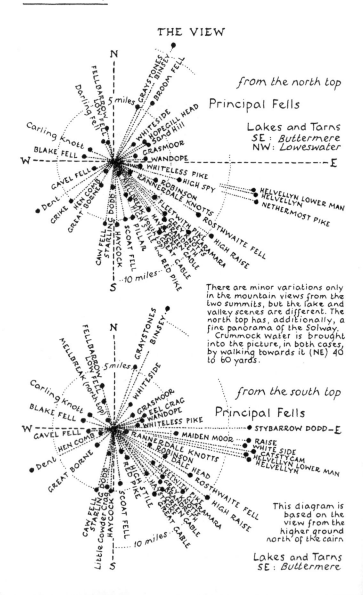

from the north top

Principal Fells

Lakes and Tarns
SE: *Buttermere*
NW: *Loweswater*

There are minor variations only in the mountain views from the two summits, but the lake and valley scenes are different. The north top has, additionally, a fine panorama of the Solway. Crummock Water is brought into the picture, in both cases, by walking towards it (NE) 40 to 60 yards.

from the south top

Principal Fells

This diagram is based on the view from the higher ground north of the cairn

Lakes and Tarns
SE: *Buttermere*

Grasmoor
from the
north top

Rannerdale from the south top
(Whiteless Pike, left background)

Middle Fell

1908'

Wasdale Head
▲ SEATALLAN ●

MIDDLE ▲
FELL
▲ BUCKBARROW
● Greendale

● Strands

MILES

0 1 2 3 4

Bowderdale

from Wast Water

NATURAL FEATURES

Many of the lesser fells of Lakeland make up for their lack of height by an aggressive fierceness of expression that seems more appropriate to greater mountains and by an intimidating ruggedness and wildness of terrain that makes their ascent rather more formidable than their size and altitude would suggest. Middle Fell, overlooking Wast Water, comes into this category. Tier above tier of hostile crags, steep slopes overrun by tumbled boulders, vegetation masking pitfalls and crevices : these are the features that rule out, at a glance, any possibility of a simple climb either from the lakeside or from Nether Beck at its eastern base, these being the two aspects that face the traveller along the valley. Nor, if one ventures up by Greendale Gill, on the west, does the scene relent, although a route here presents itself. It is only on the short side of the fell, where there is a high saddle connecting with Seatallan, that a weakness in the fell's armour becomes apparent and the climb to the cairn is comfortable. As a viewpoint for the Wasdale fells, the summit is magnificently placed, and it is fitting that a reward such as this should be earned only by effort.

Waterfalls, Nether Beck

*Middle Fell
from the headwaters
of Nether Beck*

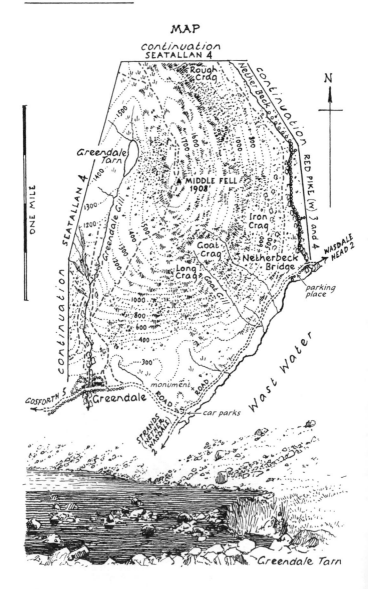

MAP

continuation
SEATALLAN 4

Rough
Crag

N

continuation
SEATALLAN 4

Nether Beck

continuation RED PIKE (w) 3 and 4

1500

1400

Greendale
Tarn

1300

1200

Greendale Gill

1700

1600

1000

800

▲ MIDDLE FELL
1908'

Iron
Crag

Goat
Crag

Long
Crag

Goat Gill

Netherbeck
Bridge

WASDALE
HEAD 2

parking
place

1500

1400

1300

1100

1000

800

600

400

300

monument

ROAD + ROAD

Wast Water

car parks

GOSFORTH 5

Greendale

STRANDS
(NETHER
WASDALE)
2

ONE MILE

Greendale Tarn

ASCENT FROM WASDALE
(GREENDALE)
1650 feet of ascent : 1½ miles

Watch for the bifurcation at 700': the uphill branch to the right (which is taken) is an offshoot of the original path for Greendale Tarn. The summit track ascends a green slope first, then a patch of boulders, and continues all the way to the summit. The gradient is now easy, all the rock outcrops are avoided, and after a simple climb that will seem longer than expected the summit cairn is reached on the Wasdale edge of a small plateau.

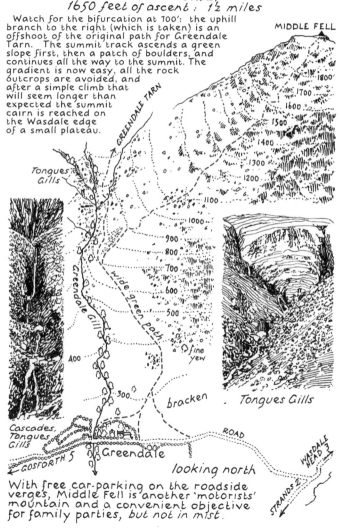

MIDDLE FELL

GREENDALE TARN

1800
1700
1600
1500
1400
1300
1200
1100
1000
900
800
700
600
500
400
300

Tongues Gills

Greendale Gill

Wide green path

fine yew

bracken

Tongues Gills

Cascades, Tongues Gills

← GOSFORTH 5

Greendale

ROAD

looking north

WASDALE HEAD 3

STRANDS 2

With free car-parking on the roadside verges, Middle Fell is another 'motorists' mountain and a convenient objective for family parties, *but not in mist.*

THE SUMMIT

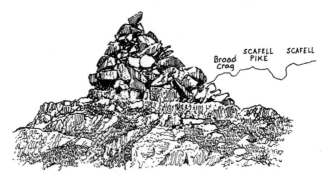

The summit-cairn crowns a small rocky mound on the Wasdale edge of a grassy depression on the top of the fell, and although it is a splendid vantage point there is little in the immediate vicinity to suggest the rocky nature of the slopes just below.

DESCENTS: In clear weather, easy descents may be made to join the path going down to Greendale south-west, or north to the marshy flats above Greendale Tarn; in other directions lies trouble. Keep to grass, skirting innumerable low crags. *In mist use only the south-west route*: the slope is gentle (bear right if steep ground is encountered) and longer than expected (nearly a mile) before the path on the east side of Greendale Gill is joined.

RIDGE ROUTE

To SEATALLAN, 2266': 1½ miles
    N, NNW and SW
    Depression at 1550'
    750 feet of ascent

This is not so much a ridge route as a passage from one fell to another, keeping to the height of the land.

There is no path at first, but two faint ones soon appear, running parallel to each other and eventually merging. The combined path does not follow the ridge, but drops down to the left and leads to a juicy depression. Step gingerly across this, taking either of the two paths, preferably the one on the left. Swing left to the shoulder of Seatallan and go up this on good turf to the top.

ONE MILE

THE VIEW

The most extensive views are not necessarily the finest, and here, from Middle Fell, is a charmer restricted in distance by the Wasdale mountains, which, however, compensate for the deficiency by their own striking appearance. Wast Water is seen full length, backed by the Screes, and, beyond, Black Combe fills up the horizon southward.

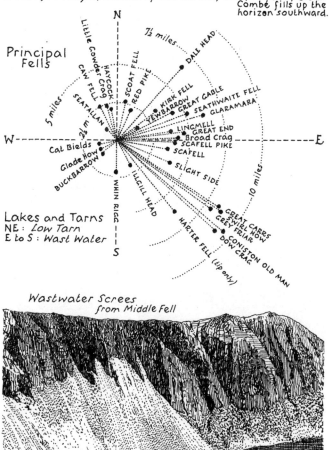

Principal Fells

7½ miles

5 miles

N

Little Cowder Crag
HAYCOCK
CAW FELL
SCOAT FELL
RED PIKE
DALE HEAD
SEATALLAN
KIRK FELL
YEWBARROW
GREAT GABLE
SEATHWAITE FELL
GLARAMARA
LINGMELL
GREAT END
Broad Crag
SCAFELL PIKE
SCAFELL
Cat Bields
Glade How
BUCKBARROW
SLIGHT SIDE
WHIN RIGG
ILLGILL HEAD
GREAT CARRS
GREY FRIAR
CONISTON OLD MAN
HARTER FELL (tip only)
DOW CRAG

10 miles

W ———— E

S

Lakes and Tarns
NE : Low Tarn
E to S : Wast Water

Wastwater Screes from Middle Fell

Pillar

2927'

from Brin Crag, Brandreth

NATURAL FEATURES

Great Gable, Pillar and Steeple are the three mountain names on Lakeland maps most likely to fire the imagination of youthful adventurers planning a first tour of the district, inspiring exciting visions of slim, near-vertical pinnacles towering grandly into the sky.

Great Gable lives up to its name, especially if climbed from Wasdale; Pillar has a fine bold outline but is nothing like a pillar; Steeple is closely overlooked by a higher flat-topped fell and not effectively seen.

Pillar, in fact, far from being a spire of slender proportions, is a rugged mass broadly based on half the length of Ennerdale, a series of craggy buttresses supporting the ridge high above this wild north face; and the summit itself, far from being pointed, is wide and flat. The name of the fell therefore clearly derives from a conspicuous feature on the north face directly below the top, the most handsome crag in Lakeland, originally known as the Pillar Stone and now as Pillar Rock. The Rock, despite a remote and lonely situation, had a well-established local notoriety and fame long before tourists called wider attention to it, and an object of such unique appearance simply had to be given a descriptive name, although, at the time, one was not yet needed to identify the mountain of which it formed part. The Pillar was an inspiration of shepherds. Men of letters could not have chosen better.

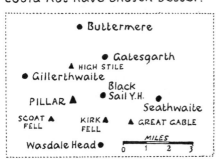

The north face of the fell has a formidable aspect. Crags and shadowed hollows, scree and tumbled boulders, form a wild, chaotic scene, a setting worthy of a fine mountain.

continued

NATURAL FEATURES

continued

Pillar is the highest mountain west of Great Gable, from which it is sufficiently removed in distance to exhibit distinctive slopes on all sides. It dominates the sunset area of Lakeland superbly, springing out of the valleys of Mosedale and Ennerdale, steeply on the one side and dramatically on the other, as befits the overlord of the western scene. A narrow neck of land connects with a chain of other grand fells to the south, and a depression forms the east boundary and is crossed by Black Sail Pass at 1800', but elsewhere the full height of the fell from valley level is displayed. Some of the streams flow west *via* Ennerdale Water and some south *via* Wast Water, but their fate, discharge into the Irish Sea from the coast near Seascale, is the same, only a few miles separating the two outlets.

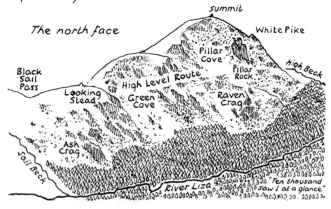

Afforestation in Ennerdale has cloaked the lower slopes on this side in a dark and funereal shroud of foreign trees, an intrusion that nobody who knew Ennerdale of old can ever forgive, the former charm of the valley having been destroyed thereby. We condemn vandalism and sanction this mess! Far better the old desolation of boulder and bog when a man could see the sky, than this new desolation of regimented timber shutting out the light of day. It is an offence to the eyes to see Pillar's once-colourful fellside now hobbled in such a dowdy and ill-suited skirt, just as it is to see a noble animal caught in a trap. Yet, such is the majesty and power of this fine mountain that it can shrug off the insults and indignities, and its summit soars no less proudly above. It is the admirers of this grand pile who feel the hurt.

A Pillar Rock
portfolio

from the east

Pillar 5

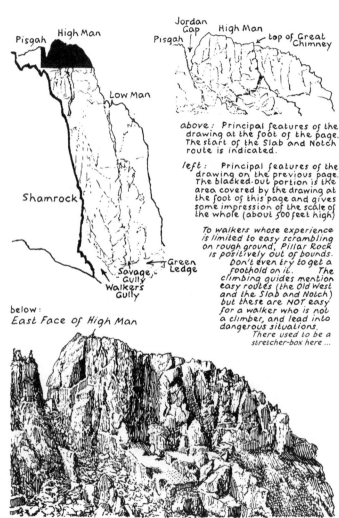

Pisgah — High Man

Low Man

Shamrock

Savage Gully

Walkers Gully

Green Ledge

Jordan Gap

Pisgah — High Man — top of Great Chimney

above: Principal features of the drawing at the foot of the page. The start of the Slab and Notch route is indicated.

left: Principal features of the drawing on the previous page. The blacked-out portion is the area covered by the drawing at the foot of this page and gives some impression of the scale of the whole (about 500 feet high)

To walkers whose experience is limited to easy scrambling on rough ground, Pillar Rock is positively out of bounds. Don't even try to get a foothold on it. The climbing guides mention easy routes (the Old West and the Slab and Notch) but these are NOT easy for a walker who is not a climber, and lead into dangerous situations. There used to be a stretcher-box here ...

below:
East Face of High Man

as seen from the Shamrock Traverse.

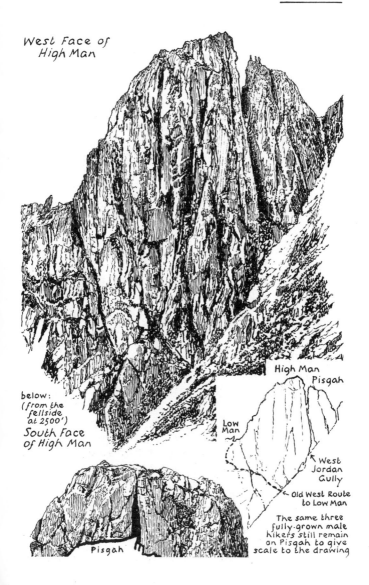

West Face of
High Man

below:
(from the
fellside
at 2500')
South Face
of High Man

Pisgah

High Man
Pisgah

Low
Man

← West
Jordan
Gully

← Old West Route
to Low Man

The same three
fully-grown male
hikers still remain
on Pisgah to give
scale to the drawing

MAP

ONE MILE

E n n e r d a l e

River Liza

felled area

felled area

SCARTH GAP

felled

500

1000

1100

1300

1200

1500

1500

1400

1300

1200

1100

1000

900

2000

White Pike

Pillar Rock

Hind Cove

PILLAR 2927

2700

2600

2500

2400

2300

2200

2100

2000

1500

1000

900

800

Windgap Cove

Wind Gap

continuation SCOAT FELL →

continuation on opposite page

continuation SCOAT FELL →

Moredale Beck

continuation RED PIKE (W) 4

fold

N

High Beck

Low Beck

The Bridges over the River Liza

As the trees in the Ennerdale plantations grow in height, so they grow in density. forming a dark and impenetrable jungle open to the sky only where roads have been slashed through for the forestry vehicles or in the avenues or firebreaks left unplanted.   Only in these cuttings can a walker now make headway, and it has become more and more important for those who climb Pillar from Ennerdale, or descend to this valley, to know exactly where the footways are in relation to the bridges over the Liza, which cannot easily be waded or forded.   A former footbridge 300 yards upstream from High Beck has done, but there are others along the base of the mountain. The Irish bridge near the head of Ennerdale Water is nearly always crossable, but, if it is not, there is a footbridge only a quarter of a mile upstream. A further two miles up the valley is a concrete road bridge, and this is useful for the direct ascent *via* Pillar Cove.   Next, two-thirds of a mile further, is the memorial footbridge, provided mainly to facilitate the approach to Pillar Rock from Buttermere.   The last, in open country beyond the plantations, is the much-used footbridge at the foot of Black Sail Pass.

MAP

Black Sail is the most remote youth hostel in the Lake District, being 6 miles along the valley from the public car park at Bowness Point. The hostel is open to all but it is advisable to book well in advance.

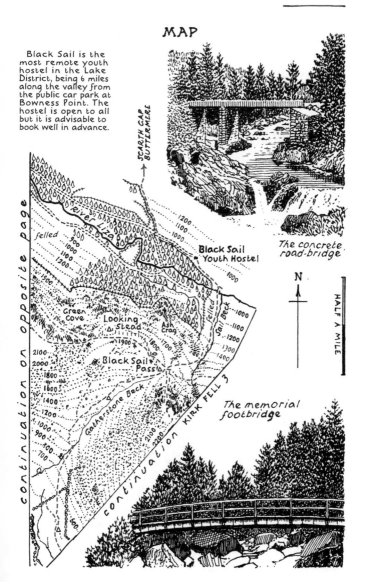

The concrete road-bridge

The memorial footbridge

SCARTH GAP BUTTERMERE

River Liza

felled

Black Sail Youth Hostel

Green Cove

Looking Stead

Ash Crag

Black Sail Pass

Gatherstone Beck

N

HALF A MILE

continuation on opposite page

continuation KIRK FELL 3

ASCENT FROM WASDALE HEAD
2700 feet of ascent
4½ miles via Black Sail Pass
3¼ miles via Wind Gap

The short cut is not really a time-saver in ascent, the better plan being to go on to the top of the pass and do the whole ridge.

PILLAR

Wind Gap

2500

2600

2500

Wistow Crags

2400

2300

2100

2000

1900

1800

1700

1600

1500

1400

1300

1200

old bield

1100

1000

900

800

looking north

At this point the High Level route goes off to the right (see next page)

Looking Stead

Black Sail Pass

grass

tarn

short cut

1500 paved

last water on the ascent

Gatherstone Beck

Indistinct track on a rising tongue of grass

E grass

Wind Gap

scree shoot

If using the Wind Gap route, be careful to identify the Gap correctly from the valley. It is clearly in sight and identifiable by its long scree-run. But note that the Gap is not the true head of the valley, this being Blackem Head away to the left, where Mosedale Beck has its source.

Too bracken

fold

Mosedale Beck

pen

800

700

600

500

400

300

The **usual route** (via Black Sail Pass and the ridge) is an excellent walk and the easiest way to any of the Wasdale summits. A good walker will do it nonstop.

The more direct **Wind Gap route** is out of favour, being more confined, less attractive in its views, and damned by an unpleasant and unavoidable scree-run.

The Wind Gap route turns (indistinctly) from the Black Sail path at the cairn at 500'.

Don't go wrong at the very start! The way lies NOT over the bridge but along the bank of the stream, passing behind the farmhouse of Row Head.

Mosedale

Wasdale Head

Row Head

Inn

ASCENT FROM ENNERDALE
(BLACK SAIL YOUTH HOSTEL)
2000 feet of ascent : 2¾ miles
(2100 feet, 3 miles by High Level Route)

The main ridge, from Black Sail Pass to the summit, is a pleasant walk without difficulty, three stony rises being succeeded by splendid turf. A line of iron posts accompanies the ridge but the path, in many places, deviates to the left.
The High Level route is a traverse across the fellside (aiming for Pillar Rock), not a way to the summit, although the two can be connected (see next page). This is a fine pedestrian way, highly recommended, rough but not difficult.

Originally the High Level Route had an awkward start. A new variation avoids the difficulty.

PILLAR

Great Doup

Pillar Rock

Hind Cove

grass

Green Cove

Robinson's Cairn

High Level Route

← detail →

△ Looking Stead

WASDALE HEAD
direct route

1900

tarn

WASDALE HEAD

1800

Black Sail Pass

1700

There is a gate at the top of the pass but only a fanatical purist would think of using it.

1600

The path avoids the actual top of Looking Stead, but walkers should not. It is an excellent viewpoint for a survey, both of the High Level route and of Ennerdale.

Main ridge:
1: zigzag path
2: direct path
High Level route:
3: original start
4: new variation
Main ridge:
5: from Black Sail

1500

1400

1300

1200

Ash Crag

1100

River Liza

Sojourners at the hostel are fortunate in having Pillar on their doorstep, and can enjoy one of the best days of their young lives by climbing it.

felled

Sail Beck

1100

1000

Black Sail Y.H.

moraines

looking west

Robinson's Cairn to the summit

The end of the Traverse with stretcher box (now gone)

Pisgah

summit

2800

Great Doup

2700 steep loose scree slope

2600 Pisgah

2500 High Man

Pillar Rock

Shamrock Traverse 2400

2300 Low Man

start of Traverse 2200

scree slope

Shamrock

2100 low rock ridge

slight descent across a bouldery hollow

High Level Route △ Robinson's Cairn

There are no difficulties or dangers on this route *provided the path is kept underfoot*. There ARE difficulties and dangers if exploratory deviations are attempted, especially on the Traverse. The walking is rough, but not steep; the track is loose and stony, but safe. The rock-scenery is magnificent.

The start of the Traverse (a wide, tilted shelf or rake)

Robinson's Cairn

—a memorial to JOHN WILSON ROBINSON, a pioneer fellwalker and rock-climber; a man sincerely devoted to the fells. A tablet, beautifully worded, is affixed to a nearby rock.

ASCENT FROM ENNERDALE
(HIGH GILLERTHWAITE)
2500 feet of ascent
3¼ miles (A) : 2¾ miles (B)

PILLAR

Pillar Rock

White Pike

line of cairns

2800
2700
2600
2500
2400
2300
2200
2100
2000

Black Crag

A

Wind Gap

2500

2700

Make the short stony detour to the top of White Pike for a good profile view of Pillar Rock.

Windgap Cove

The dark pinnacle high up on the right of Windgap Cove is Steeple

B grass

1900

1800

grass

1700

1600

A

1500

old wall (incorrectly shown as a stream on Bartholomew's map, and formerly on the 1" O.S. map. Coincidence has truly a long arm.)

1500

1400

B

High Beck

A

gate

felled

1100

looking south-east

Pillar Rock from White Pike

1000

High Beck

clearing

900

BOWNESS POINT

The diagram on this page originally showed a footbridge over the River Liza and two paths rising through the plantations, one on each side of High Beck. The footbridge has now gone and both the paths are impassable. To ascend Pillar from the Bowness Knott car park, follow the forest road for a mile and a half and turn right at the junction shown in the top left-hand corner of the map on Scoat Fell 3. On entering the plantation turn left and keep going for a further mile and a half. Immediately after crossing Low Beck turn right up an unsignposted path that is easily missed. This is an attractive woodland path alongside a steep-sided ravine and comes as a surprise. A hundred yards up the hill there is a signpost to Pillar. The route is obvious here, but it is reassuring to know that you have come the right way. When you come to a forest road turn left. From here onwards the route is shown on the diagram on this page. Thirty yards past a cleared strip take a path on the right, again unsignposted, and continue through a felled area to a gate. Above the gate, two routes are given. Route A is the more usual, and a recognised pass between Ennerdale and Wasdale, but Route B is an obvious alternative up the north-west ridge, easy to 2000' and then very stony.

ASCENT FROM ENNERDALE
(direct from THE MEMORIAL FOOTBRIDGE)

2250 feet of ascent
1¼ miles

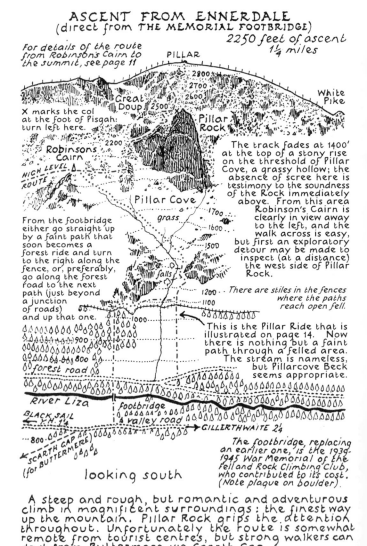

For details of the route from Robinson's Cairn to the summit, see page 11

PILLAR

2800
2700
2600
2500

White Pike

Great Doup

Pillar Rock

X marks the col at the foot of Pisgah: turn left here.

2200

Robinson's Cairn

HIGH LEVEL ROUTE

Pillar Cove

grass

The track fades at 1400' at the top of a stony rise on the threshold of Pillar Cove, a grassy hollow; the absence of scree here is testimony to the soundness of the Rock immediately above. From this area Robinson's Cairn is clearly in view away to the left, and the walk across is easy, but first an exploratory detour may be made to inspect (at a distance) the west side of Pillar Rock.

1700
1600
1500

From the footbridge either go straight up by a faint path that soon becomes a forest ride and turn to the right along the fence, or, preferably, go along the forest road to the next path (just beyond a junction of roads) and up that one.

falls

1200
1100

There are stiles in the fences where the paths reach open fell.

1000

900

800

forest road

This is the Pillar Ride that is illustrated on page 14. Now there is nothing but a faint path through a felled area. The stream is nameless, but Pillarcove Beck seems appropriate.

River Liza

BLACK SAIL *F.H. 1½*

Footbridge
valley road

GILLERTHWAITE 2¼

800

SCARTH GAP
(for BUTTERMERE)

The footbridge, replacing an earlier one, is the 1939-1945 War Memorial of the Fell and Rock Climbing Club, who contributed to its cost. (Note plaque on boulder).

looking south

A steep and rough, but romantic and adventurous climb in magnificent surroundings: the finest way up the mountain. Pillar Rock grips the attention throughout. Unfortunately the route is somewhat remote from tourist centres, but strong walkers can do it from Buttermere via Scarth Gap.

ASCENT FROM BUTTERMERE

Most walkers when planning to climb a mountain aim to avoid any downhill section between their starting-point and the summit, and if the intermediate descent is considerable the extra effort of regaining lost height may rule out the attempt altogether. A good example is Great Gable from Langdale, where the descent from Esk Hause to Sty Head is a loss of height of 700 feet and a double loss of this amount if returning to Langdale. Plus the 3000' of effective ascent, this is too much for the average walker. Distance is of less consequence. The same applies to ascent of Pillar from Buttermere. This is a glorious walk, full of interest, but it cannot be done without first climbing the High Stile range (at Scarth Gap) and then descending into Ennerdale before setting foot on Pillar. If returning to Buttermere, Ennerdale and the High Stile range will have to be crossed again towards the end of an exhausting day. There is no sadder sight than a Buttermere-bound pedestrian crossing Scarth Gap on his hands and knees as the shadows of evening steal o'er the scene. *The route is therefore recommended for strong walkers only.*

The most thrilling line of ascent of Pillar is by way of the memorial footbridge, this being very conveniently situated for the Buttermere approach ('the bridge was, in fact, provided to give access to Pillar from this direction). A slanting route down to the footbridge leaves the Scarth Gap path some 150 yards on the Ennerdale side of the pass. The bifurcation is not clear, but the track goes off to the right above the plantation, becoming distinct and crossing the fences by three stiles. The climb from the bridge is described on the opposite page. A less arduous route of ascent is to keep to the Scarth Gap path into Ennerdale and climb out of the valley by Black Sail Pass to its top, where follow the ridge on the right — but this easier way had better be reserved for the return when energy is flagging.

To find the slanting path from Scarth Gap look for the rocky knoll, with tree (illustrated) and turn right on grass above it

Via the footbridge :   3550 feet of ascent : 5¼ miles
Via Black Sail Pass : 3250 feet of ascent : 6¼ miles

Pillar Rock, from the north

The Pillar Ride

THE SUMMIT

shelter   north shelter

As in the case of many fells of rugged appearance, the summit is one of the smoothest places on Pillar, and one may perambulate within a 50-yard radius of the cairn without being aware of the declivities on all sides. There are stones, but grass predominates. The number of erections, including two wind-shelters and a survey column, testifies to the importance of the summit in the esteem of fellwalkers and map-makers.

DESCENTS :

To Wasdale Head : In fair weather or foul, there is one royal road down to Wasdale Head, and that is by the eastern ridge to join Black Sail Pass on its journey thereto. The views are superb, and the walking is so easy for the most part that they can be enjoyed while on the move. There should be no difficulty in following the path in mist — only in one cairned section is it indistinct — but the fence-posts are there in any event as a guide to the top of the Pass. The improved path from Black Sail Pass is preferable to the short cut from Looking Stead. The route into Mosedale *via* Wind Gap is much less satisfactory, and no quicker although shorter. Another way into Mosedale sometimes used is the obvious scree-gully opening off the ridge opposite the head of Great Doup, but why suffer the torture of a half-mile of loose stones when the ridge is so much easier and pleasanter?

To Ennerdale : If bound for Black Sail Hostel, follow the eastern ridge to the pass, and there turn left on a clear path. If bound for Ennerdale Youth Hostel (High Gillerthwaite) or places west, head northwest to White Pike and its ridge, which has a rough section of boulders below the Pike; but in stormy weather prefer the route joining High Beck from Wind Gap.

To Buttermere : In clear weather, the direct route climbing up out of Ennerdale may be reversed; at the forest road beyond the memorial footbridge walk up the valley for 120 yards, then taking a slanting path through the plantation on the left to Scarth Gap. In bad conditions, it is safer to go round by Black Sail Pass.

To any of the above destinations via Robinson's Cairn
Leave the summit at the north wind-shelter. Pillar Rock comes into view at once, and a path with many bends leads down to the point where the first of its buttresses (Pisgah) rises from the fellside. Here turn right (where there was once a stretcher box) and along the Traverse to easy ground and the Cairn. On no account descend the hollow to the right of Pisgah: this narrows to a dangerous funnel of stones and a sheer drop into a gully. (This is known as Walker's Gully, NOT because it is a gully for walkers, but because a man of this name fell to his death here).

PLAN OF THE SUMMIT

100 YARDS

WHITE PIKE
PILLAR ROCK
W.shelter
shelter
Great Doup
WIND GAP — 2900
2800
BLACK SAIL PASS

Pillar Rock as seen from the north shelter

RIDGE ROUTES

TO SCOAT FELL, 2760': 1¼ miles: WSW
Depression at 2480' (Wind Gap): 300 feet of ascent
A fine little journey in spectacular scenery.

After an indefinite start, a line of cairns leads down to Wind Gap, the last stage of the descent being steep and rough, but not difficult. Beyond the Gap a clear path goes up the facing slope into the boulders preceding the easy grassy promenade along the top above Black Crag. Then follows a slight loss of height before the final rise to Scoat Fell, the summit wall of which is joined in a chaotic pile of boulders.

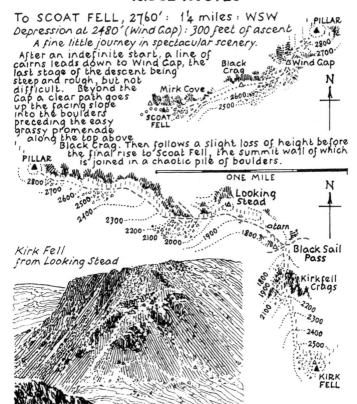

Kirk Fell
from Looking Stead

TO KIRK FELL, 2630': 2½ miles: ESE, then S
Depression at 1800' (Black Sail Pass): 850 feet of ascent
Excellent views, both near and far; a good walk

The Ennerdale fence (what is left of it) links the two tops, and the route never ventures far from it. The eastern ridge of Pillar offers a speedy descent, the path being clear except on one grassy section, which is, however, well cairned. At the Pass, the crags of Kirk Fell look ferocious and hostile, but a thin track goes off bravely to tackle them and can be relied upon to lead to the dull top of Kirk Fell after providing a minor excitement where a high rock step needs to be surmounted.

THE VIEW

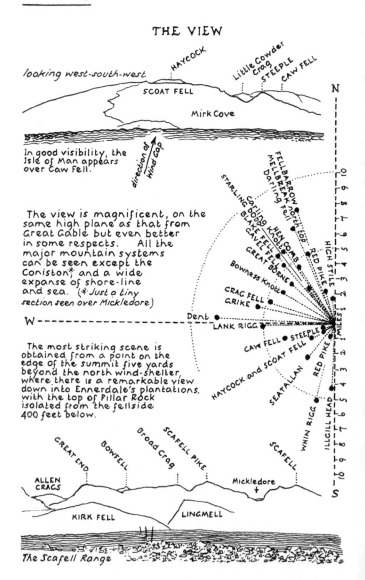

looking west-south-west

HAYCOCK

Little Cowder Crag

STEEPLE

CAW FELL

SCOAT FELL

Mirk Cove

N

In good visibility, the Isle of Man appears over Caw Fell.

direction of wind gap

The view is magnificent, on the same high plane as that from Great Gable but even better in some respects. All the major mountain systems can be seen except the Coniston,* and a wide expanse of shore-line and sea. (* *Just a tiny section seen over Mickledore*)

FELLBARROW

MELLBREAK

Darling Fell

HEN COMB

STARLING DODD

Great Borne

BLAKE FELL

GAVEL FELL

CARLING KNOTT

KNOCK MURTON

RED PIKE

HIGH STILE

Bowness Knott

GREAT BORNE

CRAG FELL

GRIKE

W

Dent

LANK RIGG

CAW FELL

STEEPLE

SCOAT FELL

HAYCOCK and SCOAT FELL

SEATALLAN

RED PIKE

WHIN RIGG

ILLGILL HEAD

S

The most striking scene is obtained from a point on the edge of the summit five yards beyond the north wind-shelter, where there is a remarkable view down into Ennerdale's plantations, with the top of Pillar Rock isolated from the fellside 400 feet below.

GREAT END

BOWFELL

Broad Crag

SCAFELL PIKE

SCAFELL

ALLEN CRAGS

Mickledore

KIRK FELL

LINGMELL

The Scafell Range

THE VIEW

Principal Fells

Lakes and Tarns

SSE : Eel Tarn
SSE : Burnmoor Tarn
WNW : Ennerdale Water
NNW : Loweswater

Innominate Tarn on Haystacks, ENE, is brought in the view by walking 10 yards from the column eastwards

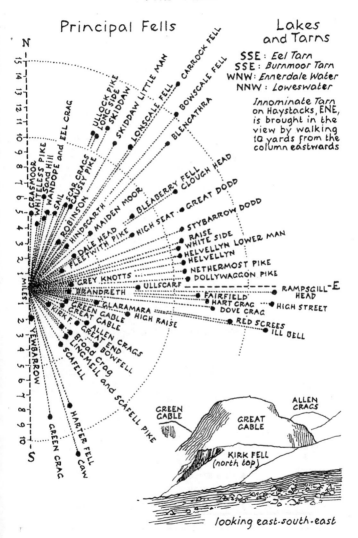

looking east-south-east

Red Pike
(Buttermere)

2479′

from Crummock Water

The duplication of place-names is a source of confusion and error.
In the Lake District there are dozens of Raven Crags and Black Crags,
many Dodds, six Mosedales, two Seathwaites, three Sourmilk Gills,
and several other instances of name-repetition in different areas.

Amongst the major fells,
there are two High Raises, two
High Pikes and two Harter Fells
— all fortunately well dispersed
in widely-separated localities.
But two Red Pikes, only three
miles apart, require distinct
identification. It is usual to
refer to the one dealt with in
this chapter, which the name
aptly fits, as the Buttermere
Red Pike, and the other, which
is higher and bulkier, but for
which the name is less suited,
as the Wasdale Red Pike.

Buttermere ●

STARLING
DODD ▲

Gatesgarth ●

▲ RED PIKE

▲ HIGH STILE

Gillerthwaite ●

▲ HIGH
CRAG

MILES

0   1   2   3

NATURAL FEATURES

The most-trodden mountain track out of Buttermere, a ladder of stones, leads to the summit of Red Pike (which itself cannot be seen from the village), and indeed this is the only tourist path permitted by the extremely steep and rough fellside on the south, overlooking the valley. Red Pike is deservedly a popular climb; the way to it is both interesting and beautiful, the summit is a graceful cone without complications, the cairn being set exactly at the head of the path; and the view is excellent. Less imposing than its near neighbour, High Stile, Red Pike is nevertheless a greater favourite with visitors (which is unjustifiable on merit).

Following the general pattern of the mountains in the High Stile series, Red Pike sends out a stony buttress to the north-east, but unlike its fellows this one succeeds a depression, the Saddle, and then rises to a subsidiary, Dodd, before plunging down to the valley, the final slope being pleasantly wooded and featuring the attraction everybody remembers Buttermere by — the long cascade of Sourmilk Gill. Westwards, Red Pike extends a curving arm trending north to Crummock, and within it nestles the heathery hollow of Ling Comb; outside its curve the fell creases into a watercourse, and here is another of Red Pike's star attractions, Lakeland's highest waterfall, Scale Force. East of the buttress, shared with High Stile, is the hanging valley of Bleaberry Comb and a secluded tarn, thought to occupy the crater of a dead volcano. To the south the fell slopes steeply down, without incident, to Ennerdale.

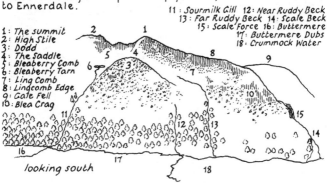

1: The summit
2: High Stile
3: Dodd
4: The Saddle
5: Bleaberry Comb
6: Bleaberry Tarn
7: Ling Comb
8: Lingcomb Edge
9: Gale Fell
10: Blea Crag
11: Sourmilk Gill
12: Near Ruddy Beck
13: Far Ruddy Beck
14: Scale Beck
15: Scale Force
16: Buttermere
17: Buttermere Dubs
18: Crummock Water

looking south

Syenite in the rock and subsoil of the fell produces the rich red colouring that has given Red Pike its name and this is particularly marked in places where surface disturbance has occurred (the stony track by the side of Scale Force is a good example), remaining brilliant until weathering results in a more sombre ruddiness.

MAP

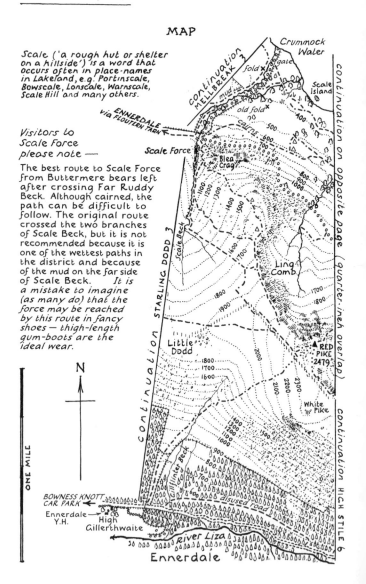

Scale ('a rough hut or shelter on a hillside') is a word that occurs often in place-names in Lakeland, e.g. Portinscale, Bowscale, Lonscale, Warnscale, Scale Hill and many others.

Visitors to
Scale Force
please note —

The best route to Scale Force from Buttermere bears left after crossing Far Ruddy Beck. Although cairned, the path can be difficult to follow. The original route crossed the two branches of Scale Beck, but it is not recommended because it is one of the wettest paths in the district and because of the mud on the far side of Scale Beck.   It is a mistake to imagine (as many do) that the force may be reached by this route in fancy shoes — thigh-length gum-boots are the ideal wear.

MAP

If the lie of the ground is favourable, a mountain stream needs little persuasion to change its course — a few boulders washed down in time of flood, landslides or erosion are common causes. Examples are many.

Note that Scale Beck reaches Crummock Water at two places 400 yards apart. The bifurcation upstream was due to storm, but in this case there has been a partial recovery and both branches carry water to the lake when the water level is high.

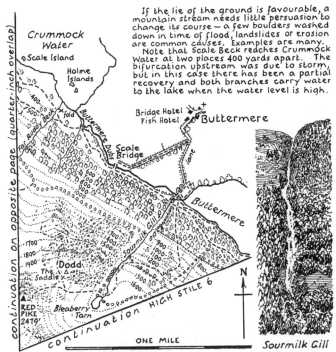

Crummock Water

Scale Island

Holme Islands

Bridge Hotel
Fish Hotel

Buttermere

Scale Bridge

Buttermere

Dodd

The Saddle

RED PIKE 2479'

Bleaberry Tarn

continuation on opposite page (quarter-inch overlap)

continuation HIGH STILE 6

ONE MILE

N

Sourmilk Gill

Scale Bridge

ASCENT FROM BUTTERMERE
via BLEABERRY TARN
2150 feet of ascent : 1¼ miles

RED PIKE

RIDGE TO HIGH STILE

Chapel
Crags

2200
2100
2000

The
Saddle

grass

Dodd

Bleaberry
Tarn

At Bleaberry Tarn, Red Pike
is seen to be aptly named,
the screes below the top
having a distinctly
ruddy colour

bilberry   1800   1700

The line of the
route is excellent,
affording superb
views, and from
Buttermere to
the Saddle the
path is kept
in an excellent
condition. BUT
the top part
of the path is
very stony
and becoming
worse annually.
It is clear from
the undisturbed
ground nearby
that the stones
have been
brought to
the surface
by the tread
of many feet.
The stones
are loose
and ready to
slide, making care
especially necessary
when descending.

1600
bilberry   1500
1400
1300
1200
1100
1000
900
gate   800
700
600
500
400

paved zig-zags

Burtness
Wood

SCARTH
GAP

Dodd
often hides Red Pike
and is mistaken for it
in views from the valley.
The summit of Red Pike
cannot be seen from
Buttermere village

the path formerly forded the
stream here, but now all trace
of the old crossing has gone,
and the path visits the tarn.

The cascades in
Sourmilk Gill are
very beautiful. The
lowest of them can
be seen from the
footbridge at the
foot of the gill, but
the whole sequence
is best viewed
from the start
of the road to
Newlands Pass
from Buttermere.

Sourmilk Gill

SCALE
BRIDGE

Buttermere Dubs

Three footbridges
and three gates give
access to the
Wood

Buttermere
(the lake)

Buttermere is
surrounded by
fine mountains,
but the challenge of
Red Pike predominates
and, as the state of
the path testifies,
it is a very popular
objective by the route here shown,
this being the most obvious and
direct way to the top.

looking
south-west

lane
(much used
by visitors)

SCALE
BRIDGE

Fish
Hotel

Buttermere

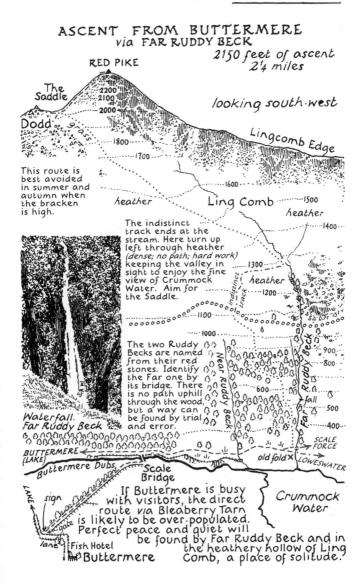

ASCENT FROM BUTTERMERE
via FAR RUDDY BECK

2150 feet of ascent
2¼ miles

RED PIKE

The Saddle

Dodd

grass

looking south-west

2200
2100
2000

1800

1700

Lingcomb Edge

This route is best avoided in summer and autumn when the bracken is high.

heather

Ling Comb

1600

1500

heather

1400

The indistinct track ends at the stream. Here turn up left through heather *(dense; no path; hard work)* keeping the valley in sight to enjoy the fine view of Crummock Water. Aim for the Saddle.

indistinct track

heather

1300

1200

1100

1000

The two Ruddy Becks are named from their red stones. Identify the Far one by its bridge. There is no path uphill through the wood, but a way can be found by trial and error.

Near Ruddy Beck

Far Ruddy Beck

900

800

fall

600

500

400

Waterfall.
Far Ruddy Beck

SCALE FORCE

BUTTERMERE (LAKE)

Buttermere Dubs

Scale Bridge

old fold ×

LOWESWATER

Crummock Water

LAKE

sign

gate

lane

Fish Hotel
Buttermere

If Buttermere is busy with visitors, the direct route *via* Bleaberry Tarn is likely to be over-populated. Perfect peace and quiet will be found by Far Ruddy Beck and in the heathery hollow of Ling Comb, a place of solitude.

ASCENT FROM BUTTERMERE
via LINGCOMB EDGE
2150 feet of ascent : 2¾ miles

RED PIKE

The Saddle

2200
2100

1900

1800

Lingcomb Edge

grass

1700

cairn on Lingcomb Edge

Lingcomb Edge, looking to Red Pike

Ling Comb

1600

1500

1300

1200

Turn up steep slope

1100

1000

900

gap

800

700

Far Ruddy Beck

600

500

three holly trees

SCALE FORCE

Scale Bridge

old fold ✕

grass

bracken

400

looking south-south-west

Scale Island

LOWESWATER

Crummock Water

If Scale Force has not already been visited, the route on the next page should be taken in preference to the one here shown.   This more direct route has some steep scrambling in lush heather above the wall, and there is not a clear path underfoot for much of the way; otherwise it is pleasant and quiet and has superb views of the Crummock district.
(In 2008 this route was so difficult to follow that it was not worth attempting.)

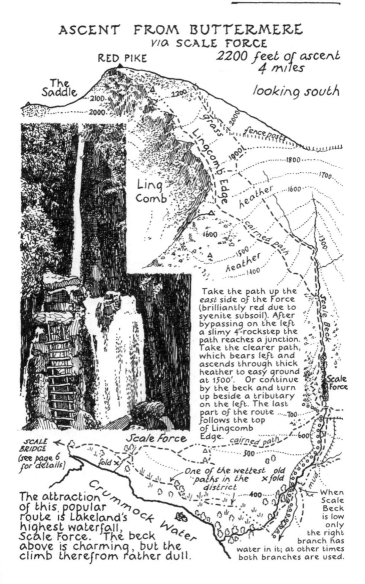

ASCENT FROM BUTTERMERE
VIA SCALE FORCE
2200 feet of ascent
4 miles

looking south

RED PIKE

The Saddle

2100
2000

2200

grass

Lingcomb Edge

fence posts

2000

1900

1800

1700

Ling Comb

1600

heather

cairned path

1600

1500

heather

1500

1400

1300

Scale Beck

Take the path up the east side of the Force (brilliantly red due to syenite subsoil). After bypassing on the left a slimy 4'-rockstep the path reaches a junction. Take the clearer path, which bears left and ascends through thick heather to easy ground at 1500'. Or continue by the beck and turn up beside a tributary on the left. The last part of the route follows the top of Lingcomb Edge.

Scale Force

700

600

Scale Force

cairned path

500

SCALE BRIDGE
(see page 6 for details)

fold

One of the wettest old paths in the district

fold

Crummock Water

400

mud

The attraction of this popular route is Lakeland's highest waterfall, Scale Force. The beck above is charming, but the climb therefrom rather dull.

When Scale Beck is low only the right branch has water in it; at other times both branches are used.

ASCENT FROM ENNERDALE
(HIGH GILLERTHWAITE)

2000 feet of ascent
1¼ miles

looking north-east

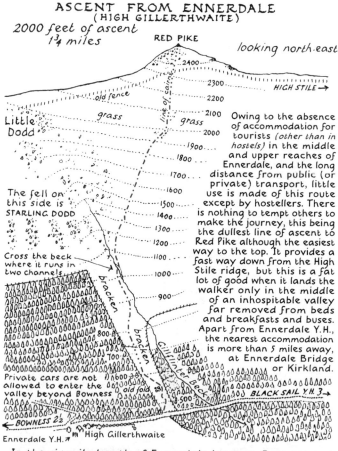

RED PIKE

HIGH STILE →

Little Dodd

grass

grass

old fence

line of cairns

2400
2300
2200
2100
2000
1900
1800
1700
1600
1500
1400
1300
1200
1100
1000
900
800
700
600
500

The fell on this side is STARLING DODD

Cross the beck where it runs in two channels

bracken

bracken

Gillerthwaite beck

old fold

Private cars are not allowed to enter the valley beyond Bowness

← BOWNESS 2½

Ennerdale Y.H.

High Gillerthwaite

BLACK SAIL Y.H. 3 →

Owing to the absence of accommodation for tourists *(other than in hostels)* in the middle and upper reaches of Ennerdale, and the long distance from public (or private) transport, little use is made of this route except by hostellers. There is nothing to tempt others to make the journey, this being the dullest line of ascent to Red Pike although the easiest way to the top. It provides a fast way down from the High Stile ridge, but this is a fat lot of good when it lands the walker only in the middle of an inhospitable valley far removed from beds and breakfasts and buses. Apart from Ennerdale Y.H., the nearest accommodation is more than 5 miles away, at Ennerdale Bridge or Kirkland.

In the six-mile length of Ennerdale between Bowness and Black Sail Youth Hostel there is only one break in the dense plantations on the north side of the rough valley road. This is a narrow strip of unplanted ground between fences rising from the road 350 yards east of High Gillerthwaite. It is the only avenue by which sheep may be brought down from the fells and may be used for the ascent of Red Pike. The path is cairned and easy to follow, mainly on grass, but tedious and unexciting, interest being restricted to the retrospective view of the Pillar Group across the valley.

THE SUMMIT

The summit projects from the main mass of the fell, boldly, like a promontory from a cliff-face, having a steep fall on three sides, a flat top, and a gentle decline to a grassy plateau southwards, which is crossed by a bounndary fence above the Ennerdale slope. A wind shelter and a large cairn occupy the abrupt corner of the promontory directly at the head of the Buttermere path. The top is grassy, with an intermingling of small outcrops and stony patches.

DESCENTS : The top is well trodden but not formed into definite tracks. Two lines of guide-cairns lead away southwards, to Gillerthwaite and to High Stile; if, in mist, doubt arises in selection, error will be revealed when the fence is reached, the High Stile route turning left in company with it, the Gillerthwaite crossing it. The Scale Force line of descent is marked by a cairn that comes into view a few yards from the summit cairn. In mist it is best to leave this route alone. The direct route down to Buttermere by way of Bleaberry Tarn is marked by a well-situated cairn. In a few yards the path splits into two, both branches being very difficult to negotiate because of loose stones. Once the Saddle is reached all the difficulties are over.

The summit, from Bleaberry Tarn

High Stile in the background

THE VIEW

Lakes and Tarns

NE : *Derwent Water*
E : *Buttermere*
E : *Bleaberry Tarn (seen a few paces east of the cairn)*
W : *Ennerdale Water*
W : *Reservoir near Dent*
NW : *Loweswater*
N : *Crummock Water*

Red Pike's view is notable for the number of lakes that can be seen, really seen and not merely glimpsed; their prominence adds an unusual beauty to the scene.

Despite High Stile's impending bulk the mountain view is quite satisfying, the Grasmoor group, seen from tip to toe, being very conspicuous.

Many detailed descriptions of this view have appeared in print, not always completely in accordance with the facts.

Principal Fells

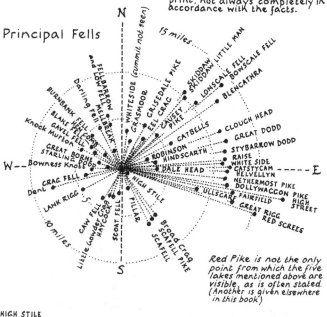

Red Pike is not the only point from which the five lakes mentioned above are visible, as is often stated. (Another is given elsewhere in this book)

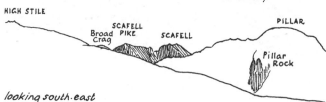

looking south-east

RIDGE ROUTES

TO HIGH STILE. 2644′ : ¾ mile : S, then SE and E.

Depression at 2300′
350 feet of ascent
Very easy, becoming rough finally

A line of marker cairns heads south to
the old fence, which may be followed
across excellent turf to the stony rise
of High Stile, but in clear weather keep
to the edge of the escarpment to get the
best views ; watch in particular for the
striking aspect of Chapel Crags from the
head of the scree-gully alongside.

ONE MILE

The ridge to High Stile

head of Chapel Crags gully

Chapel Crags

TO STARLING DODD, 2077′ : 1¼ miles : W, then WNW.

Depressions at 1880′ and 1850′
240 feet of ascent
Little of interest

Surveyed from
Red Pike, this
route obviously
is a long trudge
over grass with
no excitements.
So it proves. As
the start of a high-level
way down to Ennerdale it is better.

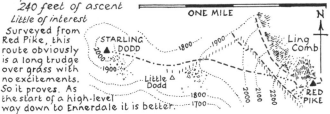

ONE MILE

Red Pike
(Wasdale)

2707'

from Over Beck

▲ PILLAR
▲ SCOAT FELL
▲ HAYCOCK ▲ RED PIKE
Wasdale
● Head
YEWBARROW ▲
●
Overbeck Bridge

MILES
0   1   2   3   4

from Black Crag

NATURAL FEATURES

There are several Mosedales, and the best-known of them, and the best, is the one branching from Wasdale Head. The circuit of the ridges around this side-valley is a succession of exciting situations and fine vantage points in rugged surroundings, and a highlight greatly enjoyed on this splendid expedition is the traverse along the crest of the mile-long escarpment of Red Pike, its top cairn dramatically poised on the brink of a wild cataract of crags forming the eastern face: this is a grim declivity falling 2000 feet to the valley, a place for adventurers or explorers perhaps but it carries no walkers' paths.   In contrast the western slopes decline more gradually over an extensive area jewelled by Scoat Tarn and Low Tarn, before coming down roughly to Nether Beck.   North, Red Pike abuts closely against Scoat Fell, and the southern boundary is formed by Over Beck.   Red Pike claims a short water frontage on Wast Water in the narrow strip of cultivated land lying between the outlets of Nether Beck and Over Beck, and only here, in the pastures and trees of Bowderdale, does the fell's fierce expression relent a little; only here does its dourness break into a pleasant smile. Just here, by the water's edge, is an oasis of sylvan beauty quite uncharacteristic of the fell towering behind, which, everywhere else, exemplifies the utter wildness and desolation of true mountain country.

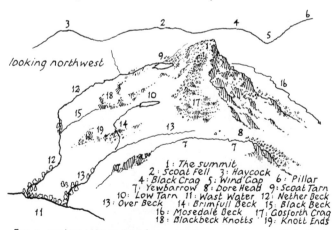

looking northwest

1: The summit
2: Scoat Fell   3: Haycock   6: Pillar
4: Black Crag   5: Wind Gap
7: Yewbarrow   8: Dore Head   9: Scoat Tarn
10: Low Tarn   11: Wast Water   12: Nether Beck
13: Over Beck   14: Brimfull Beck   15: Black Beck
16: Mosedale Beck   17: Gosforth Crag
18: Blackbeck Knotts   19: Knott Ends

For a century there has been confusion between this Red Pike and its namesake overlooking Buttermere. Confusion is worse confounded by their proximity, the summits being only three miles apart. To make a distinction, it is usual to refer to the subject of this chapter as the Wasdale Red Pike.

MAP

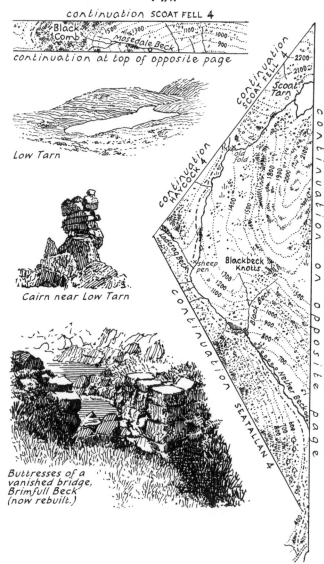

continuation SCOAT FELL 4

Black Comb 1500 1300 1100 1000 900
Mosedale Beck

continuation at top of opposite page

Low Tarn

Cairn near Low Tarn

Buttresses of a
vanished bridge,
Brimfull Beck
(now rebuilt.)

continuation SCOAT FELL 4

continuation on opposite page

continuation HAYCOCK 4

continuation SEATALLAN 4

2200
2100
Scoat Tarn
old fold
2100
2000
1900
1800
1700
1600
1500
1400
Loading Beck
sheep pen
Blackbeck Knotts
1300
1200
1100
1000
900
800
Black Beck
Nether Beck
700
600
500
400

MAP

continuation at top of opposite page

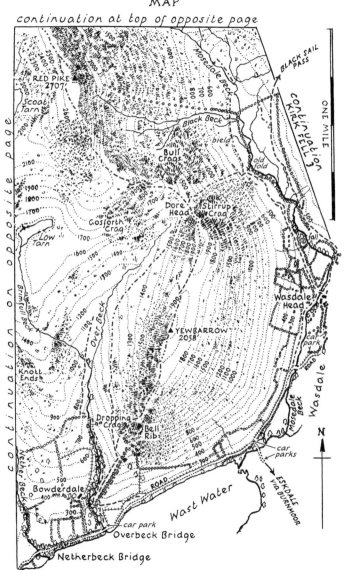

ONE MILE

continuation on opposite page

N

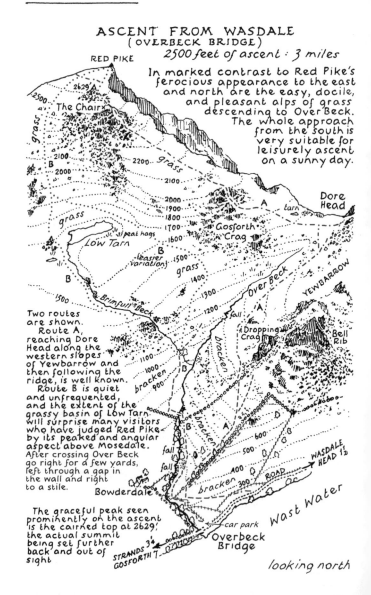

ASCENT FROM WASDALE
(OVERBECK BRIDGE)
2500 feet of ascent : 3 miles

In marked contrast to Red Pike's ferocious appearance to the east and north are the easy, docile, and pleasant alps of grass descending to Over Beck. The whole approach from the south is very suitable for leisurely ascent on a sunny day.

RED PIKE

2629

The Chair

2500

grass

2100

2000

grass

2200

grass

2100

2000

1900

1800

1700

1600

Gosforth Crag

Dore Head

tarn

A

grass

Low Tarn

peat hags

(lesser variation)

1500

1400

grass

Over Beck

YEWBARROW

B

1300

1200

Brimfull Beck

1500

fall

A

Dropping Crag

Bell Rib

1100

Two routes are shown.
   Route A, reaching Dore Head along the western slopes of Yewbarrow and then following the ridge, is well known.
   Route B is quiet and unfrequented, and the extent of the grassy basin of Low Tarn will surprise many visitors who have judged Red Pike by its peaked and angular aspect above Mosedale. After crossing Over Beck go right for a few yards, left through a gap in the wall and right to a stile.

1000

900

bracken

bracken

B

600

A

fall

WASDALE HEAD 1½

500

fall

fall

400

ROAD

300

bracken

Bowderdale

The graceful peak seen prominently on the ascent is the cairned top at 2629', the actual summit being set further back and out of sight

car park

Overbeck Bridge

STRANDS 3½
GOSFORTH 7

Wast Water

looking north

ASCENT FROM WASDALE HEAD
2450 feet of ascent : 2½ miles

Although this walk is commonly undertaken as the first part of a splendid ridge-route — the Mosedale Horse-shoe — continuing over Scoat Fell and Pillar, it is a fine expedition even if Red Pike is the only objective, for this is a fell deserving a leisurely and detailed exploration; in which event the descent by way of Low Tarn and Over Beck is recommended.

Leave Wasdale Head by the bridge at the rear of the inn and pass between walls to the open fell, the rock pinnacle on Stirrup Crag now being prominent. Keep to the path to the foot of the Dore Head slope — nothing is gained by making a rising short cut through the field of boulders, as some walkers prefer to do. Ascend to Dore Head by the grass to the right of the scree-run.

The steep climb up to Dore Head is rather overfacing after a heavy breakfast and is actually longer and more tedious than it appears to be. Under a hot sun, it calls for resolution. An alternative is available, however, this being to continue along the valley into the moist and cool recesses at the source of Mosedale Beck, where the rock scenery of Blackem Head is superb, so gaining the ridge in the depression beyond the summit. (See Scoat Fell 6 for an illustration of the route.) This devious tactic may not quite be playing the game, but all is fair in fellwalking from Wasdale Head.

looking west   This route serves to prove that the Scafells and Great Gable have not a monopoly of the best walks around Wasdale Head. The ridge of Red Pike is excellent, lovely turf alternating with a few simple scrambles on pleasant rock.

THE SUMMIT

Cairn at 2707'

The highest cairn, at 2707', is dramatically sited on the very brink of the Mosedale precipice and is so much on the edge of space that it cannot be walked round. It is a place to avoid in high wind. Yet the opposite western slope rises to the cairn in a gentle incline, carpeted with lovely turf. The transition in a matter of a few feet is a shock to the senses.

500 yards south is a larger cairn set amongst stones on an elevated plateau. This is point 2629', a typical mountain top in appearance and often regarded as the real summit.

DESCENTS : The descent from 2707' (but not from 2629') south to Overbeck Bridge via Low Tarn is, surprisingly, one of the easiest in the district, on grass throughout and gently graded, but there is no path. In mist, aim for Dore Head, keeping the escarpment on the left, and the start of the path will be found twenty yards east of the 2629' top; at Dore Head go left down the scree or the grass bank alongside, for Wasdale Head, or turn right for Overbeck Bridge. An interesting alternative is to descend from the col northwards to Scoat Tarn and Nether Beck. Do not attempt the Blackem Head

Cairn at 2629'

route into Mosedale unless it has been prospected in ascent.

THE SUMMIT

continued

The Chair

A summit feature that often escapes attention nowadays is an outcrop of rock that has been converted into a comfortable seat by the erection of a back rest and side arms of stones. This is The Chair, and a century ago was so well known that people spoke of climbing The Chair as today they speak of climbing Red Pike. It occupies a vantage point on the edge of the stony plateau of the south summit, overlooking Wast Water, and is 120 yards south of the 2629' cairn. It is within 100 yards of the Dore Head track and prominently in view therefrom but may be mistaken at a glance for a cairn. It has survived the storms of many years remarkably well, but is not proof against vandals. Please respect it.

On the ascent from Overbeck Bridge it is The Chair that is so conspicuously in view, apparently on the highest point, and not the summit cairn as may be thought.

Quite unaccountably, the ridge path prefers to skirt the highest cairn instead of visiting it.

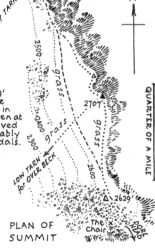

PLAN OF SUMMIT

THE VIEW

The view is good only in parts. Scoat Fell and Pillar, nearby and higher, shut out the distance northwards and have little attraction. The Scafell range, seen full length and in true perspective, is the best feature. There is a striking aerial view of Black Comb, which will impress those who have come up by this route.

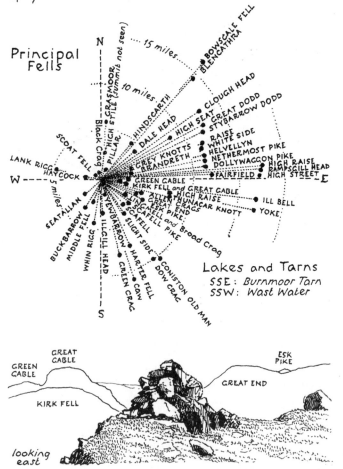

Principal Fells

N

15 miles

10 miles

BOWSCALE FELL
BLENCATHRA
CLOUGH HEAD
GREAT DODD
STYBARROW DODD
HIGH SEAT
RAISE
WHITE SIDE
HELVELLYN
NETHERMOST PIKE
DOLLYWAGGON PIKE
HIGH RAISE
RAMPSGILL HEAD
FAIRFIELD
HIGH STREET
HIGH STILE (GRASMOOR summit not seen)
HINDSCARTH
DALE HEAD
HIGH SEAT
CREY KNOTTS
GRANDRETH
Black Crag
SCOAT FELL
LANK RIGG
HAYCOCK
5 miles
W
E
GREEN GABLE
KIRK FELL and GREAT GABLE
HIGH RAISE
ILL BELL
YOKE
ALLEN CRAGS
KIRK FELL
HONACAR KNOTT
GREAT CRAGS
SCAFELL PIKE
GREAT END
SCAFELL PIKE and Broad Crag
YEWBARROW
SEATALLAN
BUCKBARROW
MIDDLE FELL
WHIN RIGG
ILLGILL HEAD
SLIGHT SIDE
HARTER FELL
CAW
GREEN CRAG
DOW CRAG
CONISTON OLD MAN

S

Lakes and Tarns
SSE: *Burnmoor Tarn*
SSW: *Wast Water*

GREEN GABLE
GREAT GABLE
ESK PIKE
GREAT END
KIRK FELL

looking east

RIDGE ROUTES

To SCOAT FELL, 2760' : ¾ mile : NNW
Depression at 2500' : 270 feet of ascent
A dull climb, but brief.

Follow the escarpment north to the depression, then go straight up the opposite slope, ignoring paths trending to the right. Bear left to avoid a rough area of boulders at the east end of the summit wall. Cross the wall (on which the cairn stands) to obtain fine views of Steeple across Mirk Cove.

ONE MILE

To YEWBARROW, 2058' : 1¾ miles : S, SE and SSW
Depression at 1520' : 680 feet of ascent
A pleasant descent followed by an arduous scramble

Down to Dore Head at 1520' everything is just fine. The south summit will have been crossed, the Chair will have been found and sat upon, two rough rocky declivities will have been negotiated without much difficulty and a good speed maintained down the easy grass slopes. But, at Dore Head, Yewbarrow looks really hostile. Steep scree and grass lead up to a barrier of rock (Stirrup Crag) that looks impassable, but grimly-determined pedestrians can force a way up a series of cracks following evidences of the sufferings of those who have gone before. After 40 yards of toil there is sudden relief as grass is met again, and easy walking across a wide depression and up the opposite slope leads to the summit. Anxiety then shifts to the job of getting off safely... which is another story in another chapter.

If there are no witnesses about to tell of their shame, timid walkers may avoid Stirrup Crag entirely by taking the Overbeck path from Dore Head for quarter of a mile until beyond the boulders, then slanting up grass to the depression on Yewbarrow (route indicated on map above).

Stirrup Crag and Dore Head, as seen from the slopes of Red Pike

Scoat Fell

2760'

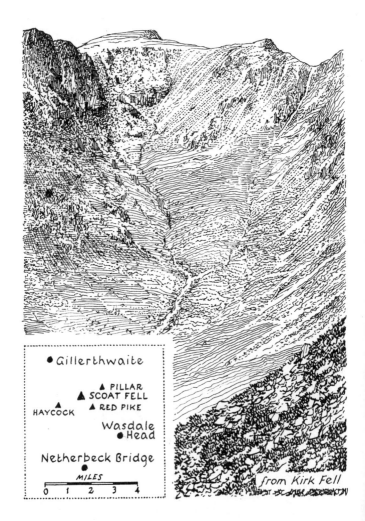

Gillerthwaite

▲ PILLAR
▲ SCOAT FELL
HAYCOCK ▲ ▲ RED PIKE

Wasdale
Head

Netherbeck Bridge

MILES
0 1 2 3 4

from Kirk Fell

NATURAL FEATURES

Although often climbed from Wasdale as a part of the 'Mosedale Horse-shoe', Scoat Fell has no fan club and few devotees, for the long plateau forming the top compares unfavourably with the more shapely summits of other fells even easier of access from Wasdale Head; and, moreover, a massive stone wall following the watershed impedes freedom of view and freedom of movement: the top of a mountain is never improved by man's handiwork, only a simple cairn being acceptable.

Yet Scoat Fell triumphs over its disabilities, and provides magnificent mountain scenery on all sides. The mile-long escarpment facing Ennerdale, between Wind Gap and Mirklin Cove, is tremendously exciting, wild and desolate terrain, interrupted only by a thin arête linking with Steeple, a subsidiary pinnacle of remarkable proportions towering gracefully across the void. All along here is scenery of high quality.

The fell descends broadly to Ennerdale in grass and heather slopes between Deep Gill and High Beck, and is afforested below 1200 feet; on the Wasdale side, where Red Pike soon obstructs the descent, the upper reaches of Nether Beck and Mosedale Beck form the boundaries.

Scoat Tarn is shared with Red Pike, but two lesser sheets of water, Tewit Tarn (which is now completely covered in vegetation) and Moss Dub, a valley pool in the Ennerdale forest, are within the territory of Scoat Fell exclusively.

Steeple (left) and Scoat Fell, looking across Mirklin Cove

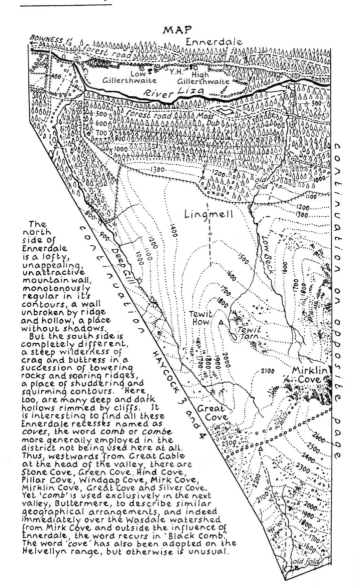

MAP

The north side of Ennerdale is a lofty, unappealing, unattractive mountain wall, monotonously regular in it's contours, a wall unbroken by ridge and hollow, a place without shadows.

But the south side is completely different, a steep wilderness of crag and buttress in a succession of towering rocks and soaring ridges, a place of shuddering and squirming contours. Here too, are many deep and dark hollows rimmed by cliffs. It is interesting to find all these Ennerdale recesses named as coves, the word comb or combe more generally employed in the district not being used here at all. Thus, westwards from Great Gable at the head of the valley, there are Stone Cove, Green Cove, Hind Cove, Pillar Cove, Windgap Cove, Mirk Cove, Mirklin Cove, Great Cove and Silver Cove. Yet 'comb' is used exclusively in the next valley, Buttermere, to describe similar geographical arrangements, and indeed immediately over the Wasdale watershed from Mirk Cove and outside the influence of Ennerdale, the word recurs in 'Black Comb'. The word 'cove' has also been adopted on the Helvellyn range, but otherwise is unusual.

MAP

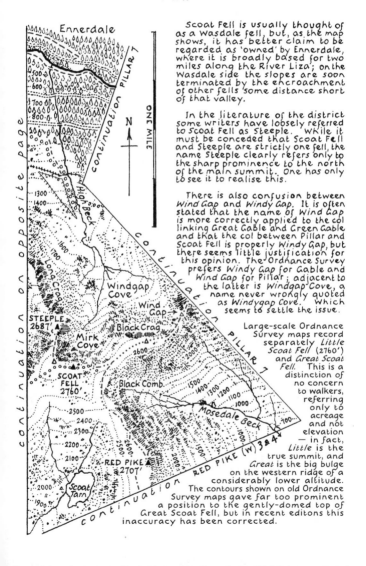

Scoat Fell is usually thought of as a Wasdale fell, but, as the map shows, it has better claim to be regarded as 'owned' by Ennerdale, where it is broadly based for two miles along the River Liza; on the Wasdale side the slopes are soon terminated by the encroachment of other fells some distance short of that valley.

In the literature of the district some writers have loosely referred to Scoat Fell as Steeple. While it must be conceded that Scoat Fell and Steeple are strictly one fell, the name Steeple clearly refers only to the sharp prominence to the north of the main summit. One has only to see it to realise this.

There is also confusion between *Wind Gap* and *Windy Gap*. It is often stated that the name of *Wind Gap* is more correctly applied to the col linking Great Gable and Green Gable and that the col between Pillar and Scoat Fell is properly *Windy Gap*, but there seems little justification for this opinion. The Ordnance Survey prefers *Windy Gap* for Gable and *Wind Gap* for Pillar; adjacent to the latter is *Windgap* Cove, a name never wrongly quoted as *Windygap* Cove. Which seems to settle the issue.

Large-scale Ordnance Survey maps record separately *Little Scoat Fell* (2760') and *Great Scoat Fell*. This is a distinction of no concern to walkers, referring only to acreage and not elevation — in fact, *Little* is the true summit, and *Great* is the big bulge on the western ridge of a considerably lower altitude. The contours shown on old Ordnance Survey maps gave far too prominent a position to the gently-domed top of Great Scoat Fell, but in recent editons this inaccuracy has been corrected.

ASCENT FROM WASDALE
(NETHERBECK BRIDGE)
2550 feet of ascent : 4¼ miles

HAYCOCK

SCOAT FELL

looking north

Route A is normally used in the ascent of Haycock, but is also convenient for Scoat Fell (best views on the far side of the wall). But Route B is better because of the visit to Scoat Tarn, a gem in a wild setting.

old fold

Scoat Tarn

RED PIKE

split boulder Scoat Tarn

Ladcrog Beck

sheep pen

Netherbeck

A fair path proceeds along the west side of Nether Beck to 1400', where the routes diverge. This path leaves the road a quarter-mile from Netherbeck Bridge. Cutting across from the bridge is not recommended because of thick bracken and marshy ground.

falls

parking place

WASDALE HEAD 2

Netherbeck Bridge

ROAD

STRANDS 2¾
GOSFORTH 6½

Wast Water

On Route B : looking back to Scoat Tarn from 2400'

This is the easiest line of approach to Scoat Fell from any direction, there being no steep gradients. The biggest attraction en route is Scoat Tarn, the grandest of the western tarns, and itself sufficient to justify the walk.

ASCENT FROM WASDALE HEAD
2500 feet of ascent : 3 miles

looking west

The gradual climb alongside Mosedale Beck (pathless, on grass) is very pleasant, and eagerness is added to the march by the promise of exciting ground ahead manifested by the beetling crags of Red Pike, which grow more impressive with every step. When the rowan-bedecked gorge and upper waterfall are passed, these crags in full view and present a remarkable sight, falling in bewildering confusion from the summit ridge. The stream bifurcates in a grassy hollow and further progress appears barred by a long low wall of rock beyond, but note on the left of this a straight boulder-strewn rake leading directly to the skyline and flanked by a succession of cliffs on both sides. Go up this, keeping to the right to avoid the worst of the boulders (two detours on grass are possible), finally passing through a narrow rock gateway to emerge on the ridge exactly in the depression between Red Pike and Scoat Fell, the summit of the latter being only ten minutes distant on the right.

YEWBARROW rises on this side

Y Boulder is named on O.S. maps. It is the shortest place name in the Lake District.

starry saxifrage

Botanists will enjoy this flowery route and should particularly look amongst the wet rocks and mossy recesses for *saxifraga stellaris* when commencing the ascent of the rake.

Leave Wasdale Head by the bridge behind the inn and keep Mosedale Beck on the right throughout to its source.

Scoat Fell is usually reached from Wasdale Head via Dore Head and Red Pike, or via Pillar, i.e. as part of a ridge-walk, but illustrated here is a direct way, little-known and unfrequented, that climbs out of Mosedale through the magnificent rock scenery of Blackem Head and provides a route onto the ridge much more exciting than the usual tedious ascents of Dore Head and Wind Gap.

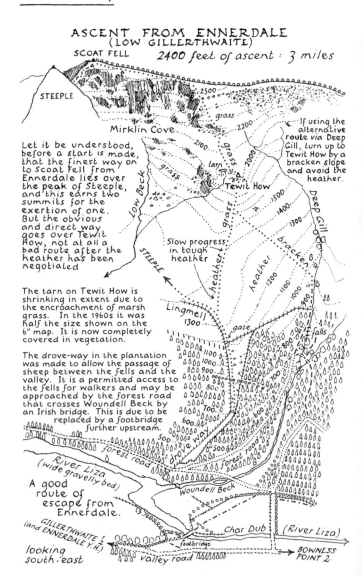

ASCENT FROM ENNERDALE
(LOW GILLERTHWAITE)
2400 feet of ascent : 3 miles

SCOAT FELL

STEEPLE

Mirklin Cove

2500

grass

2200

2100

grass

2000

tarn

Tewit How

1500

1400

1300

Deep Gill

If using the alternative route via Deep Gill, turn up to Tewit How by a bracken slope and avoid the heather.

Low Beck

Let it be understood, before a start is made, that the finest way on to Scoat Fell from Ennerdale lies over the peak of Steeple, and this earns two summits for the exertion of one. But the obvious and direct way goes over Tewit How, not at all a bad route after the heather has been negotiated

The tarn on Tewit How is shrinking in extent due to the encroachment of marsh grass. In the 1960s it was half the size shown on the 6" map. It is now completely covered in vegetation.

The drove-way in the plantation was made to allow the passage of sheep between the fells and the valley. It is a permitted access to the fells for walkers and may be approached by the forest road that crosses Woundell Beck by an Irish bridge. This is due to be replaced by a footbridge further upstream.

STEEPLE

Slow progress in tough heather

heather

heather

grass

bracken

1200

1100

1000

900

Lingmell
1300

gate

800

700

Falls

600

500

forest road

drove way

1100

1000

900

800

700

600

500

forest road

River Liza
(wide gravelly bed)

A good route of escape from Ennerdale.

Woundell Beck

GILLERTHWAITE 1
(and ENNERDALE Y.H.)

Char Dub

(River Liza)

looking south-east

footbridge

Valley road

BOWNESS POINT 2

THE SUMMIT

Walkers who insist on summit cairns being sited precisely on the highest part of a summit have suffered a frustration here, for the exact spot representing the maximum altitude of Scoat Fell is fully occupied by a solid bit of wall. Not to be thwarted, however, our purists have had the enterprise to build a cairn on the top of the wall at this point, and so erected an edifice unique in Lakeland. But less meticulous visitors will generally accept as the summit the prominent cairn on open ground near the angle of the wall, where the cliffs of Mirk Cove terminate in a gentle slope leading to the Steeple arete: this is a few feet lower.

HAYCOCK

Great Scoat Fell

Wall

The top of the fell, stony in places, is an easy parade in the proximity of the wall but one is always conscious of the profound abyss of the northern coves close at hand and the gullies biting deeply into the edge of the plateau. Striking views are obtained by keeping along the rim of the cliffs and by following some of the headlands until they drop into space.

DESCENTS: For Ennerdale, in clear weather, the Steeple ridge is best, followed by the beautiful woodland path that accompanies Low Beck, but in mist prefer a route (there is no path) over Tewit How or by Deep Gill, turning down the easy slope beyond Mirklin Cove. For Wasdale, the Red Pike ridge is the finest route if it can be seen, but in mist accompany the wall WSW to the Haycock col, where a grass slope left descends to Nether Beck, which can be followed by an indistinct path on the west bank down to the road at Netherbeck Bridge.

Direct descents into Mirk and Mirklin Coves are dangerous.

PLAN OF THE SUMMIT

quarter mile

ENNERDALE

STEEPLE

TEWIT HOW

DEEP GILL

Mirklin Cove

Mirk Cove

PILLAR and WIND GAP

SCOAT TARN direct

RED PIKE and WASDALE

HAYCOCK

N

THE VIEW

Only Pillar of the nearer fells overtops Scoat Fell and although it takes a big slice out of the distance there is enough left to see to occupy the attention for a long time on a clear day.   The summit wall is an obstruction, preventing a comprehensive view in all directions.

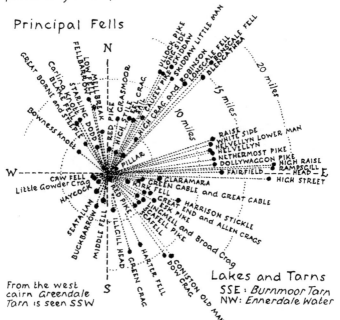

Principal Fells

Lakes and Tarns
SSE: Burnmoor Tarn
NW: Ennerdale Water

From the west cairn Greendale Tarn is seen SSW

Some readers have written to claim that they have identified fells additional to those named on the diagrams of views in these books. This may well be so. The diagrams, as stated, show only the *principal* fells in view. Generally, in the case of a summit of low altitude, the list will be complete, but where a view is extensive, or where several fells appear in a tight group, it becomes impossible to indicate every one in the limited space available and a selection must be made: in such circumstances lower intermediate heights may be excluded to give preference to those forming the skyline; or, again, where only a very small section of a fell can be seen, and then only in favourable conditions, it may be omitted rather than cause confusion, possibly, by including it. With regard to tarns, often these are indistinguishable from their surroundings, especially when of only slightly less elevation, and in many cases will be noticed only when illuminated by sunlight. (Which will account for any omissions of tarns in these views, for the author's wanderings have not always been accompanied by sunshine!)

RIDGE ROUTES

A pre-requisite of a good mountain, from a walker's point of view, is that its summit should be the place of convergence of ridges from all directions, and Scoat Fell, which certainly is a good mountain, measures up to this requirement. Its four ridges all lead to the tops of other fells and provide splendid walks in exciting surroundings.

To STEEPLE, 2687': ¼ mile: N
Depression at 2620'
70 feet of ascent
Ten enjoyable minutes

Unless time is pressing, this short walk should not be omitted even if it is intended to leave Scoat Fell by another route.   Easy ground north of the cairn at the angle of the wall leads in a hundred yards to the top of the arete and the start of a distinct track. If, in mist, this cannot be found, do not proceed. Normally the way is clear and without difficulty.

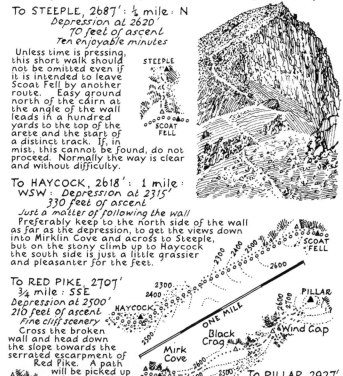

To HAYCOCK, 2618': 1 mile:
WSW: *Depression at 2315'*
330 feet of ascent
Just a matter of following the wall
Preferably keep to the north side of the wall as far as the depression, to get the views down into Mirklin Cove and across to Steeple, but on the stony climb up to Haycock the south side is just a little grassier and pleasanter for the feet.

To RED PIKE, 2707'
¾ mile : SSE
Depression at 2500'
210 feet of ascent
Fine cliff scenery
Cross the broken wall and head down the slope towards the serrated escarpment of Red Pike.   A path will be picked up but when it trends right keep straight on or the top cairn will be by-passed.

To PILLAR, 2927'
1¼ miles : ENE
Depression at 2480' (Wind Gap)
500 feet of ascent
Grand, just grand
Big boulders make hard going at first, but then follows a grassy traverse to the fine cairn above Black Crag. More boulders must be crossed on the descent to Wind Gap. The facing slope is very rough but soon eases. Cairns lead to the top.

Seatallan 2266'

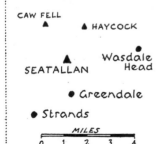

CAW FELL ▲

▲ HAYCOCK

▲ SEATALLAN

● Wasdale Head

● Greendale

● Strands

MILES

0 1 2 3 4

from below Scoat Tarn

NATURAL FEATURES

When the organisers of a local mountain race selected the top of Seatallan as a check-point, some of the contestants confessed that they had never before heard of the fell, and it is probably true to say that the name is not generally known to walkers who have not yet based their activities on Wasdale Head.

Seatallan, formerly known as Seat Allan, forms a steep western wall to the quiet valley of Nether Beck for much of its length, exhibiting thereto a rocky slope above which the summit rises in easier gradients to a graceful cone. Northwards, the curve of the skyline, after a sharp initial fall, sweeps up to the more bulky Haycock; southwards are the two subsidiary heights of Middle Fell and Buckbarrow, both craggy, arresting the decline of the ground to Wast Water. In line with Middle Fell from the summit, hidden in an upland combe, is Greendale Tarn.

It is to west and southwest, in the territory of Copeland Forest, that Seatallan shows its most innocuous slopes, extensive grass sheepwalks that descend gradually to Nether Wasdale and Gosforth, where the River Bleng, by a remarkable change of course, defines the boundaries of the fell on three sides. In this area, a wealth of timber old and new is provided by woodlands and plantations in a pleasant rural setting.

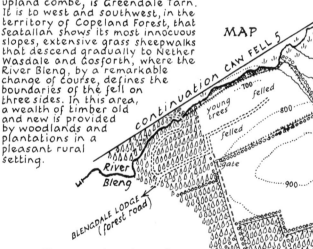

MAP

continuation CAW FELL 5

continuation on following page

700

felled

young trees

800

felled

River Bleng

gate

900

BLENGDALE LODGE (forest road)

Hollow Moor

N

The grass lane here shown is the best way to reach the open fell of Seatallan from Gosforth: it is direct and quiet. It leaves the road to Wasdale at the top of Wellington Brow.

GOSFORTH 2²

grass lane

ONE MILE

MAP

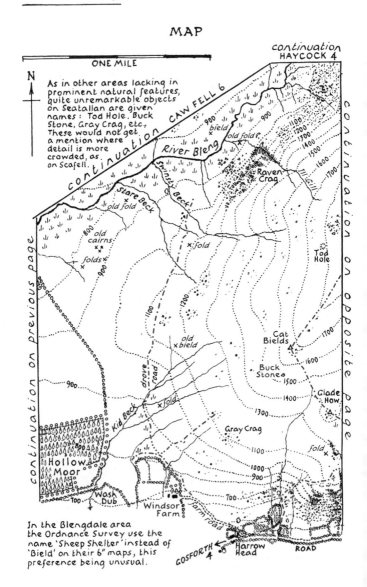

continuation HAYCOCK 4

continuation on opposite page

continuation on previous page

continuation CAW FELL 6

ONE MILE

N

As in other areas lacking in prominent natural features, quite unremarkable objects on Seatallan are given names: Tod Hole, Buck Stone, Gray Crag, etc. These would not get a mention where detail is more crowded, as on Scafell.

River Bleng

bield
old fold

Raven Crag

old fold

Stare Beck
old fold

Swinsty Beck

old cairns

folds

fold

Tod Hole

Cat Bields

old bield

Buck Stones

Glade How

drove road

fold

Gray Crag

fold

Kid Beck

Hollow Moor

Wash Dub

Windsor Farm

farm road

GOSFORTH 4

Harrow Head

ROAD

In the Blengdale area the Ordnance Survey use the name 'Sheep Shelter' instead of 'Bield' on their 6" maps, this preference being unusual.

MAP

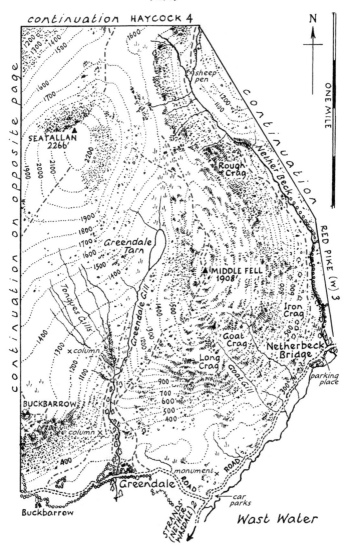

continuation HAYCOCK 4

N

ONE MILE

continuation on opposite page

SEATALLAN
2266'

sheep
pen

Rough
Crag

continuation Nether Beck

RED PIKE (w) 3

Greendale
Tarn

MIDDLE FELL
1908'

Tongues Gills

Greendale Gill

Iron
Crag

×column

Goat
Crag

Netherbeck
Bridge

Long
Crag

Goat Gill

parking
place

BUCKBARROW

column ×

monument ×

ROAD

car
parks

Buckbarrow

Greendale

STRANDS
(NETHER
WASDALE) 2

West Water

ASCENT FROM NETHER WASDALE

2150 feet of ascent
4 miles from Strands
(4½ via Buckbarrow)

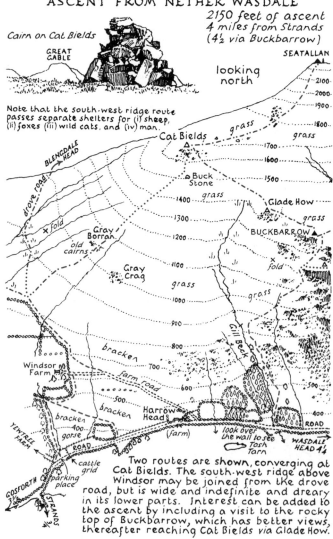

Cairn on Cat Bields

GREAT GABLE

SEATALLAN

looking north

Note that the south-west ridge route passes separate shelters for (i) sheep, (ii) foxes (iii) wild cats, and (iv) man.

BLENGDALE HEAD

drove road

Cat Bields

grass

grass

× fold

old cairns

Gray Borran

Buck Stone

grass

Glade How

grass

BUCKBARROW

× fold

Gray Crag

grass

grass

Gill Beck

bracken

Windsor Farm

farm road

bracken

Harrow Head

(farm)

look over the wall to see Tosh Tarn

bracken
gorse

ROAD

ROAD

WASDALE HEAD 4½

YEWTREE FARM

cattle grid

GOSFORTH 3½

parking place

STRANDS ¾

Two routes are shown, converging at Cat Bields. The south-west ridge above Windsor may be joined from the drove road, but is wide and indefinite and dreary in its lower parts. Interest can be added to the ascent by including a visit to the rocky top of Buckbarrow, which has better views, thereafter reaching Cat Bields via Glade How.

ASCENT FROM WASDALE

(GREENDALE)
2050' of ascent : 2 miles

(NETHERBECK BRIDGE)
2100' of ascent : 3 miles

SEATALLAN

2100
2000
1900
1800
1700
1500
1400
1300
1200
1100

Greendale Tarn

There is now no footbridge at the place where the gill is crossed.

Tongues Gills

Tongues Gills is a double plural: there are several tongues and gills forming magnificent ravine scenery.

MIDDLE FELL

800
700 — Tongues Gills come into view.

grass path

600
500
400
300

fine yew

bracken

ROAD

Greendale

←GOSFORTH 5¼   WASDALE HEAD→ 3½

looking north

The walk up the fell to Tongues Gills is delightful, and the grim scenery of the gills (unseen from the road) is a great surprise.

Instead of proceeding thence as far as Greendale Tarn, which is unattractive, avoid its marshy surroundings by turning up the slope of Seatallan, keeping left to avoid the summit screes.

SEATALLAN

HAYCOCK

2100
2000
1900   *grass*
1800
1700   *grass*

Lad Crag

1600
1500
1400
1300
1200

A fair path, with cairns, ascends the valley of Nether Beck. The first easy escape from the craggy confines of the valley is provided by a grass slope alongside Ladcrag Beck, at the top of which turn left for Seatallan (back towards Wast Water), the fell ahead being Haycock.

Rough Crag

1100
1000
900
800
700

Nether Beck

Cutting across to the path from the bridge is not recommended because of marshy ground and bracken.

600
500
400

fall
fall

400
300

parking place

ROAD

Netherbeck Bridge

←GOSFORTH 6½

Wast Water

WASDALE HEAD→ 2

looking north·west

Nether Beck occupies a quiet valley with pretty waterfalls, and the walk alongside is easy and pleasant. In contrast, the climb out of the valley to the top of Seatallan, on grass, will be found tedious.

THE SUMMIT

Different versions of Ordnance Survey maps describe the heap of stones variously as an 'ancient cairn' and a 'tumulus'.

Local archæologists prefer to describe it as a large tumulus sixty-seven yards in circumference.

Stones galore, all in a great heap on a felltop predominantly of soft turf, is an unnatural phenomenon that greets all visitors to Seatallan's summit. Cairns are not a fashion introduced by walkers. Shepherds built cairns as landmarks for their own guidance in bad weather long before people climbed hills for pleasure. And long before the shepherds the first primitive dwellers in the district built cairns in and around their settlements and over their burial places. The big cairn on Seatallan is attributed to the early British inhabitants and may well be thousands of years old. Nearby, on the grass, is a modern erection: S. 5762 — an Ordnance Survey column. The top of the fell is otherwise featureless. A landslip on the north side has left a fringe of crags and aretes, providing a natural quarry from which the stones of the tumulus were probably obtained.

DESCENTS: Routes of ascent may be reversed, but, *in mist*, Buckbarrow is better left severely alone.

RIDGE ROUTE

To HAYCOCK, 2618': 2 miles: NNE
Depression at 1610'
1050 feet of ascent

Easy grass leads down to and across the depression. A doubt arises as Gowder Crag is approached, but it is not formidable and a scramble over steep scree may be made frontally, or a grassy rake around to the left may be preferred.

THE VIEW

As a viewpoint Seatallan does not rank highly. From Haycock round to Scafell a mountain barrier hides most of the district, only the Coniston fells being well seen at a distance. West and south, however, there is a full and uninterrupted panorama of the coastline and the Black Combe hinterland.

Principal Fells

N

10 miles

Little Cowder Crag

CAW FELL

HAYCOCK

LANK RIGG

Dent

LITTLE SCOAT FELL

RED PIKE

Black Crag

PILLAR

GREY KNOTTS

KIRK FELL

GREEN GABLE

GREAT GABLE

GLARAMARA

HIGH RAISE

GREAT END

Broad Crag

LINGMELL

SCAFELL PIKE

SCAFELL

SLIGHT SIDE

GREAT CARRS

SWIRL HOW

GREY FRIAR

CONISTON OLD MAN

DOW CRAG

HARTER FELL

CAW

GREEN CRAG

ILL GILL HEAD

WHIN RIGG

5 miles

W — — — — — — — — — E

S

Lakes and Tarns

None from the cairn, but a short walk NE brings Low Tarn and Scoat Tarn into view directly ahead and a section of Wast Water can be seen to the right.

The Scafell range from Seatallan

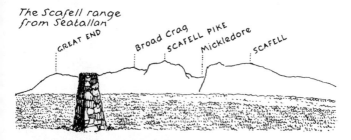

GREAT END   Broad Crag   SCAFELL PIKE   Mickledore   SCAFELL

A special feature is the symmetrical appearance of Scafell Pike, the shape of which is better emphasised from this viewpoint than from any other. The summit is seen midway above the steep twin flanking profiles of Dropping Crag and Pikes Crag.

Starling Dodd

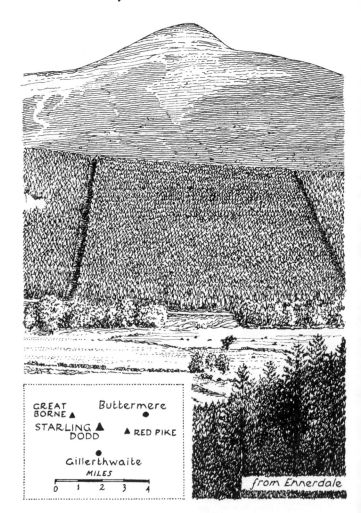

GREAT
BORNE ▲   Buttermere
                      ●

STARLING ▲   ▲ RED PIKE
   DODD

        Gillerthwaite
             ●
         MILES

   0   1   2   3   4

from Ennerdale

NATURAL FEATURES

Starling Dodd, between Buttermere and Ennerdale, is one of those unobtrusive and unassuming fells that are rarely mentioned in literature or in conversation, that never really make an impact on mind or memory, that most visitors to the district know vaguely, from a study of maps, without ever wanting to know well. Its neat rounded summit surveys exciting landscapes but remains shyly aloof as though aware of its own limited contribution to the scenery.

The fell closely overlooks Ennerdale, having on this side a steep but featureless slope, the lower part being densely planted by the Forestry Commission. Its best aspect is to the north, where the extensive plateau of Gale Fell, just below the summit, breaks suddenly into a rough drop to the desolate headwaters and marshes of Mosedale Beck. Gale Fell is bounded by Scale Beck, a place of popular resort in its lower course where Scale Force, Lakeland's highest waterfall, makes its thrilling leap in a deeply-enclosed ravine.

Starling Dodd is a point on a loosely-defined ridge, which runs west to Great Borne before dropping sharply to Ennerdale Water and east to Red Pike and the superb traverse of High Stile. It is seldom conspicuously seen in views from the valleys, being prominent only on the walk into Mosedale from Loweswater, directly in front.

Red Gill,
Mosedale

Starling Dodd
from High Beck,
Ennerdale

MAP

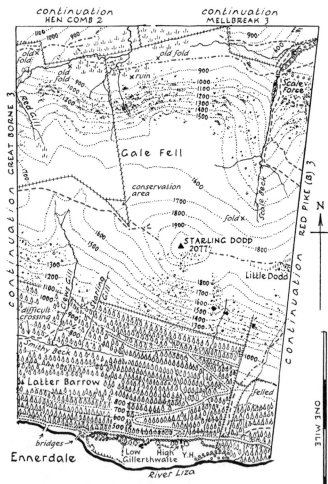

It is now almost impossible to trace on the ground the original line of the Floutern Pass route coming up from Crummock Water, although the Ordnance maps persist in recording it; the present route crosses the foot of Scale Force. Similarly, footpaths shown along the ridge of Starling Dodd should be treated with reserve.

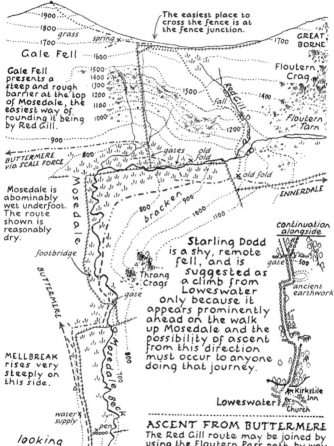

ASCENT FROM LOWESWATER
1700 feet of ascent : 4½ miles

STARLING DODD
1900
1800 grass
1700
Gale Fell
1600

The easiest place to cross the fence is at the fence junction.

1700 GREAT BORNE

Floutern Crag

1500
1400
1300
1200
1100
1000
900

Gale Fell presents a steep and rough barrier at the top of Mosedale, the easiest way of rounding it being by Red Gill.

Red Gill

fall 1400

Floutern Tarn

1200

← BUTTERMERE via SCALE FORCE

800 gates old fold

× old fold

ENNERDALE →

Mosedale is abominably wet underfoot. The route shown is reasonably dry.

Mosedale

800 bracken 900

1000 1100

continuation alongside

gate 500

footbridge

Thrang Crags

Starling Dodd is a shy, remote fell, and is suggested as a climb from Loweswater only because it appears prominently ahead on the walk up Mosedale and the possibility of ascent from this direction must occur to anyone doing that journey.

ancient earthwork

BUTTERMERE

gate

MELLBREAK rises very steeply on this side.

Mosedale Beck

800 700

Kirkstile Inn

Loweswater

Church

water supply

pen

700

looking south

600

continuation alongside

ASCENT FROM BUTTERMERE
The Red Gill route may be joined by using the Floutern Pass path by way of Scale Force from Buttermere. Or, shorter, from the Force climb Scale Beck to its source and bear right.

ASCENT FROM ENNERDALE
From High Gillerthwaite (Ennerdale Y.H.) use the zigzag forest road or the gap between the plantations. (See the map on the opposite page.)

THE SUMMIT

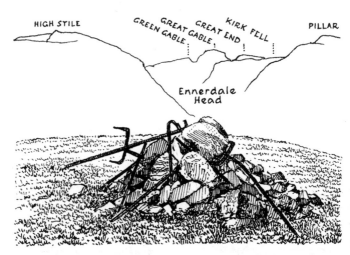

On the way to the top there are slight traces of a former fence, and one wonders what has happened to the iron posts which usually survive long after the wires have gone. Upon arrival at the summit the question is partly answered, for several of them now reinforce the two summit cairns. The top is smooth and grassy, with a little gravel, and except for the cairns, is quite featureless.

DESCENTS : *For Buttermere*, descend north-east, joining the path from Red Pike alongside Scale Beck. *For Loweswater*, reverse the route of ascent *via Red Gill (see previous page). For Ennerdale Bridge*, traverse Great Borne in clear weather, but in mist go down by Red Gill to join the Floutern Tarn route. *For Ennerdale Youth Hostel or Black Sail*, contour Little Dodd to join the public footpath through the forest from Red Pike.

RIDGE ROUTE

TO RED PIKE, 2479' : 1¼ miles : E, then ESE
Depressions at 1850' and 1880' : 650 feet of ascent
Easy walking on grass, steepening towards the finish

In the depression before Little Dodd is a curious hollow with a pool in it, like a bomb crater, and just beyond the rise is a strange field of boulders, these being the only features of note.

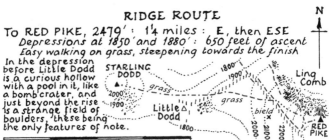

THE VIEW

The best feature of a moderate view is Ennerdale Water, strikingly seen in its entirety except for a small part hidden behind the intervening Bowness Knott.   Of the mountain array, Pillar and Company are the most impressive and, if not in too deep shadow, this is an excellent place to study the topography of the group.

Principal Fells

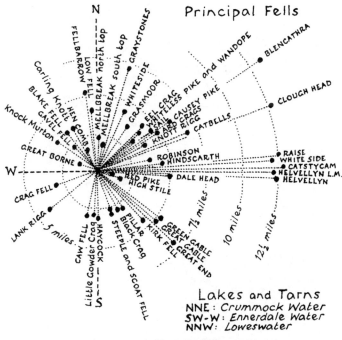

Lakes and Tarns
NNE: Crummock Water
SW-W: Ennerdale Water
NNW: Loweswater

RIDGE ROUTE

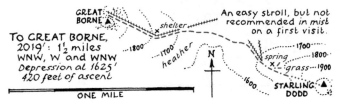

GREAT BORNE ▲
shelter ×

An easy stroll, but not recommended in mist on a first visit.

TO GREAT BORNE, 2019': 1½ miles WNW, W and WNW
Depression at 1625'
420 feet of ascent

1800
1700 heather
1600

N

1700
1800
spring × grass 1900

STARLING DODD ▲

ONE MILE

Steeple

2687'

from Windgap Cove

• Gillerthwaite

STEEPLE ▲   ▲ PILLAR
         ▲ SCOAT FELL
         ▲
HAYCOCK   ▲ RED PIKE

         Wasdale
         • Head

Netherbeck Bridge
         •

MILES
0   1   2   3   4

NATURAL FEATURES

The unknown man who first named this fell was blessed both with inspiration and imagination. Few mountains given descriptive names have fared better. Steeple is a magnificent choice. Seen on a map, it commands the eye and quickens the pulse; seen in reality, it does the same. The climbing of Steeple is a feat to announce with pride in a letter to the old folks at home, who can safely be relied upon to invest the writer with undeserved heroism. Fancy our Fred having climbed a steeple!

This fell, however, is no slender spire. A cross-section of the summit-ridge is not like this ∧ but this ⋀. It is a fine pointed peak nevertheless, one of the best. If the west face was as steep as the east and the south ridge as long as the north, Steeple would provide a great climb. What spoils it is its close attachment to the bulkier Scoat Fell, to which it is linked by a short arete and which is not only higher but completely dominant.

Steeple in fact is no more than an excrescence on the side of Scoat Fell, and only its remarkable proportions have earned it a separate identity. The east crags in particular, forming a half-mile escarpment above Windgap Cove, give a fine airiness to the summit and to the rocky spine of the ridge climbing out of Ennerdale to reach it. This is first-rate mountain country. The short drop west to Mirklin Cove is less fearsome, but rough. Boundary streams Low Beck and High Beck both flow into the Liza, so that Steeple is wholly a fell of Ennerdale.

The north ridge

summit

Scoat Fell

The upper part of
the north ridge

Steeple, as seen
from Scoat Fell
across Mirk Cove

MAP

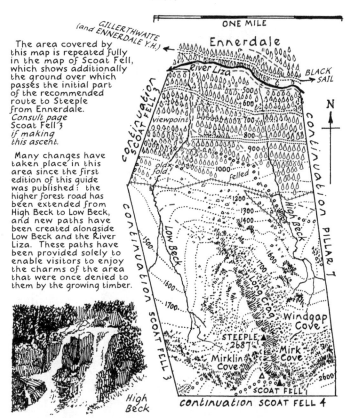

ONE MILE

GILLERTHWAITE
(and ENNERDALE Y.H.)

Ennerdale

River Liza

BLACK SAIL

N

continuation SCOAT FELL 3

viewpoint

old fold!

felled

continuation PILLAR 7

500
600
700
800
900
1000
1200
1300
1400
1500
1600
1700
1800

High Beck

Low Beck

Long Crag

Windgap Cove

STEEPLE
2687

Mirk Cove

Mirklin Cove

SCOAT FELL
2600

continuation SCOAT FELL 3

continuation SCOAT FELL 4

High Beck

The area covered by this map is repeated fully in the map of Scoat Fell, which shows additionally the ground over which passes the initial part of the recommended route to Steeple from Ennerdale. Consult page Scoat Fell 3 if making this ascent.

Many changes have taken place in this area since the first edition of this guide was published: the higher forest road has been extended from High Beck to Low Beck, and new paths have been created alongside Low Beck and the River Liza. These paths have been provided solely to enable visitors to enjoy the charms of the area that were once denied to them by the growing timber.

Low Beck and High Beck are joyful streams on the last half-mile of their descent to join the River Liza, leaping and tumbling in lovely cascades down the fern-clad ravines they have carved out of the fellside. Not so very long ago, growing plantations hid them from the sight of travellers in the valley and muted their merry music. Except where the forest roads crossed their courses (on concrete bridges that have not the beauty bridges should have) they could neither be properly seen nor easily reached. Things are not what they used to be in Ennerdale, and they never will be, but in recent years improvements have been made. Nowadays it is possible to follow the banks of Low Beck by a public footpath, and the viewpoint shown on the map is one of the finest in the district. It deserves to be better known.

ASCENT FROM ENNERDALE
(LOW GILLERTHWAITE)
2350 feet of ascent : 3 miles

STEEPLE

SCOAT FELL

Mirk Cove

Mirklin Cove

Long Crag

Windgap Cove

A succession of towers on the final 500' of the ridge promises excitement, but there are no difficulties. The climb is unexpectedly easy, and mainly on grass.

← At the top of a low rock barrier (climbed by a simple gully in the middle) there is a first view of the upper part of the ridge rising to the sharp summit. This is a good moment.

← Head for the boulder slope and follow up a line of route-marker cairns.

heather 1500

1400

Leave the path 100 yards after crossing Low Beck and turn up the grass.

Low Beck

old wall

In order to make their plantations appear more natural the Forestry Commission have added extensions with scattered trees and areas left unplanted. The limit of such an extension is marked by this fence.

SCOAT FELL VIA TEWIT HOW

Deep Gill

heather

1400 heather
Lingmell
1300

The drove way in the plantation was made to allow the passage of sheep, and is the only unplanted strip of ground on the south side of the forest. It is a permitted way of access to the fells for walkers. It may be reached from Bowness Point by crossing the River Liza by an Irish bridge, turning left at the start of the plantation and crossing Woundell Beck by another Irish bridge (which will soon be replaced by a footbridge fifty yards upstream).

1200 gate
1100
1000
900
old wall
800
700
600
500 drove way

↓ falls

forest road

River Liza (wide gravelly bed)

A fine climb, even yet!

Woundell Beck

GILLERTHWAITE ½ (and ENNERDALE Y.H.)

400 Char Dub (River Liza)

footbridge

valley road

looking south-east

BOWNESS POINT 2

THE SUMMIT

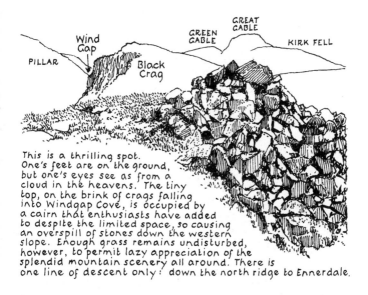

PILLAR — Wind Gap — Black Crag — GREEN GABLE — GREAT GABLE — KIRK FELL

This is a thrilling spot.
One's feet are on the ground,
but one's eyes see as from a
cloud in the heavens. The tiny
top, on the brink of crags falling
into Windgap Cove, is occupied by
a cairn that enthusiasts have added
to despite the limited space, so causing
an overspill of stones down the western
slope. Enough grass remains undisturbed,
however, to permit lazy appreciation of the
splendid mountain scenery all around. There is
one line of descent only: down the north ridge to Ennerdale.

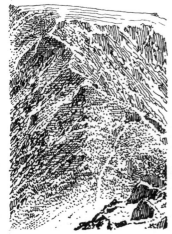

RIDGE ROUTE

To SCOAT FELL, 2760': ¼ mile
        S, but start W
    Depression at 2620'
    140 feet of ascent
    Every step is a joy.
    The arête leading on to Scoat
Fell is in clear view, with a path
winding up it, from the summit
of Steeple, but the col below it
cannot be reached by a beeline;
instead, first go a few paces to
the west and pick up a distinct
track that swings
round to the col.
    The arête is easy,
safe in mist, finely
situated, and ends
on the flat top, the
cairn being directly
ahead (100 yards).

STEEPLE

SCOAT FELL

QUARTER·MILE

THE VIEW

Although the view is greatly circumscribed by the loftier and impending masses of Scoat Fell and Pillar, there is to be seen more than Steeple's subservient position on the north side of the watershed would lead one to expect. West and north the scene is uninterrupted and there is a good sweep of mountainous country to be seen eastwards. The view of Ennerdale, where the lake is displayed almost entirely, is excellent, but visitors are likely to be impressed most of all by the craggy hollows of Mirk and Mirklin Coves nearby.

Principal Fells

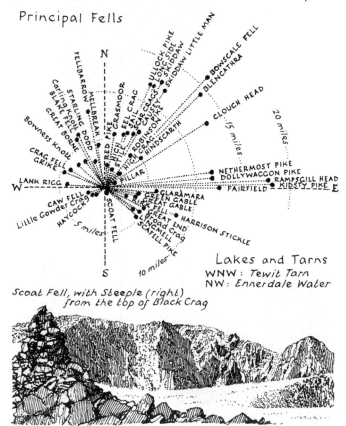

Lakes and Tarns

WNW : Tewit Tarn
NW : Ennerdale Water

Scoat Fell, with Steeple (right)
from the top of Black Crag

Steeple, east face,
from Black Crag

Yewbarrow

2058'

RED PIKE ▲

YEWBARROW ▲ · Wasdale Head

▲ MIDDLE FELL
● Bowderdale

MILES
0 1 2 3 4

from Netherbeck Bridge

NATURAL FEATURES

Many mountains have been described as having the shape of the inverted hull of a boat, but none of them more fittingly than Yewbarrow, which extends along the west side of Wasdale for two miles as a high and narrow ridge, the prow and the stern coming sharply down to valley level with many barnacled incrustations. These latter roughnesses make the long summit rather difficult of attainment from either end, while the steep sides also deter ascent, so that Yewbarrow is not often climbed although it is a centre-piece of magnificent fell country and commands thrilling views. Nor is the ridge itself without incident, one feature in particular, Great Door, being a remarkable cleft where the crest narrows at the top of the craggy declivity above Wastwater.

Yewbarrow's western side is well defined by Over Beck, which comes down from Dore Head, the col linking the fell with Red Pike and the Pillar group. At one time, Dore Head had the reputation of providing the best scree-run in the district on its northern side, descending to Mosedale, but generations of booted scree-runners have scraped the passage clean in places and left it dangerously slippery.

left: Dropping Crag

below: Dropping Crag and Bell Rib, on the approach up the south ridge.

The 'avoiding tactic', to skirt the precipitous upper rocks of Bell Rib, is indicated by a dotted line.

above:

Great Door, as it is seen on the descent of the south ridge. The line of escape from this *impasse* is indicated (→)

The South Ridge

right : Just before reaching Great Door on the descent, a similar cleft is met which might be mistaken for it; this, however, is rounded without difficulty.

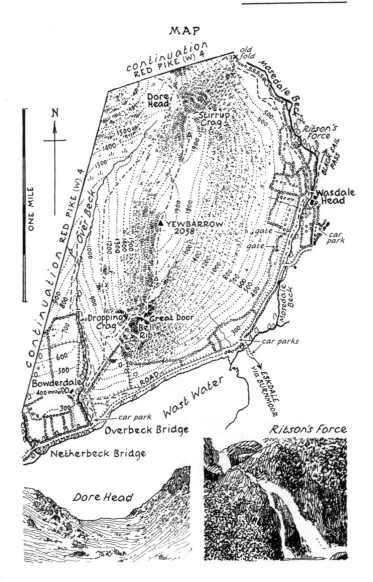

MAP

continuation
RED PIKE (W) 4

old
fold

Mosedale Beck

Dore
Head

Stirrup
Crag

Ritson's
Force

N

BLACK SAIL PASS

Wasdale
Head

1500
1400
1300

Over Beck

continuation RED PIKE (W) 4

▲ YEWBARROW
2058

gate

car
park

gate

600
500

Dropping
Crag

Great Door
Bell
Rib

ROAD

Mosedale Beck

car parks

ESKDALE VIA BURNMOOR

Bowderdale

600
500
400
300

Wast Water

car park

Overbeck Bridge

Netherbeck Bridge

ONE MILE

Dore Head

Ritson's Force

ASCENT FROM WASDALE
(OVERBECK BRIDGE)
1900 feet of ascent : 1½ miles

Very prominent in the early stages of the ascent is the towering pinnacle of Bell Rib, directly astride the ridge. Bell Rib cannot be climbed by a non-expert, and maps that show a path straight up it are telling fibs.

From the wall take the slanting track towards Dropping Crag and scramble up the steep but easy grass to the right of it, entering higher a constricted gully full of loose stones, where progress is better on the simple rocks to the left. At the top of the gully, on an open slope, climb half-right to reach the ridge exactly, suddenly and dramatically at Great Door: a thrilling moment. The top of Bell Rib is here only a few rocky yards away on the right.

Turn left, now on a path, following the ridge to the summit.

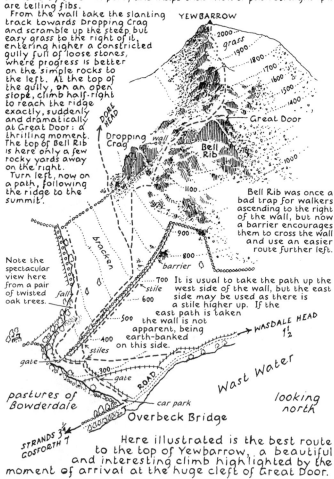

Note the spectacular view here from a pair of twisted oak trees.

Bell Rib was once a bad trap for walkers ascending to the right of the wall, but now a barrier encourages them to cross the wall and use an easier route further left.

It is usual to take the path up the west side of the wall, but the east side may be used as there is a stile higher up. If the east path is taken the wall is not apparent, being earth-banked on this side.

pastures of Bowderdale

Wast Water

looking north

Here illustrated is the best route to the top of Yewbarrow, a beautiful and interesting climb highlighted by the moment of arrival at the huge cleft of Great Door.

ASCENT FROM WASDALE HEAD
1900 feet of ascent : 2½ miles

Start the climb to Dore Head from the path at the foot of the slope below it ; short cuts across the boulders are not rewarding. Keep to the grass on the right of the scree-run.

From Dore Head, Stirrup Crag looks very formidable, and the upper band of rock unassailable, but getting up it is nothing more than a strenuous exercise in elementary gymnastics and unusual postures. The way lies within the confines of rocky cracks and chimneys, and there is no sense of danger or indecent exposure.

Follow the trail of blood left by the author, or, if the elements have removed this evidence of his sufferings, the debris of dentures, bootsoles, etc., left by other pilgrims, and step happily onto the pleasant top. Between this point and the summit of the fell is a wide depression.

Those of faint heart may avoid Stirrup Crag entirely by proceeding from Dore Head towards Over Beck, turning up a grass slope to the depression when the boulders cease.

For such, the author bled in vain.

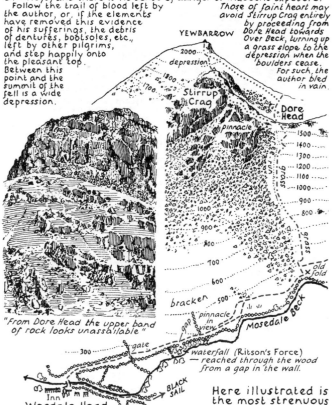

"From Dore Head the upper band of rock looks unassailable"

waterfall (Ritson's Force) — reached through the wood from a gap in the wall.

Here illustrated is the most strenuous route to the top of Yewbarrow, a tiring plod up to Dore Head being followed by an energetic scramble up a rocky rampart.

looking south-west

THE SUMMIT

KIRK FELL — GREAT GABLE — HELVELLYN — GLARAMARA

After the agonies and perils of the ascent it is an anticlimax to find the summit a peaceful and placid sheep pasture, an elevated field, with the cairn crowning a rocky outcrop.

DESCENTS: The usual descents by way of the ridge, north or south, encounter rock and need care. The south ridge, at first easy, narrows to the width of the path at Great Door in exciting surroundings. The natural continuation of the ridge lies up the facing rocks onto the top of Bell Rib, *but do NOT venture into this bad trap*; instead, at this point, turn down the slope ON THE RIGHT into a short rocky gully where loose stones are a menace and skirt the lower buttresses of Bell Rib to regain the ridge at a wall, whence an easy slope leads down to Overbeck Bridge. The north ridge route crosses a depression, rises to the cairned top of Stirrup Crag, and then drops steeply and sharply down a series of rocky cracks in the crag for a few desperate minutes: a bad passage, but neither dangerous nor difficult if care is taken. If all goes well, Dore Head, immediately below, is then soon reached at the top of the scree-run into Mosedale. Those who do not fancy steep rocks can avoid Stirrup Crag entirely by slanting down left from the depression; *in bad conditions, this is the best way off the fell.*   A descent may be made direct to Wasdale Head from the summit cairn, but note that the only gate in the intake wall is that shown on page 4.

RED PIKE

The x Chair

Dore Head   Stirrup Crag

N

YEWBARROW

The use of the Bottom in Mountaineering.

A fellwalker's best asset is a pair of strong legs; next best is a tough and rubbery bottom. In ascent this appendage is, of course, useless, but when descending steep grass or rocks such as are met on the ridge of Yewbarrow the posterior is a valuable agent of friction, a sheet-anchor with superb resistance to the pull of gravity.

RIDGE ROUTE

TO RED PIKE, 2707'
1¾ miles: NNE, NW and N
Depression at 1520'
1350 feet of ascent

Reach Dore Head over Stirrup Crag or by the variation, as described above; then follow the fair track up the opposite slope. An excellent journey.

HALF A MILE

THE VIEW

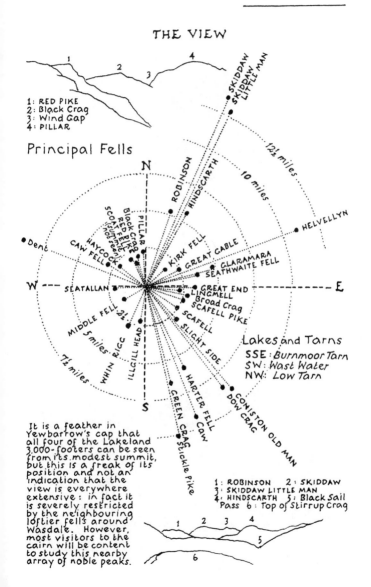

1: RED PIKE
2: Black Crag
3: Wind Gap
4: PILLAR

Principal Fells

SKIDDAW
SKIDDAW LITTLE MAN

12½ miles

10 miles

HELVELLYN

ROBINSON
HINDSCARTH

N

PILLAR
Black Crag
SCOUT (SOUTH)
RED PIKE
SCOTT (SOUTH)
RED PEAK (NORTH)

HAYCOCK
CAW FELL

Dent

KIRK FELL
GREAT GABLE
GREAT GABLE
CLARAMARA
SEATHWAITE FELL

W --- SEATALLAN
GREAT END
LINGMELL
Broad Crag
SCAFELL PIKE
E

SCAFELL

MIDDLE FELL 2½
SLIGHT SIDE

WHIN RIGG
ILLGILL HEAD
5 miles

7½ miles

HARTER FELL
Caw

S

CONISTON OLD MAN
DOW CRAG

GREEN CRAG
Stickle Pike

Lakes and Tarns

SSE: Burnmoor Tarn
SW: Wast Water
NW: Low Tarn

It is a feather in Yewbarrow's cap that all four of the Lakeland 3,000-footers can be seen from its modest summit, but this is a freak of its position and not an indication that the view is everywhere extensive: in fact it is severely restricted by the neighbouring loftier fells around Wasdale. However, most visitors to the cairn will be content to study this nearby array of noble peaks.

1: ROBINSON   2: SKIDDAW
3: SKIDDAW LITTLE MAN
4: HINDSCARTH   5: Black Sail
Pass 6: Top of Stirrup Crag

the
Wasdale
slope

Stirrup Crag

Dore
Head

Mosedale

First time we've
seen him with
a cap on

He must be
going bald
or something

from Gatherstone Head

THE WESTERN FELLS

Some Personal notes
in conclusion

When I came down from Starling Dodd on the 10th of September 1965 I had just succeeded in obtaining a complete view from the summit before the mist descended, after laying patient siege to it through several wet weekends, and in so doing I had concluded the field-work for my last book with only one week left before the end of the summer bus service put the fell out of reach. Thus a 13-year plan was finished one week ahead of schedule. Happy? Yes, I was happy, as anyone must be who comes to the end of a long road ahead of the clock. Sorry? Yes, I was sorry, as anyone must be who comes to the end of a long road he has enjoyed travelling. Relieved? Yes, I was relieved, because a broken leg during these years would have meant a broken heart, too.

I think I must concede that the scenery of the western half of Lakeland (dropping a vertical through High Raise in the Central Fells) is, on the whole, better than the eastern, although it has nothing more beautiful than the head of Ullswater. This is not to say that the fellwalking is better: it is more exciting and exacting but the Helvellyn and High Street ranges in the east are supreme for the man who likes to stride out over the tops all day. Those who prefer to follow narrow ridges from summit to summit are best catered for in the west. The southern half, too, is generally finer than the northern, so that the highlights of the district are to be found mainly in the southwestern sector, from the Duddon to Whinlatter. But it is all delectable country..... One advantage I found in roaming around the western Fells is that they are still free from the type of visitor who has spoiled Langdale and Keswick and other places easier of access. Wasdale Head and Buttermere are beginning to suffer from tourist invasion, but on the tops one can still wander in solitude and enjoy the freedom characteristic of the whole district before somebody invented the motor car.

I promised to give my opinion of the six best fells. I should not have used the word 'best', which suggests that some are not as good as others. I think they are all good. The finest, however, must have the attributes of mountains, i.e., height, a commanding appearance, a good view, steepness and ruggedness : qualities that are most pronounced in the volcanic area of the south-western sector. I now give, after much biting of finger-nails, what I consider to be the finest half-dozen:

Be quick, turn over

SCAFELL PIKE
BOWFELL
PILLAR
GREAT GABLE
BLENCATHRA
CRINKLE CRAGS

These are not necessarily the six fells I like best. It grieves me to have to omit Haystacks (most of all), Langdale Pikes, Place Fell, Carrock Fell and some others simply because they do not measure up in altitude to the grander mountains. There will be surprise at the omission of Scafell, the crags of which provide the finest sight in Lakeland, but too much of this fell is lacking in interest. It would be seventh if there were seven in the list. Contrary to general opinion (which would favour Great Gable), the grandest of the lot is Scafell Pike. Of the six, all are of volcanic rock with the exception of Blencathra.

The six best summits (attributes: a small neat peak of naked rock with a good view) I consider to be

DOW CRAG, Coniston
HARTER FELL, Eskdale
HELM CRAG, Grasmere
EAGLE CRAG, Langstrath
SLIGHT SIDE, Scafell
STEEPLE, Ennerdale

All these, except Steeple, are accessible only by scrambling on rock. The top inches of Helm Crag are hardest to reach.

The six best places for a fellwalker to be (other than summits) because of their exciting situations, and which can be reached without danger, are

> STRIDING EDGE, Helvellyn
> First col, LORD'S RAKE, Scafell
> MICKLEDORE, Scafell
> SHARP EDGE, Blencathra
> SOUTH TRAVERSE, Great Gable
> SHAMROCK TRAVERSE, Pillar

Of course I haven't forgotten Jack's Rake on Pavey Ark. I never could. But this is a place only for men with hair on their chests. I am sorry to omit Great Slab and Climbers Traverse on Bowfell.

The finest ridge-walks are, I think,

THE FAIRFIELD HORSESHOE (Ambleside)
THE HIGH STREET RANGE (Garburn-Moor Divock)
THE MOSEDALE HORSESHOE (Wasdale Head)
CAUSEY PIKE — WHITELESS PIKE
GRISEDALE PIKE – WHITESIDE
ESK HAUSE – WRYNOSE PASS, via Bowfell
THE ESKDALE HORSESHOE (Slight Side-Bowfell)
THE HELVELLYN RANGE (Grisedale Pass-Threlkeld)
THE HIGH STILE RIDGE, with Haystacks
CATBELLS - DALE HEAD - HINDSCARTH - SCOPE END
THE CONISTON ROUND (Old Man - Wetherlam)
(not in order of merit)

In my introductory remarks to Book One I described my task in compiling these books as a labour of love. So it has been. These have been the best years for me, the golden years. I have had a full reward in a thousand happy days on the fells. But, unexpectedly, it has been a profitable venture for me in terms of money, bringing me a small fortune, simply through the continued support of the many kind readers who have both bought and recommended the books. It is money I have not spent and do not want. One surely does not wish to be paid in cash for writing a love-letter! There is, or soon will be, enough to build and equip an Animal Welfare Centre in Kendal, and the Westmorland Branch of the R.S.P.C.A. have accepted for this purpose a gift which is really donated by the readers of these books. Every true fellwalker develops a liking and compassion for birds and animals, the solitary walker especially for they are his only companions, and it seems to me appropriate that this windfall should be used to provide a refuge in Lakeland where ailing and distressed creatures can be brought for care and attention. I thought you would like to know this. You have provided the bricks.

If Starling Dodd had been the last walk of all for me, and this the last book, I should now be desolate indeed, like a lover who has lost his loved one, and the future would have the bleakness of death. I have long known this and anticipated it, and sought desperately in my mind for some new avenue along which I could continue to express my devotion to Lakeland within the talents available to me. I am in better case than the lover who has lost his loved one, for my beloved is still there and faithful, and if there were to be a separation the defection would be mine. But why need this be the last book? Within a year I shall be retired from work (on account of old age!), but I can still walk, still draw, still write; and love itself is never pensioned off ..... so there must be other books ..... In this series I have crowded details of the fells into some 2000 pages, but as much as I have included has been omitted through lack of space. I would like now, in a more leisurely fashion, to continue acquaintance with the fells, and, out of consideration for my white hair, explore the valleys and daleheads more. What I have in mind is A LAKELAND SKETCHBOOK, which, all being well, could be the start of a new series that would aim to show the best of Lakeland in pictures and, by indicating the changes taking place in the district, in valley and on fell, serve to supplement the present series of guidebooks. I also have a good title for another book: FELL WANDERER, and might do this first if I can think of something to write about — personal experiences on the fells perhaps — not, definitely not, an autobiography (as if I dare! Let me keep my friends!). In between times I am pledged to do A PICTORIAL GUIDE TO THE PENNINE WAY, and have had four collaborators, four good men and true, sweating their guts out during the past year to provide a mass of detail and resolve certain doubts and generally smooth my own journey subsequently. This will be a unique book the way I plan it: you will start it at the bottom of the last page and you will read upwards and forwards to the top of the first, which is something that even the Chinese never thought of doing. It will seem logical, however, when you see it, and there is no question of your having to stand on your head.

Regretfully, I reject suggestions of a Book Eight: 'The Outlying Fells'

.... So this is farewell to the present series of books.

The fleeting hour of life of those who love the hills is quickly spent, but the hills are eternal. Always there will be the lonely ridge, the dancing beck, the silent forest; always there will be the exhilaration of the summits. These are for the seeking, and those who seek and find while there is yet time will be blessed both in mind and body.

I wish you all many happy days on the fells in the years ahead.

There will be fair winds and foul, days of sun and days of rain. But enjoy them all.

Good walking! And don't forget — watch where you are putting your feet.

AW.

Christmas. 1965.